10
CHRISTIANS
EVERYONE
SHOULD KNOW

· · · · · · · · · · · · · · · · · ·

Lives of the Faithful and What
They Mean to You

JOHN PERRY
editor

THOMAS NELSON
Since 1798

NASHVILLE   DALLAS   MEXICO CITY   RIO DE JANEIRO

Published in Nashville, Tennessee, by Thomas Nelson. Thomas Nelson is a registered trademark of Thomas Nelson, Inc.

Abridged from *Saint Patrick*, © 2010 by Jonathan Rogers; *Galileo*, © 2011 by Mitch Stokes; *Anne Bradstreet*, © 2010 by Master Sales, Inc.; *John Bunyan*, © 2010 by Kevin Belmonte; *Johann Sebastian Bach*, © 2011 by Rick Marschall; *Jane Austen*, © 2009 by Peter Leithart; *D. L. Moody*, © 2010 by Kevin Belmonte; *George Washington Carver*, © 2011 by John Perry; *Sergeant York*, © 2010 by John Perry; *William F. Buckley Jr.*, © 2010 by Jeremy Lott.

Thomas Nelson, Inc., titles may be purchased in bulk for educational, business, fund-raising, or sales promotional use. For information, please e-mail SpecialMarkets@ThomasNelson.com.

Library of Congress Cataloging-in-Publication Data

10 Christians everyone should know : lives of the faithful and what they mean to you / John Perry, editor.
    p. cm.
Includes bibliographical references (p.   ) and index.
ISBN 978-1-4002-0361-1
1. Christian biography. I. Perry, John, 1952- II. Title: Ten Christians everyone should know.
BR1700.3.A15 2012
270.092′2--dc23
[B]

2012010092

Printed in the United States of America

12 13 14 15 16 QG 6 5 4 3 2 1

CONTENTS

EDITOR'S INTRODUCTION

The impact of Christianity on Western culture has never depended on the quality of a twenty-minute Sunday sermon. Its tectonic, world-changing power flows instead from the words and deeds of those who believe in Christ and follow Him with all their hearts. God sent His Son to earth in human form to demonstrate how the godly must live. Through the lives of the faithful, the world sees the teaching and the promise of the Christ they serve. It is through them that Christianity makes its mark on the world.

Just as Christ was a humble man, a carpenter and not a king, many of history's most admirable and influential Christians have come from what the world considers a lowly station. Others were high-born, and many more lived and worked in the teeming, anonymous middle of humanity, blooming where they were planted. That being the case, we might encounter great Christian figures in any stratum of society, anywhere in the world, in any historical age. That brings us to the stories of the ten men and women in the book you now hold in your hands.

It would be almost impossible to imagine ten people more different from each other than these. There is the aristocrat and the orphan; the great man of learning and the wilderness housewife; the father of twenty and the lonesome spinster; a soldier, a shoe salesman, a millionaire publisher, and a maker of pots and pans. This variety gives us the first truth of Christian living: anybody, anywhere can be a champion of the faith, an example and inspiration to all who follow. Anne Bradstreet was a busy wife and mother with a houseful of children in the wilderness of colonial America. Yet her Christian poetry was so heartfelt and compelling, so universal in its appeal, that she became the first published poet in the New World and the first woman ever to be published in both England and America. Beginning his life as a slave and an orphan, George Washington Carver ended it as a beloved international celebrity who never tired of telling the world about his Creator and God's love for every living thing.

Another lesson these figures remind us of is that being a Christian doesn't necessarily make life easier; in fact, it often makes it harder. Saint Patrick felt a calling to minister to the very people who had kidnapped him from a life of ease and plenty. Galileo and Bunyan were imprisoned for daring to express Christianity as they knew it rather than bow to demands of the religious hierarchy. To these believers, faith was more important than freedom, more important than the comfort and safety of their families, even more important than their lives. As Christ had sacrificed Himself for them, they were willing to give all they had in His service.

Christians living and working outside church walls show us, too, that some of the most effective sermons aren't sermons at all. Bach was inspired by his faith to write music that has in turn inspired countless millions. D. L. Moody did some of his most powerful evangelizing not preaching in great churches packed to the rafters, but befriending ragged street children in a Chicago railyard. William F. Buckley never delivered a sermon, yet a Christian worldview informed his erudite, witty, and influential output in print and broadcasting for nearly half a century.

We see as well that Christianity is timeless. This is good news for those of us who fear for the future of the faith in this so-called "post-Christian" era. Saint Patrick was born in the fifth century AD. William Buckley died in 2008. As different as their worlds were—and as different from the worlds of Galileo or Austen—they nonetheless faced some of the same obstacles. Christianity goes against the most deeply ingrained tendencies of the human heart. We are by nature hopelessly self-centered. As Jeremiah 17:9 warns us, "The heart is deceitful above all things, and desperately wicked." Scanning the headlines of today's newspaper or news website will bear this out. Chances are that every tragedy reported there is the result of someone taking what he doesn't have simply because he wants it. Robbery, rape, war, kidnapping, embezzlement, and all the rest come from the deceit and wickedness within.

Christianity, on the other hand, teaches us to be humble, selfless, and sacrificial in our lives. Humankind alone has no power to overcome our dark natural tendencies; only the divine power of God through Christ makes it possible. From the time of Christ to our own, the world has remained a treacherous and unwelcoming place. The obvious way to deal with it is to practice treachery in return. Christ, through His followers, teaches us that the better way is through kindness and compassion. It lightens our burden in this life and readies us for the unalloyed joy of the next.

Saint Patrick and Mr. Buckley, and everyone in between, had to deal with the same treacherous world populated by the same wicked hearts. And so in this fundamental way, Roman Britain and twenty-first-century New York City put up the same barriers to Christian living. And the same faith, courage, and willingness to sacrifice achieve the same God-given success in overcoming them.

One of the great gifts of history is that since the moment humankind appeared on earth, human nature hasn't really changed. This means that knowing the past gives us a window on understanding the future. Look at the decision a historical figure had to make, the choice that was made, and the results that followed. Anyone facing a similar decision today can learn from what happened then. Thus the more kinds of people we know of and the more we know about them, the better equipped we will be to make our own choices. Nine hundred years before Christ, King Solomon observed, "There is nothing new under the sun" (Ecclesiastes 1:9). These ten inspired and inspiring Christians, scattered across time and place, are proof of Solomon's wisdom, faithful guides from the past helping us thread a pathway through the future.

In sum, our band of brothers and sisters here leaves us with two spiritual markers.

One: No Excuses. However modest your means or circumstances, no worldly limitations need keep you from knowing Christ and sharing His message. You have no education? Sergeant York never made it past the third grade. No platform for evangelism? Anne Bradstreet lived in obscurity in the wilds of the New World, not only laboring to make sure her children were fed, clothed, and educated, but worried about their being scalped. No spare time? Bach transformed the world of Christian music while juggling complex eighteenth-century European politics, holding down three or four jobs at a time, and fathering twenty children.

Two: No Fear. "I can do all things through Christ who strengthens me." Philippians 4:13 doesn't promise that we will do any particular thing, but that we *can* do *any* thing with Christ's help. Obstacles to living a Christian life may be huge. Yet even in the face of grave danger—whether the torture chamber of the Inquisition or the deadly fire of German machine guns—these Christians held fast. Probably none of us will face that level of physical threat. More likely we will have to endure the politics, job pressures, financial burdens, social strains, or family tragedies that are more typical of human experience. The important point is that, like our ten historic examples, we need never fear. God will save His people and honor their sacrifice.

A reader may see himself reflected more than once in these portraits. My life has been nothing like any of them, and yet there are practical connections that strengthen the spiritual ones: I sing Bach's music, carried a rifle in the infantry like Sergeant York, and exchanged letters with Mr. Buckley. Then and now, great and small, they and we are all threads in the same tapestry of faith.

Soli Deo Gloria
John Perry
Nashville
Ash Wednesday, 2012

1 | SAINT PATRICK

(ca. 380–ca. 490)

by Jonathan Rogers

*He [the Lord] watched over me before I knew him . . . and
protected me, and consoled me as a father would his son.*

—SAINT PATRICK

For more than three centuries, the Romans ruled Britain. The occupation began in AD 43, when the emperor Claudius, with a herd of war elephants, crossed the Channel from Gaul.

But by Patrick's time, Roman sway in Britain had begun to buckle beneath the constant pressure of surrounding tribes that refused to bow to the imperial yoke.

AD 367 marked the beginning of troubles that would continue more or less uninterrupted until the Roman army left Britain altogether. The "Barbarian Conspiracy"—a well-coordinated offensive by Picts, Scots, Saxons, and a tribe known as the Attacotti (who hailed from Ireland)—threw the Roman army into disarray. The barbarians pillaged, raped, and murdered civilians throughout the island.

The army managed to regain control a year or two later, sending the invaders back home. But the Barbarian Conspiracy was a sign of things to come.

Enter Patrick.

Patrick was a good Roman—a Latin-speaking son of Roman wealth and privilege—in a land from which the Roman Empire was receding, never to return. His given name was the Latin *Patricius*, which means "highborn," and indeed he was. His father, Calpurnius, was a Roman aristocrat—a landowner, town councilor, and deacon in the Roman Catholic Church.

We cannot know Patrick's exact dates. He didn't mention his birth year in any of his writings, but he may have been born as early as the 380s, and died as late as the 490s. The fact that he identified his father as a *decurion* (a Roman official) suggests that he was born toward the earlier end of this range. On the other hand, monks who claimed to have known him personally were still alive well into the sixth century, which would suggest that he lived toward the end of the fifth century. In any case, by the time he was born in Britain, the order and discipline associated with the Roman rule had clearly broken down.

In the opening lines of his *Confession*, Patrick reported that he was from a settlement called Bannaventa Burniae, but no one knows for sure where that was. There was a Bannaventa in what is now Northamptonshire, right in the heart of England, but the distance between there and the western coast would have been awfully far for Irish raiders to travel for booty. Surely, if it was susceptible to Irish pirates, Patrick's Bannaventa Burniae was in the western reaches of Britain. A map of the villas that archaeologists have identified in Britain shows a much higher concentration of villas along the Bristol Channel than anywhere else along Britain's west coast. That area, where the southern coast of Wales meets England, seems as good a guess as any for the location of Patrick's boyhood home.

LEGENDS OF CHILDHOOD

The legends describe Patrick as an extremely pious child. In one, the infant Patrick miraculously provides the holy water for his own baptism! A blind and oddly underprepared priest, realizing that he doesn't have any water on hand, takes baby Patrick's hand and makes the sign of the cross over the ground. A spring of water bubbles forth, the baptism goes forward, and the blind priest receives sight when he washes his face with the water.

Another story has the boy Patrick using drops of water to start a fire and burning chunks of ice for firewood in order to show his nurse "how possible are all things to them who believe."[1]

In many cases, the legends of Patrick illustrate and give color to the few facts we know of the saint. These stories of juvenile piety, however, flatly contradict what Patrick himself wrote. "I did not, indeed, know the true God," he said of his sixteen-year-old self.[2] Elsewhere he wrote, "I did not then believe in the living God, nor had I believed, since my infancy."[3] This from a man whose father was a deacon and his grandfather a priest.

In his *Confession*, Patrick wrote of some sin that, he said, "I had perpetrated . . . in one hour—in my boyhood because I was not yet . . . [self-controlled]. God knows—I do not—whether I was then fifteen years old at the time."[4]

What sin, committed in a single hour by a fifteen-year-old boy, would be so serious that he would still consider it significant so many years later? Sexual indiscretion comes to mind; a teenager doesn't even need an hour to head down that path. But likely the only sin Patrick could be talking about is homicide. Perhaps in a moment of rage, the young Patrick impulsively killed one of the slaves who worked the family's lands. He could get away with it: after all, he was the son of the lord of the manor. But as time went on—and he found himself in the position of slave, his heart changed by the love of God—the gravity of his crime dawned on him.

SAVAGE IRELAND

Britain may have seemed uncivilized compared, say, to the parts of the Roman Empire that ringed the Mediterranean, but it was downright urbane compared to Ireland. In AD 19, the Greek geographer Strabo wrote of Ireland, "The people living there are more savage than the Britons, being cannibals as well as gluttons. Further, they consider it honorable to eat their dead fathers and to openly have intercourse, not only with unrelated women, but with their mothers and sisters."[5] Though he admitted that he had no reliable witnesses to confirm these calumnies against the Irish, he reasoned that since other barbarians were "known" to practice cannibalism, he could be confident in his characterization of the Irish.

Strabo was writing three or four hundred years before Patrick, at a time when even Britain seemed to be beyond the end of the world. But Roman attitudes toward the Irish hadn't necessarily changed much by Patrick's time. Consider what Saint Jerome had to say in the early fifth century:

> I myself as a young man in Gaul saw the Atticoti, a British people, feeding on human flesh[.] Moreover, when they come across herds of pigs and cattle in the forests, they frequently cut off the buttocks of the shepherds and their wives, and their nipples, regarding these alone as delicacies.[6]

Jerome was in Gaul in 367, the year of the Barbarian Conspiracy in Britain. It is possible that he saw Irish raiders who had crossed the Channel to extend their pillage into Gaul. But did he actually encounter Irishmen feeding on human flesh? It seems more likely, says author Philip Freeman, that Jerome encountered "rough-and-ready foreign soldiers having fun with a gullible Roman youth over a meal of mutton stew."[7]

The Irish were a Celtic people who migrated to the island from the Continent (or perhaps from Britain) no later than the fourth century BC. The Celts dominated large swaths of Europe during the Iron Age, from Asia Minor to the Iberian Peninsula to Gaul (modern-day

France) and Britain. The Romans who first encountered the Celts were struck by their warlike spirit.

Caesar's campaigns in Gaul in 58–51 BC marked the end of the Celtic ascendancy in northern Europe. As the centuries progressed, the Celts succumbed to the civilizing influence of their Roman conquerors. Throughout the Continent, the wild Celts became good Romans. And they made their own contributions to the empire as soldiers, as artisans, and as orators.

The Irish, however, on their remote, green island, were a sort of time capsule of Iron Age Celtic culture. In the absence of significant external forces, their tribal, agricultural, warlike society stayed very much the same for a very long time.

⁕

It was by conquering that the Roman army brought a new social order to the Celts of the Continent and Britain. It was by retreating that they brought a new social order to the Celts of Ireland. The army's departure from Britain—and the power vacuum it created— was the outside impetus that finally brought significant change to Ireland's centuries-old, Iron Age society. Liam de Paor wrote:

> This is what constitutes an "heroic age": that a people subsisting stably on pasture and tillage, with a simple system of customary law and an already established social hierarchy, is provided with an opportunity to prey on a rich, highly organized and prestigious civilization. And in the heroic age of the fourth and fifth centuries in Ireland, chieftains who could organize well-equipped raiding bands [and] arrange shipping . . . were able to enrich themselves with loot and slaves.[8]

Raids and battles had always been a fact of Irish life, but until now they had only shifted wealth and relative power from one part of the island to another. They had never tilted the social equilibrium the way the sudden influx of wealth from Roman Britain did. A new class of warrior kings was emerging.

Across the Irish Sea, these seismic shifts would have the most direct and personal effect imaginable on a teen named Patrick.

Kidnapped

"I was taken into captivity in Ireland with many thousands of people . . . ," wrote Patrick in his *Confession*, "for quite drawn away from God, we did not keep his precepts, nor were we obedient to our priests."[9]

Continuing, he wrote, "And the Lord brought down on us the fury of his being, and scattered us among many nations, even to the ends of the earth."[10] He was speaking quite literally. So far as he knew, Ireland was indeed the end of the earth. There was nothing beyond but ocean. Writing fifty years or more after that dreadful day, Patrick could see that his capture by Irish pirates was the first step in his lifework of bringing salvation to the ends of the earth.

In his writings, Patrick had more to say about the internal or spiritual facts of his slavery than he did about the external, physical facts. He never named his master or gave any other details about him (later tradition identifies him as a petty king named Miliucc). Neither did he say where he spent his years of servitude. It was probably somewhere near Ireland's west coast; when he escaped, he had to travel two hundred Roman miles to catch a ship headed toward Britain—which, presumably, would be leaving from Ireland's east coast. Later in life, when he received the call to return to Ireland, he said he heard "the voice of those . . . who [lived] near the wood of Foclut, which is near the Western Sea."[11] Scholars associate the wood of Foclut (or Voclut) with the Wood of Fochoill, in County Mayo, in the northwest portion of Ireland.

Patrick could hardly have experienced a more complete reversal of fortune. The aristocratic Roman—likely from a family that had slaves of its own—was out of the comfort of the villa and slaving in a sheep pasture in a barbarian country.

Patrick's outward reversal resulted in an inward reversal that was no less dramatic. There in the meadow, away from home and stripped of everything—including the organized religion of his forefathers—Patrick turned at last to the God he had heard about all his life.

> There the Lord opened my mind to an awareness of my unbelief, in order that, [perhaps], I might remember my transgressions and turn with all my heart to the Lord my God, who had regard for my insignificance and pitied my youth and ignorance. And he watched over me before I knew him, . . . and he protected me.[12]

Growing up in church, Patrick had paid little or no attention to the things of God. The Creator hadn't seemed very real or relevant or necessary in his earlier life of ease. But isolated in a field full of sheep in the lush, green hills of western Ireland, Patrick felt a holy zeal beginning to burn in him, and it would eventually transform all of Irish culture.

For all its disadvantages, the shepherd's life leaves plenty of time to think and pray, and Patrick used his time to great advantage: "More and more did the love of God, and my fear of him and faith increase," Patrick wrote, "and my spirit was moved so that in a day [I would say as many as] a hundred prayers, and in the night a like number."[13]

It was this fervent inner life that got Patrick through the physical hardships of his everyday life. More than tolerating his difficult duties, he rejoiced through them, springing to life in the morning. "I would wake up before daylight to pray, in the snow, in icy coldness, in rain, and I used to feel neither ill nor any slothfulness, because . . . the Spirit was burning in me."[14]

Patrick viewed both his kidnapping and slavery as God's direct work. God wished to draw Patrick to Himself. So rather than growing bitter, Patrick allowed God's chastisement to do its work in him. His enslavement, he believed, was a hard mercy, but a mercy nonetheless.

Those years, from age sixteen to twenty-two, laid an unassailably strong foundation for Patrick's future ministry.

⤷✦⤶

After six years of slavery, Patrick had the first of the many dreamvisions that he describes in the *Confession*. In his sleep, he heard a voice saying, "Soon you will depart for your home country." Not long afterward, he heard another voice: "Behold, your ship is ready." So he left: "I turned about and fled from the man with whom I had been for six years."[15]

The ship that awaited Patrick was two hundred miles away. It is hard to imagine how an escaped slave could have made it that far across a landscape like that of fifth-century Ireland. According to Liam de Paor, "Numerous undrained lakes and river valleys and lowlands created many watery wildernesses in which the traveling stranger would be almost literally at sea."[16] The impossible topography (and the fact that there were no roads) would have been only the beginning of Patrick's problems. The dangers from the people he met would have been terrifying, with new dangers each time he entered a different settlement. Every word Patrick spoke would have revealed his foreignness—and vulnerability. Like escaped slaves throughout history, he likely traveled at night. But how did he navigate strange bogs, forests, and rivers in the dark? And with no money, how could he feed himself on such a long journey?

Not surprisingly, Patrick attributed his success and safety to the guiding hand of God. "[He] directed my route," he wrote.[17]

When Patrick finally arrived at the sea, the ship he sought was getting ready to sail. After a three-day journey, the ship made landfall, though whether in Britain or in Gaul remains under scholarly debate.

A LIFE-CHANGING DREAM

"After a few years," Patrick wrote matter-of-factly, "I was again in Britain with my parents [kinsfolk], and they welcomed me as a son."[18] (That "after a few years" evidently referred to the time since he left Britain in the raiders' boats. At that point in Patrick's story, it couldn't possibly have been "a few years" since he left Ireland.) The fact that these people received Patrick *as a son* may suggest that the relatives were not his parents; it would be redundant to say that parents welcomed their own son "as a son." Whoever they were, Patrick's family probably never expected to see him again. In their joy they said the sort of things one would expect them to say. As Patrick phrased it, "[They] asked me, in faith, that . . . I should not go anywhere else away from them."[19]

It is a touching scene of domestic happiness—and it is shattered in the very next line:

In a vision of the night, I saw a man whose name was Victoricus coming as if from Ireland with innumerable letters, and he gave me one of them, and I read the beginning of the letter: "The Voice of the Irish"; and as I was reading . . . I seemed at that moment to hear the voice of those who were beside the forest of Foclut . . . , and they were crying as if with one voice: "We beg you . . . that you shall come and shall walk again among us." And I was stung intensely in my heart so that I could read no more.[20]

Consider for a moment the hardships Patrick had just escaped in Ireland. Now he was being called upon to turn around and go back. The vision may not have come as immediately after Patrick's return as it comes in the *Confession*, but for most former slaves, anytime would be too soon to return to the place of their enslavement.

Patrick's "Voice of the Irish" dream is one of the best-known episodes in his biography. But there are actually two dreams associated with his call back to Ireland. In the second, he heard the voices of the highly educated, and he couldn't make sense of a word they were saying: "[In] most [learned] words . . . I heard [those whom I] could not understand."[21]

The way back to Ireland would lead Patrick first through training for the priesthood. Judging from the way these two visions play out—and from Patrick's almost obsessive concern with his own lack of education—it was priestly training, not Ireland, that held real terror for Patrick.

Though he was at least twenty-two at the time, his education would have been at most that of a sixteen-year-old. If he felt educationally inferior to the people with whom he would study for the priesthood, he had good reason. The truly surprising thing is the extent to which that feeling of inferiority was expressed in the pieces Patrick wrote in middle age.

PATRICK TELLS HIS STORY

Both the *Confession* and the *Epistle* begin with self-deprecation that goes well beyond the conventional and seems to reflect genuine self-consciousness. In the first line of the *Epistle* Patrick described himself as "unlearned."[22] He was addressing pirates and slave traders, by the way; surely he didn't need to be too self-conscious about his scholarship. The *Confession* begins, "I, Patrick, a sinner, a most simple countryman, the least of all the faithful and most contemptible to many . . ."[23] Patrick's awareness of his inadequacy had been paralyzing. "For some time I have thought of writing," he said, "but I have hesitated until now, for truly, I feared to expose myself to the criticism of men, because I have not studied like others."[24] And that is just the tip of the iceberg. He devoted a good five paragraphs to analyzing the implications of his ignorance on the churchmen who were his original audience.

Some of his fellow churchmen, it seems, came out of the womb speaking (and, apparently, writing) the most high-flown academic Latin. But not Patrick. "My idiom and language have been translated into a foreign tongue . . . It is easy to prove from a sample of my writing."[25] Latin was Patrick's native tongue, but his vernacular Latin would have been quite different from the academic Latin to which he was referring. The Latin of the academics truly would be an alien language to one—even a native Latin speaker—who had never been trained by a rhetor. And that rhetoric education is exactly what Patrick missed in the years of his enslavement.

He was correct in saying that his academic shortcomings could be proven by the flavor of his writing. Latin experts point out errors and infelicities throughout Patrick's writings, and even in translation there are places where it is clear that Patrick's writing is a little clumsy.

R. P. C. Hanson speaks of Patrick as "acutely, perpetually, embarrassingly conscious of his lack of education."[26] It becomes almost equally embarrassing for the reader as Patrick continues: "So, consequently, today I feel ashamed and am mightily afraid to expose my ignorance, because, [not] eloquent, with a small vocabulary, I am unable to explain as the spirit is eager to do."[27] This was not only a matter of class-consciousness. Patrick felt the frustration of a stutterer. He had so much going on inside—so much desire, so much heart—but his language just couldn't keep up.

That is where Patrick's weakness became his strength. He testified to the works of God not because he was eloquent, but because he couldn't help it.

Why did God use Patrick to reach the people at the very ends of the earth? Because Patrick was sufficiently humble to serve the very barbarians whom the more sophisticated churchmen of his day wanted nothing to do with—and he was sufficiently rustic to relate to them. Whether or not Patrick understood this when he was first called back to Ireland, he clearly understood that Christ would be with him, praying on his behalf and answering his own prayers. So he moved forward.

Patrick wrote virtually nothing about his training for the priesthood. There were no seminaries in the fifth century, so he would have trained under a bishop in a mentor setting. In the absence of other evidence, it would seem apparent that he trained in Britain. The fact that his father and grandfather were both connected to the British church increases that likelihood. The later legends, however, often have him training in Gaul under Bishop Germanus of Auxerre; that, too, is a reasonable possibility.

Patrick's path toward the post of bishop would have been a long one. If he began his training at twenty-two or twenty-three, it would have been seven or eight years before he was even appointed a deacon (thirty was the minimum age for a deacon). He would have been a priest some years after that, and he was probably no younger than fifty when he was appointed bishop. The legends all portray Patrick as already being a bishop when he went back to Ireland. Yet given the tremendous amount he accomplished in Ireland, it seems more likely that he started working there as a younger man.

Whatever the case, at some point in Patrick's ministry, he gave a convoluted account of a humiliating incident in which, said he, "I was attacked by a goodly number of my elders, who [brought up] my sins against my arduous episcopate."[28]

DISGRACED BY ELDERS, EXONERATED BY GOD

The incident hinges on a betrayal by Patrick's "close friend."[29] We discussed Patrick's boyhood sin—possibly homicide—earlier. He confessed this offense to a friend, most likely a fellow priest-in-training, many years later, before becoming a deacon. Thirty years later (whether thirty years after the sin or thirty years after the confession is unclear), when Patrick's elders sought an occasion against him, his old friend obliged them. He dredged up the old sin that Patrick had confessed in confidence and, as he put it, "in the anxiety [of] my sorrowful mind."[30]

Apparently it was just what Patrick's enemies needed. He wasn't even present for the trial, which took place in Britain. Evidently he expected his friend to plead his case in his absence. The friend reassured Patrick that everything was going to be all right. But during the trial things didn't go as Patrick had expected. The friend, it seems, turned state's evidence. Patrick asks, "How did it come to him, shortly afterwards, to disgrace me publicly, in the presence of all, good and bad, because previously, gladly and of his own free will, he pardoned me?"[31]

Reproved by the elders, Patrick was subjected to "disgrace and scandal."[32] In the middle of his public humiliation and private pain, God came to Patrick again in a dream. In this dream Patrick saw the official document of censure that had been drawn up against him. Then he heard the voice of God: "We have seen with displeasure the face of the chosen one divested of [his good] name . . . He who touches you, touches the apple [i.e., pupil] of my eye."[33]

This is a remarkable moment. The document of censure, that artifact of the Church hierarchy held in front of Patrick's face, is nullified by God Himself with a direct word that short-circuits the whole apparatus of church leadership. *God* sides with Patrick against his elders.

Throughout his career, Patrick trusted his direct line to God more than he trusted the leadership of his superiors. This attitude would be a source of ongoing trouble for Patrick (including the trouble that led to his writing the *Confession*); but without it, he would have never begun the work of bringing the Irish to Christ.

IRELAND REBORN

When Patrick finally made it back to Ireland, what did his work there look like? In the legends, the triumph of the gospel is a fore-gone conclusion. But it is hard to believe Patrick's mission to the Irish could have gotten off to a roaring start. Nothing in Patrick's writings indicates that the Irish had been so obliging. In fact, he remarked in the *Epistle* that some of the Irish looked down on him. Perhaps more of them were able to resist Patrick's eloquence than the legends would have us believe.[34]

Nevertheless, Patrick made it clear that he experienced incredible success as an evangelist in Ireland: "[God] granted me so much grace, that through me many people would be reborn in God, and soon . . . after confirmed, and that clergy would be ordained everywhere for them, the masses lately come to belief."[35] In another place Patrick wrote that he baptized "so many thousands of people."[36]

No one had ever done what Patrick was doing in Ireland. Never before had a Catholic clergyman gone out among the pagans and seen mass conversions. Patrick's efforts don't appear to have been entirely grassroots. He cultivated relationships with kings and their families. And Patrick's program included a great deal of travel. "I went about among you, and everywhere for your sake," he said, "in danger, and as far as the outermost regions beyond which no one lived, and where no one had ever penetrated before, to baptize or to ordain clergy or to confirm people."[37]

Bribery was part of the program too. "From time to time I gave rewards to the kings," he wrote, "as well as making payments to their sons who travel with me."[38] Those kings' sons would have been bodyguards who protected Patrick as he traveled.

Patrick's interactions with Irish kings and their families yielded more than safe passage. In some cases they yielded converts. "Where they never had any knowledge of God . . . , they are lately become a people of the Lord, and are called children of God[.] The sons of the Irish [Scotti] and the daughters of the chieftains are to be seen as monks and virgins of Christ."[39]

For the most part Patrick spoke of his Irish converts collectively; the one individual he mentioned was "a most beautiful, blessed, native-born noble Irish [Scotta] woman of adult age whom," he said, "I baptized." A few days after her baptism, this woman said that she had received a prophecy advising her to become a "virgin of Christ." Six days later, "she took the course that all virgins of God take, not with their fathers' consent but enduring the persecutions and deceitful hindrances of their parents."[40]

A king with a beautiful daughter would expect to benefit from her marriage. A good marriage was an excellent way for him to make alliances, increase his fortune, and consolidate his power. Quite apart from the usual shock of having a daughter announce that she is devoting herself entirely to a novel religion, the land-owning parents of a "virgin of Christ" would have had a whole other portfolio of concerns. The pressures on such a young woman would have been tremendous.

The plight of Patrick's pious noblewoman fired the imagination of storytellers in the Patrician tradition. In several legends the

15

beautiful daughters of kings refuse marriage for the sake of God and are punished by their parents. The best known is the story of Monesan from Muirchu's *Life*. In her pursuit of truth, Monesan chooses virginity and stands firm in spite of all: "The more she was wet through with drenchings of water, the less she could be compelled against her will. Indeed, between floggings and dowsings with water, she still contrived to ask her mother and her nurse if they knew who made the wheel with which the world is provided with light."[41]

⸙

While Patrick cultivated relationships with the rich and powerful, it is clear from his writing that his evangelism did not hinge on influence peddling. He was a pastor, a shepherd, first and last, and the road was not always easy: "After hardships and such great trials," he rejoiced, "after captivity, after many years, he [has given] me so much favour in these people."[42] He found favor with them because he showed them a respect that they may not have expected from a representative of the civilized world. "[To] the heathen among whom I live," he said, "I have . . . always shown them trust."[43] That must have been a remarkable thing for the people he served, especially considering that he had once been their slave and had learned firsthand how dangerous they could be.

In a culture of violence, Patrick brought a message of peace. And in a world of arbitrary pagan gods, Patrick brought the message of a personal God who loves His people, even to the extremity of losing His life. In fact, Patrick would have been happy to be martyred for the sake of Christ and his beloved Irish. What he couldn't bear was the thought of being parted from those he was sent to serve. "May it never befall me to be separated by my God from his people whom he has won in this most remote land. I pray God that . . . he will deign that I should be a faithful witness for his sake right up to the time of my passing."[44]

There is something compelling about the stubborn gratitude and equanimity that Patrick's enslavement nurtured in him. He had been imprisoned, robbed, threatened, and mocked. He'd been betrayed by his dearest friend and punished by a church hierarchy that didn't understand him. As he wrote the *Confession*, he was in trouble again. "I certainly am wretched and unfortunate," he said. "Even if I wanted wealth I have no resources . . . Daily I expect to be murdered or betrayed or reduced to slavery if the occasion arises." And yet, in spite of all, he wrote, "But . . . poverty and failure suit me better than wealth and delight." Why? Because, he affirmed, "Christ the Lord was poor for our sakes."[45]

Patrick must have looked like Christ to the people of Ireland. Like the Savior, he lowered himself for their sake, giving up his rights and privileges, to willingly serve where he might have been served. No amount of eloquence could make the same impact.

A Passion for His People

Of Patrick's writings, his *Letter to the Soldiers of Coroticus* is the one in which his pastoral spirit is most evident. Ironically, that pastoral tenderness finds expression in hot-burning anger against men who have grievously wronged a group of Patrick's beloved converts.

Coroticus was a British warlord, one of the petty tyrants who came to power throughout Britain in the years after the Roman army left. He directed a raid on the Irish coast in which a group of freshly baptized Christian converts, still wearing their baptismal robes, were attacked; some were killed and some were carried back to Britain as slaves.

The irony wouldn't have been lost on Patrick. Just as he had been carried from Britain to Ireland by Irish raiders, now, decades later, members of his flock had been carried across the Irish Sea in the other direction, by British raiders.

But there was another, uglier irony at work here. Coroticus wasn't a pagan warlord descending on Christian victims. He was himself a professing Christian. The thought of a Christian conducting piratical raids on anyone was horrifying enough, but to think he would prey on fellow Christians was more than Patrick could bear.

As soon as he heard about the raid, Patrick sent a priest to Coroticus's soldiers bearing a letter, "to see," he said, "if we might claw something back from all the looting, most important, the baptized captives whom they had seized."[46] The soldiers laughed in the priest's face.

The epistle we know as *A Letter to the Soldiers of Coroticus* is a second letter, not the first one that the priest delivered directly.

The *Letter*, or *Epistle*, is a document of excommunication, though Patrick would have had no official authority to excommunicate a Christian belonging to a British diocese. But he believed his authority came directly from God, not from a church hierarchy. His letter was a rebuke not only to Coroticus and his men, but also to the leadership of the British church, who, Patrick was convinced, didn't care enough about their fellow Christians in Ireland to do anything about the depredations of a British Christian against them.

Those people whom Coroticus had murdered and enslaved meant everything to Patrick: for them, he wrote, "I have forsaken my country and parents, and would give up even life itself."[47] The page burns with Patrick's passion for the people of Ireland. They were the only offspring he would ever have.

The Irish believers were no longer foreigners to Patrick, but fellow citizens. The British soldiers, on the other hand, supposedly Patrick's brothers in Christ, were no such thing. "I am not addressing my own people," he said, "nor my fellow citizens of the holy Romans, but those who are now become citizens of demons by reason of their evil works."[48] Patrick was hinting at excommunication with this language. These allegedly Christian soldiers, to Patrick, had left the kingdom of God and had proven to be under Satan's authority.

When Patrick actually articulated the "excommunication" that he'd been hinting at, it was a strange excommunication indeed. He wrote, "Let every man know who fears God that they are estranged from me, and from Christ my God, whose ambassador I am."[49]

Having declared Coroticus and his soldiers to be outcasts, Patrick named the sins for which they were cast out: patricide and fratricide.[50] By calling the raiders patricides, he may have been suggesting that they had actually killed *him*, Patrick, or Patricius.

Nearing the end of the letter, Patrick mourned his loss:

O beautiful and well-beloved brethren and children! whom I have brought forth in Christ in such multitudes, what shall I do for you? . . . The wicked have prevailed over us. We have become outcasts. . . . They think it an indignity that we have been born in Ireland . . . Therefore I grieve for you—I grieve, O my beloved ones![51]

Note Patrick's full identification with his people. He felt the same injustices that they felt. And he resented the fact that the British were treating the Irish as subhuman. They had one God, he said.[52] So why were the Irish Christians still on the outside?

Ever the pastor, Patrick moved from mourning and resentment to comfort and the hope of heaven.

But, on the other hand, I congratulate myself I have not labored for nothing—my journey has not been in vain . . . Thanks be to God, ye who have believed and have been baptized have gone from earth to paradise. . . . Truly, you shall reign with the apostles and prophets and martyrs, and obtain the eternal kingdom.[53]

It is the grand reversal: the victim has become the victor. The murdered converts, he said, would one day reign on high, while outside "the . . . murderers . . . shall have their part in the everlasting lake of fire."[54] Furthermore, he assured them, they would someday sit in judgment of Coroticus and his men!

Reading Patrick's *Epistle*, it is not hard to see why the Irish loved him. He was a bulldog on behalf of his people. And he was a pastor in every sense.

In the Footsteps
of the Apostle

We could hardly overestimate the uniqueness of Patrick's work among the Irish. As a pioneering missionary, his only real precedent was the apostle Paul. When he took it upon himself to make disciples among the Irish, he became, so far as we know, Western Christendom's first missionary to the world beyond the bounds of the Roman Empire.[55]

For five centuries after Paul's missionary journeys—until Pope Gregory the Great set out to evangelize Britain's pagan Anglo-Saxons in 596—the barbarians beyond the Roman frontier still didn't figure in the Church's plans, except as foes of the faith. For Patrick to reach out to these barbarians as he did was almost as radical as Paul's outreach to the Gentiles.

In its first two centuries, the Christian faith was viewed as a threat to Roman civilization. By the second half of the fourth century, however, the Church had come to be viewed as the guardian and sole guarantor of Roman civilization. The work of Constantine the Great, who had established Christianity as Rome's state religion after his conversion in AD 312,[56] did much to strengthen Christianity throughout the civilized world. By the end of the fourth century, the Church was as big as all the empire—but, it appeared, no bigger.

The Church had never reached out to the "outer barbarians" before Patrick because they didn't see any point. "What place would God have in a savage world?" wrote one church official. "How could the Christian virtues survive among barbarians?" wrote another.[57]

And Patrick's experience as a youth would seem to prove the bishops' point: a boy is snatched away from his Christian home, removed from civilized Christian society, and enslaved in a dark world of paganism and error. These barbarians were seen as enemies to the gospel. So when the Church sent Patrick to Ireland, it wouldn't have been so he could convert the barbarians. He would have been sent to minister to the few Christians who were already there.

It appears that Patrick's refusal to go along with the program was the occasion for his writing the *Confession*. He was in self-defense mode in this piece, justifying the work he was doing in Ireland.

Reading the *Confession*, one gets the impression that Patrick's opponents were throwing a number of charges against him to see which would stick. In the fourth paragraph of the *Confession*, Patrick launched, almost without warning, into a full-blown creed (had someone challenged his theological orthodoxy?):

> For there is no other God, nor ever was before, nor shall be hereafter, but God the Father, unbegotten and without beginning, . . . his son Jesus Christ, who manifestly always existed with the Father . . . All things . . . were made by him. He was made man, conquered death and was received into Heaven, to the Father who gave him all power over every name in Heaven and on Earth and in Hell, so that every tongue should confess that Jesus Christ is Lord and God, in whom we believe. And we look to his imminent coming again, the judge of the living and the dead . . . And he poured out his Holy Spirit on us . . . which makes the believers . . . into sons of God and co-heirs of Christ . . . , and we worship one God in the Trinity of holy name.[58]

Patrick's ideas about the barbarians went against the received orthodoxy of his day. But when it came to theology, he wanted to be sure his readers knew that he adhered to a strict Trinitarian orthodoxy.

The widespread assumption in Patrick's time was that once the gospel had spread to the whole world, Christ would come back in glory. By Patrick's time, the gospel had indeed spread to the whole of what most Romans considered "the world." The Roman Empire was thoroughly Christian.

Patrick had a bigger vision than that.

"I have made you a light for the Gentiles," he had read in Acts 13:47, "that you may bring salvation to the ends of the earth" (NIV). That was the work Patrick was about—bringing salvation to the uttermost "ends of the earth." In his mind, Ireland *was* the very end of the inhabited world. To the west and to the north, he knew of no more people.

Patrick lived his whole life in the belief that he was living near the end of time. In his youth, watching the breakdown of Roman order, it wouldn't be hard to believe. Being forced out of that world and into one that was even less civilized would have felt truly apocalyptic. Later, having taken the gospel across the western threshold of the empire, Patrick believed he had taken a major step toward bringing about the end of time and ushering in the kingdom of God. Quoting Jesus from Matthew 24:14, he wrote, "This Gospel of the Kingdom shall be preached throughout the whole world . . . and then the end of the world shall come."[59]

Here is one of the paradoxes of Patrick's character: he was a thoroughly humble man, yet he believed he was the very instrument by which God was completing human history. That, in the end, was Patrick's authority for this most unorthodox mission of his: his work represented the fulfillment of prophecy. Invoking Scripture again, he wrote:

And in Hosea he says: "Those who are not my people I will call my people, and those not beloved I will call my beloved, and in the very place where it was said to them, You are not my people, they will be called 'Sons of the living God.'"

So, how is it that in Ireland, where they never had any knowledge of God but, always, until now, cherished idols and unclean things, they are lately become a people of the Lord, and are called children of God?[60]

It is a beautiful vision for his people, the Irish people. They were *not* beloved, but they were *God's* beloved! They had been told—by the very people who claimed to speak for God—that they were not God's people, but now they were being called God's *children*. Patrick marveled that he had been a part of such a reversal.

Before the Irish, no people had ever submitted to the gospel who had not first submitted to Rome. But when Saint Patrick came to the Irish, they saw in him—in his very presence among them as their former slave—that forgiveness was possible, that hardship need not result in bitterness, and that the meek just might inherit the earth after all. It was a gospel that made sense to them. They paused long enough to listen.

And to change.

To learn more about Saint Patrick, read Jonathan Rogers's *Saint Patrick* (Nashville: Thomas Nelson, 2010) from the Christian Encounters Series.

2 | GALILEO
(1564–1642)

by Mitch Stokes

I do not feel obliged to believe that the same God who has endowed us with sense, reason, and intellect has intended us to forgo their use.

—GALILEO

According to Italian custom, we know Galileo by his first name—but then again, he was one of a kind. Besides, Galileo's first name is also his last—Galileo Galilei—and perhaps a man with two first names need only go by one of them.

Galileo could trace his ancestry back to the 1200s, to a Florentine named Giovanni Bonaiuti.[1] Giovanni's great-grandson, Galileo Bonaiuti, was a man of distinction—an official at the University of Florence and a member of Florence's governing council. When he died around 1450, a proud relative considered Galileo worthy to be the founder of a new and eminent Florentine family.[2] On Bonaiuti's tombstone was inscribed *Galileis de Galilei, at one time Bonaiutis*. The name stuck.

Eighty years later, in 1520, Vincenzio Galilei was born in Florence, the seat of the Renaissance in northern Italy. Vincenzio and his son, our Galileo, would always be proud of their citizenry, and Galileo would refer to himself as "a noble Florentine" on his books' title pages.

Vincenzio was a talented musician who studied music theory under the Venetian master Gioseffo Zarlino. After Vincenzio finished his music studies in Venice in 1561 or 1562, needing additional income, he traveled to Pisa to trade wool.[3] There he met Giulia Ammannati, and in July 1562 they married.

The couple settled in the countryside near Pisa, where Vincenzio established a small music school, also continuing his work in cloth trading.

⁓

The Leaning Tower of Pisa is the campanile—the freestanding bell tower—of Pisa's cathedral. In the cathedral's baptistry, on February 19, 1564, Vincenzio and Giulia baptized their first child four days after he was born. The reddish-haired boy was named Galileo.

We know very little about Galileo's childhood, but some things are clear. In 1574, Galileo lived in Florence, where he learned Latin and Greek, and studied the fine arts. He became an excellent musician, singer, and painter.

Literature enamored Galileo. And although he would become famous primarily for mathematics and science, Galileo would change the style of Italian literature. His scientific writings were works of art.

Sometime after 1574, Vincenzio sent Galileo to be educated at the monastery in Vallombrosa. Five years later, at age fifteen, Galileo joined the monks' order, planning to take his vows once he successfully completed his probation.

But his father wanted him to become a doctor.

ARISTOTLE'S UNIVERSE

In 1581, Galileo, by now one of seven children, moved to Pisa and enrolled in the University as an *artista*, a student of medicine and philosophy.[4] The University's medical faculty was part of the faculty of arts, which also included philosophy and mathematics.[5]

The preparatory philosophical training was an overview of European science, which meant Aristotelian physics and cosmology. This part of philosophy—what we call *science*—was actually the study of nature.

It may be surprising that the science of the medieval and Renaissance universities was largely Aristotelian, given the centrality of Christianity in Europe. Aristotle was a pagan, after all. But the scholars of the time believed that Aristotle and Christianity accorded quite well on many important issues, and Aristotelianism had become so entwined with Christian doctrine that it was difficult to tell where Christianity ended and Aristotelianism began.

❦

No other ancient thinker had constructed such an expansive, coherent, and impressive system of thought as had Aristotle. Throughout the Middle Ages, Aristotle was often simply called "the Philosopher"; there were no competitors. Scholar Stillman Drake says of the European mind-set: "If one wished to *know*, the way to go about it was to read the texts of Aristotle with care . . . [All] matters of knowledge belonged to Philosophy just as all matters of faith belonged to Sacred Theology."⁶ Therefore, knowledge of the physical universe was knowledge of Aristotle's universe.

At its most basic, Aristotle's universe is spherical, the earth resting at its center. The universe's outer boundary is an enormous, rotating crystalline sphere in which the stars are embedded. The sun and moon are fixed in their own rotating crystalline shells. Five "wandering stars" are detached from the outer sphere. The Greeks called these *planets*. The earth, in Aristotle's view, is not a planet, but an object entirely unique.

The moon's shell, said Aristotle, divides the universe into two very different realms. Below the moon's sphere is the sublunary, or *terrestrial*, realm. Beyond the lunar sphere is the heavenly, or *celestial*, realm. These two realms are composed of different material and subject to very different laws. Everything in the sublunary realm is made of the four elements: earth, air, fire, and water. The celestial realm is composed of a single, fifth element, called "aether." Beyond this realm, Aristotle taught, there is nothing, not even space.

Aristotelian philosophy absorbed Galileo as much as he absorbed it. But he wasn't uncritically accepting of everything his professors taught. In fact, Galileo earned a reputation for being obstinate, and the faculty called him "the Wrangler."

Galileo's behavior was probably a manifestation of his disdain for his teachers' demeanor: arrogant and naïvely dependent on tradition. In a later satirical poem against academic life, Galileo compared his professors to the Pharisees, clinging blindly to tradition despite conflicting evidence. Not surprisingly, Galileo didn't endear himself to the faculty of arts in Pisa.

THE CHARM OF GEOMETRY

It was in Pisa that Galileo was introduced to mathematics—but not at the university.

During the winter of 1583, Galileo, a second-year student, found Ostilio Ricci, the court mathematician of the grand duke of Tuscany, lecturing on Euclid's *Elements* to the court pages. These geometry lectures were open only to members of the Tuscan court, so Galileo could not stay to listen.[7] Unbeknownst to Ricci, Galileo hid behind a door to overhear the lesson. This became a habit.[8]

It would be difficult to overstate the *Elements'*—and therefore mathematics'—significance in Western thought. Other than the Bible, Euclid's is the most widely translated book in history.

The *Elements*, or *Stoicheia* in Greek, is a massive, thirteen-chapter collection of geometrical facts—"theorems," we call them[9] (Euclid called them "propositions"). These theorems deal with shapes: points, lines, triangles, circles. There is nothing numerical about them. The *Elements'* impressively logical structure so charmed Galileo that after overhearing Ricci's lectures, Galileo began to study Euclid on his own—avoiding nearly all other subjects. He eventually returned to Ricci with questions. And these questions genuinely impressed the old man.[10]

After Easter 1583, the Tuscan court moved back to Florence, and that summer, while at home in Florence, Galileo met often with Ricci, who became a frequent visitor to the Galilei household. In time, Ricci convinced Vincenzio to allow Galileo to study his beloved mathematics. That fall Galileo returned to Pisa and diligently neglected his medical studies.

After Mass at the Cathedral of Pisa one evening, a hanging lamp caught Galileo's attention as it swung in the breeze. Galileo noticed that while the lamp's arc decreased as it swung back and forth, the amount of time it took the lamp to travel back and forth didn't. The time of oscillation—measured against Galileo's pulse—remained constant regardless the size of the arc. (He would later use his discovery of the pendulum's isochronous behavior to develop a device to measure a patient's pulse—the *pulsilogium*.[11])

For the first time, Galileo turned his attention to motion.

To discover the cause of motion was the goal of Aristotelian science, yet Aristotle did not incorporate mathematics. In his study of nature, he used terms like *faster, slower, heavier,* and *lighter.* He used no numbers. He made up for his lack of precision by providing fundamental causal explanations. Galileo would eventually abandon the search for fundamental physical causes; his new goal would be mathematical descriptions.

꙯⁓꙯

By the end of his fourth year of study, Galileo was in a position to take a degree.[12] Yet for whatever reason, he didn't. In spring 1585, Galileo returned to Florence a college dropout. He was twenty-one and unemployed.

He immediately began looking for teaching posts in Italian universities, meanwhile offering private instruction in mathematics and philosophy. During this time Ricci introduced Galileo to another of his ancient acquaintants: Archimedes. Whereas Euclid had provided Galileo with a mathematical method, Archimedes used that method to describe nature.

Galileo gushed over Archimedes' discoveries, including his hydrostatic principle, and in 1586 he wrote his first complete scientific treatise—*La Bilancetta*, or *The Little Balance*, using Archimedes' principle.

But he still didn't have a job.

THE YOUNG PROFESSOR

Dante Alighieri was a Florentine treasure. His great poem *The Divine Comedy* (1300) is a convenient dividing line between the Middle Ages and the Renaissance. Dante's epic poem is influential, in part, because of the cosmos it presented to Europe.

In *The Divine Comedy*, Dante travels through a modified Aristotelian cosmos, one adapted to the teachings of the Church and Scripture.[13] Outside the universe is God's throne; at the cosmos's center is the earth. Below the earth's surface is hell.

In the intervening centuries, Italian scholars had pored over Dante's work, taking literary criticism so seriously that they even debated the exact dimensions of Dante's cone-shaped hell.

This hellish problem had proved recalcitrant to scholars of a literary and philosophical bent. In 1588, the famous Platonic Florentine

Academy decided to consult someone familiar with mathematics, as well as literature and philosophy. Galileo was chosen.

In his *Two Lectures to the Florentine Academy on the Shape, Place, and Size of Dante's Inferno*, Galileo argued that, given Dante's description, Lucifer's height is 1,935 arm lengths.[14] The Academy was delighted.

Galileo's name was becoming known.

❦

In 1589, the mathematics professor at Pisa stepped down. Galileo was hired to replace him. He was twenty-five, and four years out of college.

But Galileo's attitude toward academic pretension had not improved. He wrote a somewhat crude, three-hundred-line poem—*Against the Donning of the Gown*—satirizing academic ritual. Although the poem was meant only for Galileo's friends,[15] it was circulated nonetheless, winning him few friends among the faculty.

But he also wrote an excellent treatise called *De Motu*, or *On Motion*, in which he combined the study of physical causes with mathematical descriptions.

❦

In the summer of 1591, Vincenzio died at age seventy. Galileo had his father's body placed in the Basilica in Santa Croce. The oldest son, Galileo now bore the financial burden of his family's well-being. Three of his siblings had died in childhood, but there were still his mother, two sisters (Virginia and Livia), and his sixteen-year-old brother, Michelangelo. Galileo's meager salary was barely enough for a single man with no family responsibilities.

Yet for now, he managed. He was able to continue paying for Livia to live at the Convent of San Giuliano until he could ensure her a suitable marriage. Virginia was soon to be wed, and it fell upon Galileo to pay her dowry installments.

In 1592, Galileo's tenure at the University of Pisa was nearing its end. But he'd heard that at the University of Padua—possibly the most prestigious in Europe at the time—the mathematics chair was vacant.[16] Galileo visited in the fall of 1592 and won the coveted appointment, presenting his inaugural lecture on December 7.

A Revolutionary View

Like other men of learning, Galileo was expected to uphold the Aristotelian notion of the planets and their movements. (By the way, it was Aristotle's teacher, Plato, who had originally arrived at the idea of a universe with the earth at the center.) But the notion of this perfectly conceived geocentric universe had been challenged by a Polish church official and astronomer named Nicolaus Copernicus, who put the *sun* at the center of the cosmos. He also said that the earth *moved*.

Copernicus went public with his system in 1543 in his *On the Revolution of the Heavenly Spheres*, usually referred to as *De Revolutionibus*.

And Galileo adored it. Even so, it was only one area of interest to a teacher and man of learning who possessed one of the keenest minds of the era.

Not only was Galileo interested in science; its application to engineering, especially in military applications, also interested him. Around 1597, he developed a device called the "geometric and military compass"[17] that allowed engineers, soldiers, and sailors to solve any mathematical problem they were likely to encounter.[18] He made the compasses in his workshop, on the ground floor of the large house he now rented. The device was so successful that, in 1599, Galileo hired a craftsman to make them full-time.

By this time Galileo's home was also a small boarding house for students and other guests. One person who may have come to live with him was the young and beautiful Marina Gamba, whom he met in 1599.[19] Although they never married, their twelve-year love affair resulted in three children.

Galileo's first daughter, Virginia, was born in 1600, when he was thirty-six and Marina twenty-two. The parish in Padua registered Virginia as "born of fornication."[20] In 1601, Marina gave birth to Galileo's second daughter, Livia, and later, in 1606, to their third child, Vincenzio. (Galileo apparently had no sympathy for future biographers: he named his daughters after his sisters and his son after his father.)

Galileo was a Christian; therefore, it is difficult to reconcile his sexual relationship with Marina, no matter how devoted he was to her. But biographer and Roman Catholic priest Michael Sharratt has written:

> Even inveterate opponents in later controversy did not suggest that by his irregular domestic arrangements Galileo had forfeited his claim to be counted as a good Catholic. . . . "Good Catholic" did not mean "exemplary Catholic": it just meant "definitely one of us," a fact which his many clerical friends, including cardinals, never had any reason to doubt.[21]

꧁꧂

Around the summer of 1603, Galileo and two friends took an afternoon nap in a villa just outside Padua. They slept in a lower room cooled naturally by air from an underground cave. Regrettably,

> [t]his wind, being excessively cold and damp, meeting with their very lightly clothed bodies . . . while they were reposing there, gradually introduced into them so bad a quality in their limbs that . . . all fell into grave illness of which one of them died in a few days, the second lost his hearing and did not survive a great time.[22]

Galileo himself would suffer "up to the end of his life, by very severe pains and twinges that molested him bitterly . . . in various parts of his body."[23]

Most likely, Galileo and his friends had breathed harmful gases, a common problem with such "air conditioning" and the reason these sorts of ancient ventilating ducts were later sealed.[24] From that moment on, Galileo would struggle with his ailment, periodically bedridden for weeks.[25]

WORLDVIEWS COLLIDE

In 1572, when Galileo was a boy, he had seen a bright, starlike object—a *nova*—in the Mediterranean sky. Danish scholar Tycho Brahe, the most acclaimed astronomer of the second half of the 1500s, made exacting measurements of the nova and argued that it was outside the moon's sphere, in the celestial realm. Aristotelians, which included nearly everyone, found the claim scandalous. To them, the celestial realm was eternal and unchanging, so new objects were forbidden. The new object *must* be within the terrestrial realm.

In 1604, after Brahe's death, another nova appeared. Baldessar Capra and his German math tutor, Simon Mayr, were the first people in Padua to observe it. A couple of weeks later, on October 28, Galileo learned of it, too, and was riveted by the sight.[26] For the first time, he began making his own observations and measurements of the heavens.

The public was interested in novas as potential omens, giving Galileo the opportunity to present three open lectures on the subject.[27] His argument was essentially the same as Brahe's, but it found a much larger audience.

Galileo's Aristotelian friend and Paduan colleague Cesare Cremonini immediately launched into his own lectures against

Galileo's position.[28] Hiding behind a pseudonym, a common practice at the time, Cremonini also published *Discourse on the Nova*, arguing that the kinds of measurements we make in the terrestrial realm aren't applicable to the celestial realm, because the realms behave altogether differently.

Galileo responded, in his own pseudonymous *Dialogue of Cecco di Ronchitti*, that the same measurements and calculations hold for any kind of material, even aether.

In 1605, Galileo had a public exchange with another Aristotelian, Ludovico delle Colombe, who argued that the nova had always been there but was normally so small and dim that it couldn't be seen. It was magnified when a small lenslike portion in a crystalline sphere moved in between the earth and the star as the sphere rotated.[29] This was exactly the type of ad hoc Aristotelian ploy that Galileo hated.[30] He responded the following year with his *Considerations of Alimberto Mauri on some Passages in the Discourse of Lodivico [sic] delle Colombe.* After a year of searching, Colombe couldn't find anyone named Alimberto Mauri who might have written the work and correctly inferred that it was a pseudonym for Galileo Galilei.

☙❧

Meanwhile, in 1605, Galileo had accepted an invitation from the Grand Duchess Christina to tutor her son, Cosimo II, in subjects including the geometric and military compass. Three years later, during the summer of 1608, eighteen-year-old Cosimo wedded Maria Magdalena, the archduchess of Austria. Within months, Cosimo's father, the Grand Duke Ferdinando, fell ill. When he died a few weeks later, in February 1609, Cosimo assumed the throne. Galileo began to hope for the position of Tuscan court mathematician.

☙❧

The year before Cosimo became the Grand Duke, spectacle maker Hans Lipperhey had applied to the Dutch government for a patent on a device that could make distant objects appear much closer than they actually were—a "spyglass." The Netherlands denied the patent, but news of the device spread quickly, and by July 1609 Galileo had heard of it. Realizing the military value of a spyglass, especially for a maritime power such as Venice, he rushed back to his workshop in Padua to try to develop a similar instrument.[31]

After first perfecting an instrument that made distant objects seem eight times larger—an eight-power instrument—Galileo eventually made a twenty-power spyglass (the word *telescope* had not been coined yet) and pointed it at the heavens. He made a rapid series of astonishing observations in December and January. In March 1610, he published his telescopic discoveries in the pamphlet *Sidereal Nuncius*, or *Starry Messenger*.

The starry message was very bad news for Aristotelians. According to the philosophers, the moon was perfectly smooth, made out of immaculate aether. But Galileo had seen mountains and craters covering the lunar surface. He concluded that the moon was made of material similar to, and perhaps identical to, the four terrestrial elements, *not* some luminescent fifth element.

This amounted to philosophical heresy for Aristotelians.[32] Nevertheless, the desegregation of the cosmos would have one of the most profound impacts in history on the study of nature. If the heavens were like the earth, then no longer would we need one set of laws for earth and another for the heavens; a single set of physical laws would suffice.

And there was further shocking news for Aristotelians in *Starry Messenger*: Jupiter had its own satellites. Galileo reported that four little stars orbited the much larger Jovian wanderer. These additional wandering stars immediately destroyed the earth's uniqueness.

HONORS AND ENEMIES

In May 1610, Galileo wrote to Cosimo's secretary of state to follow up on his application for the position of court mathematician. He was hired, and in October began his lifelong appointment as "Chief Mathematician at the University of Pisa and Philosopher and Mathematician to the Grand Duke."[33]

We have little information about Galileo's family during this time, but we know that when Galileo moved from Padua back to Florence in September 1610, he brought his nine-year-old daughter, Livia, with him. His oldest daughter, Virginia, and four-year-old Vicenzio were living with their mother in Florence.[34] Marina Gamba married soon after Galileo moved away.

In December, Galileo received good news from the Jesuit front. An old friend, Christopher Clavius, the finest mathematician in Europe, had also seen Jupiter's satellites.

In March 1611, despite his continuing poor health, Galileo traveled to Rome and met with Clavius and the other Jesuit mathematicians. The Jesuits considered Galileo an esteemed scientist, and they honored him with an elaborate academic conference at the Collegio Romano.

While there, Galileo evidently discussed his telescopic discoveries with the man at the helm of the Collegio Romano. Sixty-eight-year-old Jesuit cardinal Robert Bellarmine was the official theologian to the pope and the leading theologian of the Counter-Reformation. An amateur astronomer himself,[35] Bellarmine wrote to Clavius and the Jesuit mathematicians, querying the legitimacy of Galileo's astonishing discoveries. Were his new inventions well founded? he wanted to know.

The mathematicians assured Bellarmine that Galileo's observations were genuine.

❦

While in Rome, Galileo was also honored by the *Accademia dei Lincei*, or Academy of the Lynx-eyed (those who can see clearly in the darkness). The Lyncean Academy, the world's first scientific society, was founded in 1603 by Prince Federico Cesi.[36] The Lynceans feted Galileo at a banquet during his stay, and it was there that someone suggested naming Galileo's spyglass a *telescope*.[37]

The trip to Rome could not have gone much better. Galileo even had an audience with Pope Paul V,[38] and in June 1611, returned to Florence a hero.

But his position of esteem would not last.

❦

In October, Cosimo gave a dinner in honor of two visiting cardinals, Ferdinando Gonzaga and Maffeo Barberini. Cosimo also invited Galileo to debate a philosophy professor from the University of Pisa on the issue of floating bodies. Galileo thoroughly trounced the visiting professor, and Cardinal Barberini, himself a student of natural philosophy, took Galileo's side.

In time, Cardinal Barberini would become Pope Urban VIII.

Barberini had come to Florence to visit two nieces at a local convent. This may have been part of the reason Galileo began to plan for his own daughters—now ten and eleven—to become nuns. At that time, half of "the daughters of Florentine patrician families spent at least part of their lives within convent walls."[39] In fact, Galileo's own sisters had, though they had both left to marry before taking vows. Joining a convent seemed to be the best course for his daughters' futures. They were illegitimate and therefore would have no real marriage prospects. Galileo's frequent bouts with illness probably added support to the argument. Also, Galileo's mother was getting too old to help him raise the girls, and his sisters had too many responsibilities of their own for him to impose two daughters on them.[40] (The next year Galileo brought his seven-year-old son to Florence from Padua.)

The girls were eventually admitted into the Monastery of Saint Matthew at Arcetri in 1613 or 1614.[41] Virginia would eventually take the name Sister Maria Celeste. Livia would later become Sister Arcangela.[42]

❦

Although Galileo's debate over floating bodies had gained him an important friend in Cardinal Barberini, it also resulted in enemies. In 1612, when Galileo finally published his views in *Discourse on objects which rest on water or which move in it*, his conclusion provoked a number of written attacks from Aristotelians.

Another of the new philosophical disputes involved the sun. The Chinese had known about sunspots for centuries, but Europe had just discovered them.[43] The same year his *Discourse on objects* appeared, Galileo argued about the nature of sunspots in a series of letters with a Jesuit astronomer from Germany, Christopher Scheiner. Scheiner believed that the spots were planets. Galileo argued that they were on the sun's surface and changed with time. He wrote his opinion in his *Letters on the Sunspots*, published by the Lyncean Academy in 1613.

SCIENCE VS. SCRIPTURE

In November 1612, Galileo heard that Dominican Father Niccolò Lorini had attacked the notion that the earth moved through the cosmos as being contrary to the Bible. Then in December of the following year, Galileo's close friend Benedetto Castelli wrote to him about a recent breakfast with the grand duke and his family at which Castelli, a Benedictine monk, was present. The philosopher Cosimo Boscaglia, whom the Medicis admired, was also there.[44]

During the meal, conversation turned to Jupiter's satellites, which Galileo had named Medicean stars in the grand duke's honor. Boscaglia acknowledged that these were real. In fact, all of Galileo's observations were real, but his interpretations of them were wrong. In particular, "the motion of the Earth . . . could not be true, . . . since Holy Scripture was clearly against this opinion."[45]

Cosimo's mother, the Dowager Grand Duchess Christina, sided with Boscaglia. She asked Father Castelli to speak on the matter as a theologian and not as a mathematician. In particular, she asked about the following passage from Joshua 10:

Then Joshua spoke to the LORD . . . and he said . . . ,

> *"O sun, stand still at Gibeon,*
> *And O moon in the valley of Aijalon."*
> *So the sun stood still, and the moon stopped,*
> *Until the nation avenged themselves of their enemies.*

Is it not written in the book of Jashar? And the sun stopped in the middle of the sky and did not hasten to go *down* for about a whole day.[46]

Castelli responded that whenever there is a question about the exact workings of nature, we should defer to those who know nature best—natural philosophers—not theologians. Then, *given these findings*, theologians should determine the meaning of such biblical passages.[47]

Although Father Castelli was confident that he had dealt decisively with the issue, Galileo was not so sure. He decided to formulate his own response.

Galileo quickly wrote a letter to Castelli on the relation between natural philosophy and Scripture. His fundamental assumption was that "the Holy Scripture can never lie or err, and that its declarations are absolutely and inviolably true."

> [Nevertheless,] some of its interpreters and expositors can sometimes err in various ways. One of these would be very serious and very frequent, namely, to want to limit oneself always to the literal meaning of the words; for there would thus emerge not only various contradictions but also serious heresies and blasphemies, and it would be necessary to attribute to God . . . even forgetfulness of things past and ignorance of future ones.[48]

It is clear, said Galileo, that Scripture doesn't always speak literally. And depending on the topic, it could be a grave mistake to take a figurative passage for a literal one.

Besides, he argued, Scripture isn't concerned with natural philosophy. Rather, "the authority of the Holy Writ has merely the aim of persuading men of those articles and propositions which are necessary for their salvation and . . . could not become credible through . . . science."[49]

"In disputes about natural phenomena," he concluded, Scripture "should be reserved to the last place."[50] That is, we should see what natural philosophy says about the technical workings of the cosmos, and then interpret Scripture accordingly.

❦

Galileo, revered though he was, was also making enemies among important people who thought his ideas were blasphemous. In December 1614, Tommaso Caccini, a Dominican colleague of Father Lorini's, delivered a fiery sermon against Galileo and condemning Copernicanism. But the Dominicans disapproved of Brother Caccini's tactics, and within a month Galileo received an official apology from a Dominican preacher-general in Rome.[51] He also received assurance from a close friend in Rome, Father Giovanni Ciampoli, that Caccini's sermon was of no real consequence. Nevertheless, Ciampoli advised Galileo not to venture into theology but to stick to mathematics:[52] "Cardinal Barberini . . . told me only yesterday evening that with respect to these opinions he would like greater caution in . . . not exceeding the bounds of physics and mathematics. For to explain the Scriptures is claimed by theologians as their field."[53]

Father Lorini saw Galileo's *Letter to Castelli* and, in February 1615, sent a copy of it to the Holy Office of the Inquisition in Rome, complaining that the "Galileists . . . trample underfoot all of Aristotle's philosophy, which is so useful to scholastic theology."[54] Lorini's letter marks the beginning of the Inquisition's official interest in Copernicanism, and the Holy Office asked its Florentine branch for the original letter to Castelli.[55]

When Galileo heard that Father Lorini had sent a copy of his *Letter to Castelli* to the Inquisition, he sent his own copy to a friend in Rome, Monsignor Piero Dini. Galileo wanted to make sure that the letter the authorities saw had not been altered. He asked Dini to give a copy to a Jesuit mathematician and, if possible, to Cardinal Bellarmine himself.

In March, the bombastic Father Caccini met in Rome with a fellow Dominican who was a member of the Inquisition. Caccini expressed his concern over Galileo's views (although acknowledging that many people regarded Galileo as "a good Catholic").[56] The next day, the Inquisition granted Caccini a hearing. The following is part of his statement:

> Galilei holds these two propositions: the earth moves . . . ; the sun is motionless. These are propositions which, according to my conscience and understanding are repugnant to the divine Scripture expounded by the Holy Fathers.[57]

After its investigation, the Holy Office concluded that Galileo and Copernicanism both needed to be watched.

꩜

But some clergy were in favor of Copernicanism. In January 1615, a well-respected Carmelite friar, Antonio Foscarini, had published a letter arguing that the Copernican view was compatible with Scripture. Bellarmine replied to Foscarini in April, mentioning the 1546 Council of Trent ruling on the interpretation of Scripture. He reminded Foscarini that "the Council prohibits interpreting Scripture against the common consensus of the Holy Fathers."[58]

꩜

Galileo saw Bellarmine's response to Foscarini and smelled trouble. In his *Letter to Castelli*, Galileo hadn't taken the time to appeal to the Church Fathers' authority. So in 1615, Galileo reworked and expanded the letter, resulting in his famous *Letter to the Grand Duchess Christina*— she, after all, had prompted the original discussion with Castelli. Among other arguments, Galileo highlighted the danger of the Church making rash pronouncements about science. Such premature declarations could seriously hurt the Church's witness to the unbelieving world. Galileo quoted Augustine, whom Catholics held in very high regard (he had dealt with issues similar to those encountering Galileo):

> The distressing thing is not so much that an erring man [i.e., the believer] should be laughed at, but that our authors [of Scripture] should be thought by outsiders to believe such things, and should be criticized and rejected as ignorant, to the great detriment of those whose salvation we care about. For how can they believe our books in regard to . . . the kingdom of heaven, when they . . . find these full of fallacies in regard to things they have already been able to observe or to establish by unquestionable argument?[59]

The Inquisition Rules

The grand duke had recommended Galileo to his cousin Allessandro Orsini, who had recently been made a cardinal.[60] Galileo asked Orsini to speak to the pope about Copernicanism.

Galileo knew he'd best have a compelling argument for Copernicanism, so in January 1616, he wrote out this argument in a letter titled *Discourse on the ebb and flow of the tides*.[61]

The following month Orsini presented Galileo's argument to Pope Paul V, who immediately determined that it was heretical.[62]

On February 19, 1616, the Holy Office of the Inquisition asked a panel of eleven theologians to judge the following Copernican theses:

The Sun is the center of the world and hence immovable of local motion.

The Earth is not the center of the world, nor immovable but moves . . . [63]

Although the consultors were experts in theology, they knew neither science nor mathematics.[64] Yet within a week the panel returned their decision: the first thesis, was "formally heretical, inasmuch as it expressly contradicts the doctrine of the Holy Scripture in many passages, both in their literal meaning and according to the general interpretation of the Fathers and Doctors."[65] The second thesis was "at least erroneous in faith."[66]

The Inquisition accepted the consultors' decision, and the pope ordered Cardinal Bellarmine to meet with Galileo privately, to inform him of the Inquisition's position. Galileo immediately accepted the Inquisition's decree. Bellarmine then gave Galileo a letter clearly stating that he might not defend or even *hold* Copernicanism.

In March, the issue moved from the Inquisition to the Congregation of the Index, a handful of cardinals that determined which works were put on the *Index of Prohibited Books.*

On March 5, 1616, the Congregation ruled that Copernicus's *De Revolutionibus* was to be suspended—just when Galileo was publicly defending it—until the proper corrections were made.

Galileo was suddenly in a dangerous position. He was now associated with a theory the Inquisition had condemned. Worse, rumors began to spread through Italy that the Inquisition had charged him with heresy. Worried about his reputation, Galileo appealed to Cardinal Bellarmine, who gave him a written affidavit fully exonerating him.[67] Galileo left Rome and returned to Florence in June 1616, before something worse happened.

⌘

Marina Gamba Bartoluzzi, Galileo's former lover and the mother of his children, died in February 1619. Galileo's mother, Giulia, died the next year.

The year after that, in 1621, the Grand Duke Cosimo passed unexpectedly at the age of thirty. Also deceased by year's end were two of the most powerful men in the Catholic Church, both extremely influential in Copernicanism's condemnation: Pope Paul V in January, and Cardinal Bellarmine that fall. Galileo himself fell ill again early in the year but by midyear had recovered and threw himself back into his work.

⌘

By the fall of 1622, Galileo had finished his work *Il Saggiatore,* or *The Assayer,*[68] a marvel of polemics and Italian prose.[69] Its stated topic was the comets of 1618. But throughout the work, Galileo also contrasted his mathematical science with Aristotle's reliance on obscure semantic and logical distinctions.

Renaissance science had degenerated into a futile game of interpreting Aristotle's texts. If there is any text that natural philosophers should read, said Galileo, it is the Book of Nature, whose author is divine. But without understanding its mathematical language, it is incomprehensible. If so, then only mathematicians can read this text and are, therefore, the only ones who can pass judgment on its interpretations. (Galileo did not come out and say this last part, but simply implied it.)

In October, Galileo sent a draft of *The Assayer* to Duke Virginio Cesarini, who forwarded it to Niccolò Riccardi, a Dominican professor of theology and consultor for the Holy Office of the Inquisition. In February 1623, Riccardi not only approved *The Assayer* but gushed over it.

The following May, Galileo's oldest sister, Virginia, died. But in this sad event, we have the first glimpse of Galileo's greatest joy: his twenty-two-year-old daughter, Virginia, now Sister Maria Celeste. In the first of more than a hundred letters from Maria Celeste to her father, she wrote:

Most Illustrious Lord Father,

We are terribly saddened by the death of your cherished sister, our dear aunt; but our sorrow at losing her is as nothing compared to our concern for your sake, . . . Thus, for the love of God, we pray you, Sire, to be consoled and to put yourself in His hands . . .

Most affectionate daughter,
S. Maria Celeste[70]

All of Galileo's letters to his daughter were, unfortunately, destroyed soon after his trial in 1633. But their relationship was undeniably close and affectionate. Maria Celeste's letters were "full of solicitude for his chronically precarious health" and "often accompanied by little presents of home-made cakes" for her father.[71] When Galileo was old, blind, and under house arrest, Maria Celeste was his chief consolation.

IN DEFENSE OF COPERNICANISM

In August 1623, Galileo heard that his longtime friend, Cardinal Maffeo Barberini, had been elected Pope Urban VIII,[72] head of the Catholic Church. He was now eager to make another trip to Rome to congratulate the new pontiff. Unfortunately, his illness delayed him and it wasn't until April 1624 that he arrived in Rome. The day after his arrival, Galileo met with the pope. Urban immediately sent an official testimonial to the grand duke expressing his admiration of Galileo's abilities.[73] Galileo's stock was quickly rising.

Over the next few months, Galileo met with Urban five more times, during which the two discussed Copernicanism. These talks inspired Galileo to write a book showing that Italy still led the world in science and that the Church opposed Copernicanism only for theological reasons, and not out of scientific ignorance.[74] The 1616 edict criticizing Copernicus had become unpopular among European intellectuals and was an obstacle to converts to Catholicism. This book could help change that.[75] The pope agreed, giving Galileo permission to write about Copernicanism as long as it was in a hypothetical way.

Later Urban presented Galileo with an ecclesiastical pension, making him a member of the clergy, which he remained the rest of his life.[76]

After returning to Florence, Galileo immediately began writing his book, which he referred to as "my dialogue on the tides" because his tidal theory was his main physical argument.[77] It took him more than five years to complete because of his on-again, off-again bouts of illness.[78]

By May 1630 Galileo's health had improved, and he left Florence with manuscript in hand, arriving in Rome two days later.

The *Dialogue on the Tides* was handed over for review by Dominican mathematics professor Raffaele Visconti. Father Visconti soon discovered that the *Dialogue* favored Copernicanism. A number of changes would be required, including a new introduction and conclusion explicitly stating the hypothetical nature of Copernicanism.[79] The pope also ordered that the title be changed[80] to simply *Dialogue*. (Since 1744, it has been known as *Dialogue Concerning the Two Chief World Systems—Ptolemaic and Copernican*.[81]) With the required changes, the *Dialogue* would officially conform to the Catholic Church's standards.

In June 1630, Galileo returned to Florence to make the necessary revisions.[82] Once these were made, he could send the book back to the Lynceans in Rome.

In August, however, the head of the Lynxes, Prince Cesi, died, leaving the Lyncean Academy rudderless. That was also when Galileo learned that the plague had entered Italy and was spreading through the peninsula. In the 1300s it had killed a fourth of Europe. Now it was back, and Galileo couldn't travel to Rome to pilot publication himself. So he got permission to publish it in Florence, which required a whole other round of licensing. The process dragged on for months.

Around this time Galileo began having problems with his eyes, sometimes severe enough to prevent him from reading and writing.[83]

Maria Celeste recommended that her father move closer so she could care for him. She found a villa for rent a short walk from the convent.[84]

Finally, on February 21, 1632, Galileo—now sixty-eight—received word that printing was complete. The *Dialogue* would begin shipping immediately.[85] The effort had taken nearly eight years.

❦

Galileo began the *Dialogue* by assuring the reader that Copernicanism wasn't condemned because the Italians (and the Church) were ignorant of science and math, but for "admirable reasons"[86]—that is, Catholic reasons. They were the very ones that Urban repeatedly gave Galileo, so Galileo made it very clear that he was in agreement.

The dialogue itself takes place among three men: Filippo Salviati is Galileo's main spokesman. He called Salviati's Aristotelian opponent *Simplicio*, the Italian name for Simplicius, the ancient and esteemed commentator on Aristotle. Simplicio's arguments are based on those of Galileo's old friend Cesare Cremonini, and on those of his Florentine enemy, Ludovico delle Colombe. The third man, a fence-sitter, is Giovanfrancesco Sagredo, named after Galileo's closest friend.

The *Dialogue*'s fictitious conversation takes place over four days. On the first day, Salviati begins by undermining important Aristotelian principles, most importantly, the terrestrial/celestial distinction. The moon's surface, for one thing, should convince the Aristotelians that the heavens were fashioned out of the same material as ordinary terrestrial objects.

During the second day, the three men discuss the rotational motion of the earth.

On day three the group considers the earth's annual trip around the sun.

The first three days are defensive, with Galileo addressing the main objections to a rotating and revolving earth. On day four, however, he goes on the offensive and offers what he considers positive support for Copernicanism: "If the Earth is at rest, the tides cannot occur, but if it moves with the motions described, they necessarily follow."[87]

To adhere to the 1616 edict, Galileo closes with an argument he borrowed from the pope, namely, that regardless how good the physical explanation of the tides is, God could have always caused them in any number of ways,[88] and "it would be excessive boldness for anyone to limit and restrict the Divine power and wisdom to some particular fancy of his own."[89]

Galileo uses Urban's argument to reduce any theory of the tides' cause, including Copernicanism, to an instrumental theory, one that may or may not actually be true. It doesn't rule out the possibility that Copernicanism is literally true, but it casts enough doubt on it to refrain from believing it. The *Dialogue*, therefore, ends in complete skepticism.

FIRESTORM

Copies of the *Dialogue* were distributed throughout Europe. In Italy, however, the plague was making distribution difficult. In fact, the first copies to arrive in Rome were the eight that a friend of Galileo's had taken with him. But these eight were sufficient to get Rome talking about the *Dialogue*. And not all the talk was good.

Yet it wasn't until Urban VIII was finally informed of the *Dialogue*'s contents that the firestorm erupted. Among the criticisms of the book was that Galileo put Urban's argument in the mouth of the debate's loser, Simplicio. Worse, in Italian *simplicio* can have the connotation of "simpleton."[90] Galileo vigorously denied that he had intended any such thing, because both *simplicio* and *simplicius*, strictly speaking, mean "good" or "simple," as in "without guile or deceit." Nevertheless, throughout the *Dialogue*'s discussion, Simplicio is cast in a less-than-favorable light; therefore, the pope reasoned, so was he. In Urban's own words, Galileo "did not fear to make sport of me."[91]

❦

The Commission of Enquiry recommended that Galileo's case be sent to the Inquisition. It was clear, the Commission said, that Galileo had argued too strongly for Copernicanism, thereby violating the 1616 edict against Copernicanism.

Worse, in the Holy Office's files on the 1616 decree, a document was found stating that, in addition to Bellarmine's warning to Galileo not to defend Copernicanism, a Dominican commissary had ordered Galileo not to teach or discuss Copernicanism in *any way whatsoever*.

Urban was livid. He never allowed Galileo to speak to him personally again.[92]

Unfortunately, the pope didn't know that Bellarmine had ordered Galileo to ignore the stronger injunction given by the commissary. Regrettably, the only witness to that—Bellarmine himself—was dead.

❦

On October 2, 1632, Galileo received orders to appear in Rome before the Inquisition to account for the *Dialogue*.[93] He was stunned. And he was gravely ill. So it was not until January 20, 1633, that he left for Rome. On the way, he was quarantined for two weeks, finally arriving in Rome on February 13.

There were three hearings, the first two in April. In the second, on April 30, Galileo confessed that, yes, in the *Dialogue*, he had overstated the case for Copernicanism, though *unintentionally*.

Some of the cardinals didn't believe him, and Galileo was questioned more and threatened with torture, though the Roman Inquisition rarely practiced torture.[94] Afterward, he was imprisoned in Rome while awaiting his third hearing.

The final hearing took place on June 21. Then he was asked, upon pain of torture, to state whether he had *really* intended to defend Copernicanism. He said that he had not. Galileo was not tortured, contrary to legend.[95] He returned to the Tuscan embassy to await his sentencing.

⁕

On June 22, Galileo finally came face-to-face with the cardinals of the Inquisition. The official verdict was that he was "vehemently suspected of heresy, namely of having believed and held the doctrine which is false and contrary to the sacred and divine Scriptures."[96] In other words, he was being charged with believing Copernicanism, even though he had indicated in the *Dialogue* that he didn't believe Copernicanism had been definitively proven.[97]

Galileo's famous abjuration came after the sentencing. Kneeling before the cardinals, Galileo read:

> I have been judged vehemently suspect of heresy, that is, of having held and believed that the Sun is the centre of the universe and immovable, and that the Earth is not the center of the same, and that it does move. Wishing, however, to remove from the minds of your Eminences and all faithful Christians this vehement suspicion reasonably conceived against me, I abjure with a sincere heart and unfeigned faith, I curse and detest the said errors and heresies, and generally all and every error, heresy, and sect contrary to the Holy Catholic Church.[98]

Had Galileo refused to recant, the Inquisition would have upgraded the charge to "proven guilty of heresy" and burned him at the stake. But he had recanted and was now silenced on Copernicanism forever; if he ever "relapsed" in any way, he would be burned alive.[99]

Although the official sentence indicated that Galileo was to be imprisoned, his sentence was immediately commuted to house arrest in the Villa Medici.[100] He was released into the custody of Archbishop Acanio Piccolomini, a fervent admirer of Galileo, in Siena.

A PRISONER OF RENOWN

Galileo left Rome on July 6, 1633, arriving in Siena three days later. For Maria Celeste, this was still too far away. In one of her letters, she wrote: "When you were in Rome, I said to myself: 'If he were only at Siena!' Now that you are at Siena I say: 'If only he were at Arcetri!' But God's will be done."[101]

God apparently wanted Galileo in Arcetri. In December the grand duke interceded on Galileo's behalf, obtaining permission for him to live in Arcetri "in solitude, without summoning anyone, or without receiving for a conversation those who might come."[102] But he was allowed to take walks in his gardens and travel to the nearby convent to visit his daughters. Nevertheless, Galileo was still a prisoner.

That winter, Galileo suffered a serious hernia. Worse, Maria Celeste had grown chronically weak during their separation. She became seriously ill, and on April 2, Galileo received the unhappy news that Maria Celeste had died. She was only thirty-three. Galileo fell into a deep depression that nearly killed him.

The previous year at Siena, Archbishop Piccolomini had encouraged Galileo to resume his work on motion to get his mind off his troubles. Galileo now turned to this remedy in the wake of Maria Celeste's death. It was finally time to write his work on terrestrial physics.

While Galileo worked on motion, some of his other works were being translated or published outside of Italy. In 1634 philosopher Friar Marin Mersenne translated Galileo's early work *Mechanics* into French. In December 1635, English philosopher Thomas Hobbes visited Galileo after reading an English translation of the *Dialogue*. The following year, Galileo's *Letter to the Grand Duchess* was published in Latin, giving it a widespread, albeit mainly academic, audience. Galileo was becoming legendary.

❦

In February 1637, Galileo finally finished his life's work on motion— *Discourses and Mathematical Demonstrations Concerning Two New Sciences*. And none too soon. In July he lost the sight in his right eye. Within months he was completely blind.

Galileo's body was suffering the indignities of old age. In February 1638, after receiving permission from the Inquisition, he traveled to Florence for medical care, where he stayed with his son, Vincenzio.

In the spring of 1638, *Two New Sciences* was published in Leiden, Holland—surprising since the Inquisition had prohibited Galileo from publishing anything ever again. Furthermore, when *Two New Sciences* arrived in Rome, Church officials permitted it to be sold,[103] likely because it didn't mention Copernicanism.

❦

In October 1639 a young mathematics student, Vincenzio Viviani came to live with Galileo as an amanuensis. In October 1641, Evangelista Torricelli, a brilliant student of Castelli's, also moved in with Galileo. Soon, despite his extremely poor health, Galileo began dictating a new dialogue, on proportions, from his bed.

Galileo never completed this final work. On January 8, 1642, his body succumbed at last to a lifetime of illness, with Viviani, Torricelli, and his son by his side.

❦

Despite Galileo's immense popularity in Europe, his death and burial were largely ignored.[104] Only a few people attended his funeral.

Galileo had wished to be buried next to his father in the Basilica of Santa Croce in Florence. Instead, his body was placed in a small chamber under the church's bell tower.[105] When the grand duke planned a mausoleum for Galileo, the pope warned that although Galileo died a "good Catholic," it would be improper to honor a man who had been "vehemently suspected of heresy."[106]

However in 1737, Galileo's tomb was built at last, near Michelangelo's and Machiavelli's tombs in Saint Croce's basilica.[107]

Through the years, new discoveries weakened the Church's die-hard mind-set against Copernicanism, and in 1822, under Pope Pius VII, *De Revolutionibus* and the *Dialogue* were ordered removed from the next edition of the *Index of Prohibited Books* (the *Index* itself was abolished in 1966).[108] In a report to Pope John Paul II in 1992, the Catholic Church declared that "subjective error in judgment" in dealing with Galileo produced "mistakes that must be frankly recognized."

The news spread around the world that after three and a half centuries, the Catholic Church had finally rehabilitated Galileo. In his commentary on the decision, the pope reminded theologians and scientists alike of their need "to have an informed awareness of the fields and limits of their own competencies."

In Galileo's time, as in ours, scientific theories and biblical interpretations will always hang in the balance.

To learn more about Galileo, read Mitch Stokes's *Galileo* (Nashville: Thomas Nelson, 2011) from the Christian Encounters Series.

3 | ANNE BRADSTREET
(1612–1672)

by D. B. Kellogg

I'll serve him here whilst I shall live,
And Love him to Eternity.

—Anne Bradstreet

A nne's story begins in Northampton, England, about sixty miles northwest of London. Born there in 1612, Anne was the second child of Thomas and Dorothy Yorke Dudley (b. 1582). They already had four-year-old Samuel.

Thomas was just a boy when his father was killed in battle, fighting for Queen Elizabeth I. His mother died when he was an early teen. Family friends provided a home for the orphan, making certain that he received a good education.

Thomas eventually became a page for a noble family in Northampton. The position was no small thing then; among other tasks, Thomas learned how to oversee an estate.

When he was twenty or twenty-one, Queen Elizabeth I commissioned Thomas as a captain to command eighty volunteers from Northampton. They joined the forces of Henry IV of France against Philip II of Spain during the six-month siege of Amiens in 1597. Henry's forces succeeded in regaining the city from the Spaniards.

In 1620, Thomas and Dorothy moved to Sempringham, where Thomas became the steward of Theophilus Clinton, the fourth Earl of Lincoln.

Sempringham proved to be a wonderful place for the Dudley children to grow up. Samuel and Anne welcomed two sisters, Patience and Sarah, before the move, and within a year, Mercy was born. The children were well acquainted with the earl's family members who lived on the main estate or nearby: the earl's mother, Elizabeth; his wife, Bridget, the Countess of Lincoln; his children; and his siblings Lady Arbella and Lady Susan, among others.

For Anne, having access to the earl's library was a delightful part of her years on the estate. Although their father did not neglect any of his children's education, he took special interest in Anne's. Father and daughter shared a love of books. Anne seemed especially taken with poetry, and it was during this time that the seeds of her own poetic inspiration and skill were planted.

Like most Puritan girls and women, Anne was taught to read so she could better understand the Scriptures and eventually teach them to her own children. Not all Puritan females were taught to write, however. Anne learned to do both well, and existing copies of her handwriting show a firm, clear hand.

The English Scriptures strongly influenced the daily life of the English people then. The Dudleys established a pattern of family prayer each day, and Thomas read psalms aloud and discussed the sermons they heard at church.[1] Anne clearly was paying attention to what she heard, and she took the lessons to heart, even as a young-ster. Years later she wrote that she became aware of her sinful ways at age six or seven. She did her best to avoid lying and disobeying her parents, but she was not always successful. When she felt overtaken with such evils, she could not rest until she confessed all in prayer to God.[2]

In 1534, King Henry VIII had made Anglicanism, instead of Catholicism, the state church of England. Reared as faithful members of the Church of England, in time the Dudley family embraced Puritanism. Briefly described, "Puritanism was a way of life based on the belief that the Bible was the word of God . . . Puritans were the Englishmen who endeavored to live according to that light." The term came to refer to English Protestants who "wished to carry out the Reformation to its logical conclusion, and purge the Anglican Church of forms and ceremonies [such as kneeling for Communion] for which there was no warrant in the Bible."[3]

Around 1624, Thomas Dudley left his job as steward for the Earl of Lincoln and moved the family to Boston, on the east coast of England in Lincolnshire. There they worshipped at St. Botolph's, pastored by Puritan John Cotton.

In time, Thomas returned to his position as steward for the Earl of Lincoln. While living on his estate, Anne was stricken with small-pox. A fever accompanied the illness, and it was apparently a close call. The deadly disease had no cure or means of prevention in the 1600s, and treatment provided little, if any, relief and probably con-tributed even more to the sufferer's weakness.

No painting exists to show us what Anne looked like, but her face must not have been scarred by the lesions. A relative wrote, "There needs no painting to that comely face, / That in its native beauty hath such grace."[4]

While recovering, Anne had plenty of time to think, and years later Anne wrote that "the Lord laid his hand sore upon me" with the smallpox, and she "confessed [her] Pride and Vanity" to him, after which she was restored.[5]

Anne felt the need to confess more to God. The stirrings began when she was "about fourteen or fifteen," when she found her "heart more carnal" and "vanity and the follies of youth" taking hold of her.[6] The stirrings most likely had to do with the handsome, dark-eyed assistant steward, Simon Bradstreet, who was nine years older than she and worked with her father.

Simon came to the estate in 1622 after earning a BA and an MA at Emmanuel College at Cambridge University, where his father, a Nonconformist minister,[7] and many of the "staunchest" early Puritans had also attended.[8] In time, a courtship began between Anne and Simon, and soon Simon asked the Dudleys for Anne's hand. The couple married in 1628. Anne was sixteen. They lived on the country estate of the Countess of Warwick, whom Simon served as steward.

A NEW HOME IN THE NEW WORLD

Anne and Simon Bradstreet settled into a comfortable routine of newlyweds on their own. But in 1630, troubles brewing on the political and religious fronts forced them to make a life-changing decision.

King Charles I, who had assumed the throne in 1625, was opposed to the Puritans. He was a proponent of High Anglican worship, and Bishop William Laud, his man in the Anglican Church, insisted on a strict Anglican ritual, much to Puritans' dismay. They feared that he meant to reintroduce elements of Catholicism into the English church.

The king and Laud began imprisoning some Puritans and taking positions away from others. Puritan clergymen were particular targets, and before 1630, at least three hundred lost their posts—more later.[9]

Within two years of Charles I's accession, some well-to-do Puritans in Lincolnshire, including Thomas Dudley, entertained the idea of planting the gospel in New England.[10] In 1629, they obtained a charter from the king's government for the area that became the Massachusetts Bay Colony. John Winthrop, a devout Puritan, was elected governor.

Simon was uncertain that leaving was a wise move for him and Anne, but the couple prayed together about it. Anne was fearful that she would not see her parents and siblings again if she and Simon remained behind in England. When Simon came to believe that even worse persecution of Puritans was imminent, he decided that he and Anne would join the migration to Massachusetts.

The Puritans who joined the Great Migration (1630–40) to New England came from all forty English counties. Most were "of the professional and middle classes," including estate owners, clergymen, lawyers, young scholars from Oxford, and many farmers.[11] Most, like Anne, never returned to England.

⊙⊶⟨⊶⟩⊙

The ship, named the *Arbella* in honor of its noblest passenger, Lady Arbella, had twenty-eight guns and a crew of fifty or more. Three other ships, the *Talbot*, the *Ambrose*, and the *Jewel*, would be in the group leaving in the spring of 1630 for New England. Seven others would follow later, including the already famous *Mayflower*.[12] Anne and Simon; Anne's parents and her siblings, ranging in age from nine to twenty-two; Governor John Winthrop with two of his sons; Rev. George Philips and his wife; and more than a dozen other passengers set sail from Southampton on March 22.[13] They took their colonial charter with them, to prevent the king from seizing it or amending it to suit his ends. (King James had been able to confiscate the charter of Virginia in 1624 because it had remained in London, and he'd made it a Crown colony. The Puritans were not about to have his successor do the same.)

While they were still in British waters, fifty-four-year-old Thomas Dudley was elected deputy governor.

As they had done in England, the passengers had twice-daily prayer, and the Reverend Philips preached two sermons on Sunday. They also had Bible studies, with which Anne's only brother, Samuel, a 1626 graduate of Emmanuel College, may have assisted.[14]

The *Arbella* dropped anchor on June 12, 1630, in Plum Cove, about three miles from Salem.[15] By June 14, the *Arbella* had anchored in Salem harbor. Over the next few weeks, the remaining ships arrived. By summer's end, the population had increased by about one thousand people.[16]

In July, Winthrop and the other leaders, dissatisfied with conditions in Salem, reloaded their ship and sailed to Charlestown to live.[17] On July 30, 1630, a covenant was drawn up to form the church in Charlestown. The people desired to unite themselves "into one congregation or Church, under the Lord Jesus Christ our Head"—not the Church of England. They would not use the repetitive prayers from the Book of Common Prayer; instead, prayers would be fresh and new.[18] And the Puritans themselves would control church policy and elect their ministers.

Over the next two days, ninety colonists signed the covenant. Thomas Dudley and Simon Bradstreet were among the first. Anne and her mother also signed. Anne later wrote that she was "joined to the church."[19] In 1630 the Charlestown church relocated to Boston, Massachusetts, (the "other" Boston) and became the First Church of Boston.[20]

The Court of Assistants met on August 23 to determine, among other things, the pay for Rev. Wilson and another minister, George Philips. Though Simon Bradstreet was the youngest assistant, he served as the secretary.[21]

The number of colonists decreased as illnesses took their lives. Many had already died at sea. Once on land, the intense summer heat, unlike anything they'd known in England, was more than many could bear. Many areas lacked fresh water, and there were mosquitoes. By the end of the year, more than two hundred new immigrants had perished.[22]

The colony lost others in the fall when about one hundred people, some fearing starvation, packed up and left for England or Ireland. As the winter approached, the notion of starving was more than a possibility. The colonists had to adjust to a diet vastly different from what they had left behind in England.

Sea bounty and wild game were available, but someone had to catch it or hunt it down. As the weather got colder, hunting and fishing became increasingly difficult.

Thanks to the Native Americans, the colonists learned about the value and versatility of corn. Anne's table often bore hominy and succotash, hoe cakes or ash cakes, and roasted corn. Wheat was unavailable early on, so the colonists used rye meal mixed with cornmeal to make bread.[23] Perhaps the most common dish was pease porridge, field peas boiled or baked to mush. Favorite foods were mushrooms and berries.[24] "Our fare be coarse in respect of what we formerly had," wrote John Winthrop; but God made it wholesome.[25]

The weather in December was unusually severe, and they were so short of food that some were gathering and eating acorns. Then in early February the *Lion* returned from England bearing grain, beef in barrels, peas, and lemon juice (to prevent scurvy).[26]

THE FAMILY CIRCLE

In fall 1630, Winthrop, the Dudleys, the Bradstreets, and the rest of the assistants had moved to Boston with plans to go to Newtowne in the spring.[27] Newtowne (present-day Cambridge) was chosen as the capital of the colony.

Anne's expectation of being able to move with Simon into a home of their own had been dashed just after the *Arbella* anchored. The Bradstreets had crowded into a dwelling in Boston with the six members of the Dudley family until houses could be built for them. Anne and Simon had been without a real home since they left England. But at last, in July 1631, the Dudleys, Bradstreets, and six other families moved into the first eight houses in Newtowne.[28]

The Dudleys' house, at the present-day corner of Dunster and

South Streets, was just a few blocks away from the Bradstreets. Anne and Simon set up housekeeping at what is now 1380 Massachusetts Avenue in Cambridge, in Harvard Square.[29] Both were frame houses covered with weatherboarding. Oiled paper covered the window spaces until leaded glass could be shipped from England. Anne's home was not as large as her mother's as wife of the deputy governor, but it was hers to run.

The furniture and other household items were sparse until more came from England. At the least, Anne and Simon had a dining table, a cupboard, stools or benches, and a bed. The stone fireplace, also used for cooking, warmed the house. Early on, Anne filled her lamps with fish oil, and her candlesticks held candles made of bayberry wax.

In November 1631, Winthrop's family arrived in the colony. Anne's brother, Samuel, lost no time in getting to know Mary Winthrop, daughter of the governor. In 1632, at age twenty-four, he married her in 1632. The young couple built a house in Newtowne.[30]

The family circle grew when Anne's sister Patience, age sixteen, married Daniel Denison in October 1632, and they, too, built a house in Newtowne. Daniel was another Cambridge graduate, and he eventually became the major general of Massachusetts Bay and served in the General Court.

೦᎒ᏋᎵᏇᎧᎧ

The first meetinghouse in Newtowne was not built until 1633. Until then, the people of Newtowne went to Boston for services. Anne was unable to travel to Boston for some time, however, because she was again beset by a disabling illness. After her recovery, Anne wrote that she had been stricken by a "lingering sickness like a consumption" complicated by "lameness." At twenty years of age, she was convinced that her mortal race was run and she was approaching "fatal Death." As with earlier illnesses, she felt that God was trying to humble her, but as she tossed on her "wakeful bed, / Bedrenched with tears," she looked up to the throne of the one who sends "help to those in misery," and he healed her, both soul and body.[31] Even as young as she was, Anne was already developing the ability to express thoughts about her spiritual journey in ways that would preserve her legacy of faith for generations to come.

PURITAN PERSECUTION YIELDS POETIC INSPIRATION

Anne's first child, Samuel, was born in 1633, five years after she married Simon. But the happiness Samuel's birth brought to his family was dampened by fresh news. Bishop Laud had become Archbishop of Canterbury and had thus gained even more power to persecute the Puritans.

For example, Laud had Puritan writer and lawyer William Prynne arrested and imprisoned for writing a pamphlet the archbishop regarded as seditious, and both of Prynne's ears had been cut off. Still, Prynne continued to write, smuggling his pamphlets out of the Tower of London. As further punishment, the stumps of his ears were shorn off and the letters *SL* (seditious libeler) were branded on his cheeks.[32] Then Prynne was confined again, and he was not freed until 1640.

John Cotton was another target of Laud, but he managed to escape, arriving in Boston, Massachusetts, with his wife and children in September 1633. A son, named Seaborn, was born on the voyage. Within a few weeks, Cotton was named teacher at the First Church of Boston, where John Wilson was the pastor.

At First Church, there were two sermons (always in English, not Latin) on Sunday, plus weekday lectures. Church members, including children, were expected to attend all meetings. Anne took infant Samuel as soon as she could leave the house.

Puritan sermons warned listeners that they must not lose the constant battle between the flesh and the spirit (see Galatians 5:17).

In her poem "The Flesh and the Spirit," Anne wrestled with that very topic. She set up the poem as two sisters, Flesh and Spirit, involved in a "deadly feud."[33] Spirit was the clear winner.

Flesh was obsessed with wealth and vanity while Spirit lived on meditation. Adam was Flesh's father, but Spirit's Father was from above.

Flesh taunted Spirit by saying:

> *Doth Contemplation feed thee so*
> *Regardlessly to let earth go? . . .*
> *Dost dream of things beyond the Moon*
> *And dost thou hope to dwell there soon? . . .*
> *For riches doth thou long full sore?*
> *Behold enough of precious store.*
> *Earth hath more silver, pearls and gold,*
> *Than eyes can see, or hands can hold.*
> *Affects thou pleasure? take thy fill,*
> *Earth hath enough of what you will.*
> *Then let not go, what thou mayest find,*
> *For things unknown, only in mind.*

Spirit responded,

> *Be still thou unregenerate part,*
> *Disturb no more my settled heart,*
> *For I have vowed (and so will do)*
> *Thee as a foe, still to pursue.*
> *And combat with thee will and must,*
> *Until I see thee laid in the dust.*
> *Sisters we are, yea twins we be,*
> *Yet deadly feud 'twixt thee and me. . . .*
> *Thy sinful pleasures I do hate,*

Thy riches are to me no bait. . . .
For my ambition lies above.
My greatest honor it shall be
When I am victor over thee. . . .
The City where I hope to dwell,
There's none on Earth can parallel; . . .
This City pure is not for thee,
For things unclean there shall not be:
If I of Heaven may have my fill,
Take thou the world, and all that will.[34]

Note, however, that the Puritans were not against having fun. Though musical instruments were not permitted in church, at home they were acceptable. Puritans also approved of sports and recreation, such as hunting, fishing, reading, skating, and archery, but games of chance, card playing, and horse racing were off-limits.[35] Dancing was not encouraged, but wasn't prohibited.

When it came to clothing, Puritans did not exist in a world of black and white, though most ministers did wear black.[36] Everyday clothing was gray, green, or dark blue, and people dressed up for special occasions—within limits. The General Court apparently thought some colonists were going overboard on finery, though, and ruled: "[N]o person . . . shall hereafter make or buy any apparel, . . . with any lace on it, silver, gold, or thread."[37] Among other forbidden clothing were double ruffles and capes. These restrictions had no effect on Anne, who was not known for ostentatious dressing.

As for holidays, Anne and other Puritans did not celebrate Christmas or Easter because Scripture did not sanction either one. And Thanksgiving was not reserved for a single day in the year; there were many "thanksgivings." In October 1633, for example, there was a general thanksgiving for a good harvest and the arrival of several ships.

Another approved and very important civic holiday was Election Day, complete with a procession of government officials. Simon Bradstreet, though still a young man, was elected as one of six selectmen to transact Newtowne business. On Election Day in summer 1634, Anne's father was elected governor of Massachusetts Bay Colony.

To that point, King Charles and Archbishop Laud had left Massachusetts alone for the most part. Then, some "dis-affected" people in England informed the archbishop that the Puritans, "among other wrong-doings, were setting up in America an independent church and state." Hearing this, the royal government stopped ships bound for Massachusetts and forced passengers to take an oath of allegiance to the Crown and to be conformed to the Anglican Prayer Book. Next, a commission, led by Archbishop Laud, was set up to prepare to take over the American colonies.[38] The leaders of Massachusetts started preparing for war against England.

In September, a letter from the Crown ordered the colony to lay its charter before the Privy Council in London, in effect turning over the government to the Crown. Charles I and the archbishop underestimated the colonists' legal expertise and understanding of delaying tactics, however. The colonists responded that only their General Court could act on the request, and its next meeting was not scheduled until September of the *next* year. Each time a demand came from the Crown, the colonists offered another valid excuse to avoid handing over the charter, and time worked in their favor.

The political situation within England soon took the Crown's attention off the colony. Laud was intensifying pressure on Puritans in England, and those not leaving for the New World were digging in to resist. Laud also attempted to make the churches in Scotland forsake Presbyterianism and conform to the Church of England. But the Scottish people opposed Laud and Charles, eventually confronting the king's troops.

ON THE FRONTIER

In the early 1630s, Anne and her family moved to Ipswich, the most remote settlement in the Massachusetts Bay Colony, about thirty miles out of Boston on the banks of a river and near the ocean. Ipswich had fresh water and good fishing, and clams were abundant from the beach. But to the north and west of Ipswich was a "wild wilderness" of "Indian trails" and wooded areas populated by wolves and bears.[39] Until fences were erected, cows had to be watched carefully to protect them from wolves.

Shortly therafter, the young wife of John Winthrop Jr. and their infant daughter died. John Jr. immediately left the colony, causing a leadership void that Thomas Dudley stepped in to fill. Until more houses could be built, the family—consisting of Thomas and Dorothy Dudley and their unmarried daughters, Sarah and Mercy; Patience and Daniel Denison; Samuel and Mary Dudley; and Anne, Simon, and two-year-old Samuel Bradstreet—lived in the good-sized home left behind by John Winthrop Jr. Anne's second child, Dorothy, was born either just before or just after the move to Ipswich.[40]

In 1635, the General Court ordered that in Ipswich no house was to be more than a half mile from the meetinghouse, where ammunition was stored and behind which was a stone fort, because of the Native American threat. The fear of attack was so great that the men took their weapons with them when they went to worship. They also established signals for public alarm: three musket shots during the day; a continual drumbeat or cannon shot at night. If someone called out, "Arm! Arm!" Anne was to grab her children and run to the fort. Anne's brother-in-law Daniel Denison, a former soldier, was appointed military leader of the community.

In 1634, a group of Europeans was killed in Connecticut by a tribe associated with the Pequots. In 1636, several colonists were attacked and killed near Block Island, also in Connecticut, by another

Pequot-related tribe. In retaliation, John Endicott led an expedition in August that burned Pequot homes and crops, but the people had fled before their arrival. Other tribes joined the colonists against the Pequots.

The threat intensified throughout the remainder of 1636 and into 1637, and that year Plymouth, Massachusetts, and Connecticut joined forces and attacked a Native American fort, killing several hundred Pequots. By 1638, the tribe was no more.

In spite of these conflicts, the Bradstreets, Dudleys, and Denisons built their homes and started new chapters in their lives in the frontier environment.

The Dudley and Bradstreet homes were considered the center of the community's action. Simon was well liked and was a significant figure in the colony and town government. He was also a devoted and loving husband and father, and Anne was passionately in love with him. Her fervor was evident in her private poetry to him:

> "TO MY DEAR AND LOVING HUSBAND"
> *If ever two were one, then surely we.*
> *If ever man were loved by wife, then thee;*
> *If ever wife was happy in a man. . . .*
> *I prize thy love more than whole Mines of gold. . . .*
> *My love is such that Rivers cannot quench,*
> *Nor ought but love from thee, give recompense.*
> *Thy love is such I can no way repay.*[41]

She and Simon had three more children in Ipswich: Sarah (1638), Simon (1640), and Hannah (1642). Anne was thirty when she had Hannah—and she was not their last child.

Simon was away so frequently on governmental business that Anne composed poetic letters to express her longing for him. In "A Letter to her Husband, absent upon Publick employment" she referred to him as "her life, her joy."[42] Two other poems, both bearing the name "Another," were equally passionate.[43]

⸎

The year after the relocation to Ipswich, the General Court appropriated funds to set up a college. Another infusion of funds came from young John Harvard, an Emmanuel graduate who lived in Charlestown. He died unexpectedly of consumption, leaving half of his estate to the colonists' college. The college was thus named for him. Harvard College opened in 1638 with nine students, in the newly named Cambridge, formerly Newtowne.[44] Thomas Dudley served on the Board of Overseers of the college until his death.

As the wilderness was being tamed and the colony's young men gained a place for advanced learning, Anne kept writing poetry. She had no expectation of fame as a poet, and surely didn't write with the idea that others would one day read and admire her lines, penned in the isolation of the New World. But verses poured out of her, straight from the heart. Her undated, thirty-three-stanza poem "Contemplations" has received the most critical acclaim over the centuries. The outer world of nature led her to reflect on her inner world and her Creator:

> I wish not what to wish, yet sure thought I,
> If so much excellence abide below;
> How excellent is he that dwells on high?
> Whose power and beauty by his works we know.

Later in the poem she reflected on man's eternal nature:

> Shall I then praise the heavens, the trees, the earth
> Because their beauty and their strength last longer . . . ?
> Nay, they shall darken, perish, fade and die,

And when unmade, so ever shall they lie,
But man was made for endless immortality. . . .

. . . [He] whose name is graved in the white stone [See Rev. 2:17.]
Shall last and shine when all of these are gone.[45]

LIFE ALL AROUND

Anne Bradstreet's "life was proof . . . that creative art may be fur-thered by religion; and that even the duties of a housewife and mother in a new country cannot quench the sacred flame," wrote Samuel Eliot Morrison.[46] Life was all around her in her growing brood of chil-dren, three under the age of five by 1638, and she had to care for them before she set pen to paper. Keeping everyone healthy and properly fed and teaching Samuel to read were just some of the items on her daily to-do list. Her children were seldom sick, but she still had to be prepared for the possibility.

Some colonial illnesses were the same as those in England, but others were new to Anne. One of the most serious and common ill-nesses of New England children was what their parents referred to as a "griping of the belly" accompanied by fever and/or chills, fol-lowed by severe dysentery. There were also colds, influenza, worms, chin cough (whooping cough), scrofula, and croup (the term used for laryngitis, diphtheria, or strep throat). Smallpox epidemics were sporadic, but from 1644 to 1649 outbreaks were almost constant in Massachusetts. Colonists contracted cholera from contaminated water.

A handful of doctors lived in Massachusetts Bay Colony, but for the most part, women, especially midwives, took care of the colo-nists' health needs. New England women had to learn from Native Americans about treatments and new plants and herbs that did not grow in Old England.[47]

Proper nutrition was one way to keep the colony well. By 1638, the colonists' diet improved significantly from what it had been in 1630. Many vegetables and grains thrived, among them corn, lettuce, carrots, parsnips, and wheat. Cheese and butter were common, cod was abundant, and colonists hunted wild game and raised domestic turkeys. In the better houses, beef, mutton, lamb, pork, ham, bacon, and smoked and dried fish were also available.[48] Fruit, including apples and pears, was preserved and dried.

Household baking was reserved for one day a week. On Saturday, Anne cooked the brown bread and baked beans for meals on Sunday because Puritans did not work on Sunday. (This was the origin of Boston baked beans.) Other days she or her servants roasted meat on a spit near the open fire.[49]

In addition to cooking, Anne oversaw the care of the livestock, especially when Simon was away, as well as soap and candle making, sewing, and laundry. Most of the colonists' clothing was imported in the early days, but eventually Anne and the other women were responsible for spinning, weaving, and making clothing of wool or flax. Anne probably did not do most of this work herself because she had servants. Samuel had chores too.

Teaching her children to read and write was another of Anne's duties, one she probably enjoyed. One scholar believes that much of her poetry was a teaching aid for her children, and that may be one reason she wrote it in the first place.[50]

The year 1640 was momentous for the Dudleys and Bradstreets, and for England. Anne had her second son, named after her husband; and King Charles I convened Parliament for the first time in years to raise money to fight the Scots opposing his church-related policies.

Another problem arose for the king with the division of Puritans and Anglicans, and by 1642 a civil war raged throughout the kingdom. The Roundheads, consisting of Puritans, militant Parliament members, merchants, and most citizens from southern and eastern

England, opposed the king. The Cavaliers—Catholics, nobles, about half of Parliament, and most of the northern and western population in England—supported the king. The war lasted seven long years.

Anne felt so strongly about the events unfolding in England that she wrote the well-known "A Dialogue between Old England and New; concerning their present Troubles, Anno, 1642,"[51] in response. Meanwhile, the New England leaders responded by forming a confederation of United Colonies—Plymouth, New Haven, Connecticut, and Massachusetts. Their "Articles of Confederation" were drafted in 1643.

❧

Anne's mother died suddenly on December 27 at age sixty-one, most likely from a heart attack. Dorothy and Thomas had been married forty years. Most of what we know about Dorothy's personality comes from Anne's description in "An Epitaph on my dear and ever honoured Mother Mrs. Dorothy Dudley." She was a "Worthy Matron of unspotted life," a loving mother, and an obedient wife, who was "Religious in all her words and ways." Dorothy Dudley left a "blessed memory" at her death.[52]

The next year, sixty-eight-year-old Thomas Dudley married a widow who lived in Roxbury. Within a year of the marriage, Thomas had another daughter, Deborah, and he and his new wife also had two sons, Joseph, born in 1647, and Paul, born in 1650.

Soon after Anne's mother's death and her father's remarriage, Simon made up his mind to move his family to Andover, yet another wilderness area. Andover was about sixteen miles farther inland than Ipswich and twenty miles or so directly north of Boston. Anne and her family established themselves in present-day North Andover. Few families were in Andover then, so it would have seemed deserted compared to Ipswich, then the second largest town in the colony, with more than eight hundred residents.[53] Yet Anne must have felt some consolation because her sister Mercy and her family had preceded her. Mercy became the bride of town clerk John Woodbridge in 1639, and they lived in Newbury. John was the leader of a group that settled in Andover in 1641. By then, he and Mercy had two daughters, Sarah and Lucy.

The Bradstreets did not move until 1644, but Simon soon became the most distinguished citizen and biggest property owner. He owned five hundred acres in Salem and more land in Topsfield, Watertown, Cambridge, and Boston. In addition to his government work, he built the first sawmill in Andover, and he owned saltworks at Nahant and ironworks in what is now Boxford.[54]

With his comfortable income, Simon was able to build a nice two-story home for Anne and the children, better than the Ipswich dwelling and complete with imported windows.

Just after their move, in 1645, Anne gave birth to a daugher named Mercy, after Anne's sister. Her two boys and four girls now ranged in age from a few weeks to twelve years.

Anne's ability to manage her younger children's education and keep the household running smoothly was well known among family and friends. And somehow Anne managed to extend hospitality to guests, even with her less-than-adequate staff. Many women in Andover followed her example.

In 1647, Anne's sister Sarah died. That same year, John Woodbridge took her sister Mercy and their four children to England, where he was to be the chaplain to the parliamentary commissioners trying to negotiate with the king to end the civil war. Negotiations failed in late 1648, and in early 1649, Charles I was tried for treason, found guilty, and beheaded on January 30. Parliament abolished the monarchy and took over the government of the Commonwealth of England. A series of battles with Charles II, who refused to accept the abolition of the monarchy, ensued.

The Woodbridges remained in England until after the Restoration; John spent the years serving as a minister. The family, having grown by several children, returned to New England in 1673, too late to see their beloved Anne alive again. But John Woodbridge had succeeded in a historic achievement for his poetic sister-in-law in her thirty-eighth year: the publication of *The Tenth Muse Lately Sprung Up in America*.[55]

The Tenth Muse

When John and his family had sailed for England in 1647, he had taken Anne's manuscript of poems with him. He managed to get it—a *Puritan* woman's work, written in *New* England—published by a well-known publisher in England, Stephen Boswell, in 1650.

The 1650 edition of Anne's poems filled 207 pages, and the title page read, *The Tenth Muse Lately Sprung Up in America, or Severall Poems, compiled with great variety of wit and learning, full of delight . . . by a Gentlewoman of those parts.* There were two other major editions of her work before the nineteenth century: the second edition, printed in Boston by John Foster in 1678, contained her additions and corrections and some poems found after her death; the third edition was printed in Boston in 1758. Prose pieces found in Anne's small manuscript book, which had been held by her descendants, were published in *The Works of Anne Bradstreet in Prose and Verse*, edited by John Harvard Ellis in 1867.

In his preface for the 1650 edition, John Woodbridge confirmed that the author was indeed a woman "honoured and esteemed," where she lived for, among other things, "her pious conversation" and "discreet managing of her Family occasions." He also stated that he had published the poems without her knowledge.

Doctor and minister John Rogers, who married Elizabeth Denison, the only daughter of Anne's sister Patience, was the president of Harvard College. His poetic commentary on Anne's work was included in the second edition of Anne's poems. Anne used the second edition's prologue to graciously yet firmly address her critics, asking for fair treatment as a woman:

> *Let Greeks be Greeks, and women what they are*
> *Men have precedency and still excel,*
> *It is but vain unjustly to wage war;*
> *Men can do best, and women know it well*
> *Preeminence in all and each is yours;*
> *Yet grant some small acknowledgment of ours.*

To compose her long poems, all ambitious projects, Anne had to understand science, history, the Bible, and literature. She also had to keep a keen eye on nature and on the political wranglings in both Massachusetts and England.

The *Tenth Muse* begins with four long poems: "The Four Elements," "Of the Four Humours in Man's Constitution," "The Four Ages of Man," and "The Four Seasons of the Year." Each had a religious or moral component.

"The Four Elements" is a conversation of fire, air, earth, and water as they "did contest / Which was the strongest, noblest and the best." Air was last to speak. "I am the breath of every living soul," it declared. The other elements could not top that.

"Of the Four Humours in Man's Constitution" focused on the four humors of choler, blood, melancholy, and phlegm, which have to be in balance if someone is to have good health.

Anne's playful and serious sides are evident in the lines of "The Four Ages of Man" as she takes readers through "Childhood and Youth, the Manly & Old Age."

"The Four Seasons of the Year" lets us hear and visualize the countrysides of England and New England. Anne wrote so well that she has readers sweating in the summer sun and shivering in the winter cold.

Anne ended the group of poems with one obviously intended for her father, signed "Your dutifull Daughter. A. B."

In "The Four Monarchies," Anne marched through ancient history, rhyming all the way. It was her longest poem in *The Tenth Muse* and relied heavily on Sir Walter Raleigh's *The History of the World* (1614).

A change of pace from the long poems was a poem for her father, straight from the heart.

Guillame de Salluste Du Bartas, a French poet, was a favorite of Anne's, and in 1641, she composed "In honour of Du Bartas," in which she wrote that his lines "dazzled" her.

Two other short poems are noteworthy here, because they are so different from the long ones. The first is "David's Lamentation for Saul and Jonathan," based on 2 Samuel 1:19 when David mourned the deaths of both men. The second is "The Vanity of All Worldly Things," wherein she wrote that all is vanity—except

> *that living Crystal Fount,*
> *Who drinks thereof, the world doth naught account. . . .*
> *This pearl of price, this tree of life, this spring*
> *Who is possessed of, shall reign a King. . . .*

We do not know how many copies of Anne's books were sold, but some historians believe that most Puritan homes in New England had a copy.[56] A bookseller catalog for William London noted in 1658 that hers was one of "the most vendible books in England."[57]

A VESSEL FIT FOR GOD

In 1653 Anne's father died. In response, Anne wrote "To the Memory of my dear and ever honoured Father Thomas Dudley Esq; Who deceased, July 31, 1653, and of his Age, 77" and presented her "Lamentations" for her father, in which she listed his merits: a founder of New England who "spent his state, his strength, and years with care / That After-comers in them might share. / True Patriot of this little Commonweal."[58]

Dudley had spent twenty-three years of his life managing the affairs of the Massachusetts Bay Colony, and had lived to see the births of all of her children. Anne and Simon had had two more sons, Dudley in 1648 and John in 1652. Thomas Dudley also saw Anne's oldest child, Samuel, graduate from Harvard in 1653.

Anne's daughter Dorothy married Seaborn Cotton, a Harvard graduate, in the summer of 1654. As a magistrate, Dorothy's father, Simon, performed the ceremony. The young couple moved to Connecticut and then to New Hampshire, where Seaborn served as a minister. Anne's children were starting to leave the nest.

Anne's health, never vigorous, was threatened again when she suffered almost a year of debilitating illness beginning in summer 1656. Her youngest child was just four. "After much weakness and sickness," she wrote, " . . . the Lord was pleased . . . to manifest his Love to me. . . . God doth not afflict willingly . . . [I]f he knows that weakness and a frail body is the best to make me a vessel fit for his use, why should I not bear it, not only willingly but joyfully?"[59]

The next spring, Anne was sick almost the entire time until May 11, with only a few respites. She said, "That which I now chiefly labour for is a contented, thankful heart under my affliction and weakness, being it is the will of God."[60]

In late September she wrote, "It pleased God to visit me with my old Distemper of weakness and fainting, but not in that fore manner sometimes he hath." She trusted that he brought that upon her because of his abundant love for her "straying Soul which in prosperity is too much in love with the world. I have found by experience I can no more live without correction than without food."[61]

Within two months, she wrote a poem about her son Samuel, who had sailed for England on November 6 to be trained in medicine.[62] Anne's poem was really more a prayer asking God to keep him safe and to bring her son back to her. Composing the poem for Samuel must have sparked the idea of writing one about all of her children. By June of 1658, she was ready with comments about her "eight birds hatched in one nest, / Four Cocks there were, and Hens the rest."

⤞⤝

While Anne had her eyes on domestic and health concerns, Simon and the courts had to rule on intrusion into the colony by Anabaptists and Quakers. The General Court ordered the banishment of Anabaptists in 1644 and in 1658 ordered the same for Quakers.[63] The law deemed the Quakers "a cursed sect of heretics" who considered themselves "immediately sent of God, and infallibly assisted by the spirit to speak." They wrote "blasphemous opinions" of "government and the order of God in church and commonwealth, speaking evil of dignities, reproaching and reviling magistrates and ministers" in order to turn the people from the true faith to their "pernicious ways."[64] Anyone caught teaching Quaker doctrine or importing, circulating, or concealing Quaker books could be fined, imprisoned, or whipped, or could have their ears cropped. If they repeated their crime, they could be imprisoned and then banished from the town. If they came back, the penalty was death.

One woman executed in the colony was Mary Dyer. Mary Dyer, a Puritan-turned-Quaker, was ordered to leave the colony for presenting her faith, but she refused. She was whipped, convicted of blasphemy, and thrown out of the colony. When she came back, she was condemned to death. She was hanged in 1660.[65]

The English government took notice of the colony's mistreatment of Quakers. As a result, the well-being of the colony in general and of prosecutor Simon Bradstreet in particular were threatened.

LORD MAKE ME READY

From January to May 1661, Anne was "by fits very ill and weak." But, she wrote, "it pleased the Lord . . . to hear my Prayers, and to deliver me out of adversity." She had barely recovered when Simon suffered a "burning Ague"[66] in June. He got well; then their daughter Hannah nearly died from a fever. That same year, much to Anne's relief, Samuel Bradstreet finally returned from his medical training in England to start his practice in Boston. She had not seen him for four years.

In the spring of 1660, the British monarchy had been restored with the coronation of King Charles II. But the Massachusetts colonists were uncertain what to expect from their new ruler. Rather than wait for him to make the first move, they appointed a committee to develop a state paper to deliver to him. Simon Bradstreet drew up the document, which set forth the rights and liberties of the colony under the charter, followed by a declaration of allegiance, loyalty, and duty to the king.

In time, Charles II's government demanded a response from Massachusetts about the persecution of Quakers and other complaints lodged against the colony.[67] Simon Bradstreet, Rev. John Norton, and John Hull, head of the colony's mint, took the case to England, setting sail on February 10, 1662, and reaching London in April. Immediately Anne started writing poems about her beloved Simon and asked the Lord to keep him safe.[68]

Anne had more reason to fear for Simon's safety in England than perhaps she realized. He and Norton could have been prosecuted there by relatives of the Quakers who had been executed in Massachusetts. Nevertheless, Simon returned safely to New England on September 3, having received "fair promises of a full grant" of their "whole desire in the country's behalf" from the king.[69]

Anne's "Verses on the Burning of the House, July 10, 1666" conveyed her terror and chagrin on that fateful day when a fire destroyed her home. Anne had been revising her *Tenth Muse*, and she lost all of her revisions in the blaze. We do have "The Author to Her Book" that summed up her comments on the first edition. "An Apology" from Anne, which appeared in the second edition of her book, indicated her efforts to finish the Roman section of "The Four Monarchies." She was unwilling to attempt to do more.

A new house, built like the first, was completed in 1667, yet Anne probably did not enjoy it. She suffered physically and emotionally for the remaining years of her life.

Samuel Bradstreet married Mercy Tyng in 1662, not long after his return from England. But a string of heartbreaking losses followed within the next few years. In 1664 Samuel and Mercy had their first child, Elizabeth, who died tragically only a year and a half later. Next, Anne's namesake, Anne, died of a fever when she was three and a half, in June 1669. Then Simon's namesake died at one month old in November 1669.

In September 1670 Samuel sailed for Jamaica, leaving his young daughter, also named Mercy, in Anne and Simon's care. Samuel's wife delivered another child, followed by an agonizing week "in pain and woe, / And then her sorrows all at once did go." The baby, another Anne, died before she did. Little Mercy, born in 1667, remained with her Bradstreet grandparents as long as Anne lived.

Anne and Simon's daughter Mercy was still at home, and she helped her parents care for niece Mercy. Before long, however, she had to oversee her mother's care. Anne suffered more fevers and fainting spells, and her body became frailer and frailer. For the last two years of her life, she was almost an invalid.

A few months before Anne's death, her daughter Dorothy Cotton passed away. Then consumption took Anne herself, on September 16, 1672, at the age of sixty.

We do not have to wonder what Anne was thinking at the end of her life or what she really believed, because she left a record. These writings—seventy-seven "Meditations Divine and Moral," along with a commentary about her faith—appeared posthumously in the 1678 edition of her book.

In the following poem, written August 31, 1669, Anne conveyed how ready she was to join her Bridegroom:

> As weary pilgrim, now at rest,
> Hugs with delight his silent nest . . .
> > his dangers past, and travails done . . .
> A pilgrim I, on earth, perplexed
> > with sins, with cares and sorrows vexed
> By age and pains brought to decay
> > and my Clay house mouldering away. . . .
> No fainting fits shall me assail
> > nor grinding pains my body frail. . . .
> A Corrupt Carcass down it lies
> > a glorious body it shall rise. . . .
> Lord make me ready for that day
> > then Come, dear bridegroom, Come away.[70]

No one thought to keep a record of her burial place, or it has been lost. Some think she was buried in Roxbury with her parents. The North Andover Historical Society believes her final resting place was in the Old Burying Ground in Andover. But no one knows.

Four years after Anne's death, Anne's beloved husband, Simon, now seventy-three, remarried. He was elected deputy governor, then governor of Massachusetts. After more than sixty years of public service, Simon died at age ninety-four, the last survivor of the founders who came from England in 1630. He was buried at Salem.

The young couple who sailed from England on the *Arbella* in 1630 left their indelible marks on the New World, Simon in government, Anne in poetry, and together in their many remarkable descendants, including poets, preachers, teachers, lawyers, writers, and physicians. (Anne and Simon eventually had more than forty grandchildren!)

Today, a stained glass window in St. Botolph's Church, Boston, in Lincolnshire, England, honors Anne by depicting her in Puritan dress. Imagine what she would have thought—pure, humble Anne Bradstreet, memorialized for all time in beautiful multicolored stained glass.

To learn more about Anne Bradstreet, read D. B. Kellogg's *Anne Bradstreet* (Nashville: Thomas Nelson, 2010) from the Christian Encounters Series.

4 | JOHN BUNYAN

(1628–1688)

by Kevin Belmonte

Revere the man, whose PILGRIM marks the road,
And guides the PROGRESS of the soul to God.

—William Cowper

The name of the tiny village of Harrowden, England, comes from the Anglo-Saxon word *Hearg-dūn*, meaning "Temple Hill." It was in this "one-street"[1] hamlet of thatched cottages and whitewashed walls that John Bunyan was born in the late summer or early autumn of 1628. Today, checkerboard cornfields close by bear witness to the region's agricultural past and present. It is in one of these cornfields that a stone marker can be found—a rough-hewn, red stone reminder of Harrowden's greatest claim to fame. The legend on the stone reads simply: "This stone was erected in the Festival of Britain Year to mark the birthplace of John Bunyan, 1628–1688."

But the nearby village of Elstow, one mile southwest, is the place most closely associated with the years of Bunyan's youth. There, in the abbey church of St. Mary and St. Helena where he and his family worshipped, the Norman-era font in which he was baptized still remains. Also in Elstow was a village green. At its center, still present today, is the pedestal and broken stem of the ancient stone market cross around which fairs, relished by the villagers of Elstow and beyond, were held in May.

On Elstow Green, each year of his boyhood, Bunyan would have observed "the merchants, jugglers, actors and rogues who attended the fairs"—scenes that later found such vivid expression in Bunyan's *The Pilgrim's Progress*—a work that would become one of the most important in all of English religious literature. On this green, Bunyan and other young people of the village would have danced and played sports for hours. There were spirited contests of football (soccer),[2] trapball, Northern murr, and spell.[3] A good athlete, Bunyan was particularly skilled in the game of tipcat—a form of rounders (a predecessor of baseball) played with a piece of wood instead of a ball.[4]

Other elements of the local landscape shaped Bunyan's life and fixed themselves in his memory. Elstow Brook is a rivulet he would have known well. He and his family would have crossed it countless times as they walked the mile to Elstow village and the abbey church from their home.[5] He would also have been familiar with the River Great Ouse in Bedford.

Bunyan's family had ancient connections to Elstow. Records show that in 1199 a worthy named William Bonyun rented land from the Abbess there.[6] Other curious spellings of the Bunyan surname appear down through the years. In 1603 the Vicar of Elstow registered one infant's birth under the name Thomas *Bonnionn*[7]— our Bunyan's father.

Thomas and Margaret (neé Bentley) Bunyan were married in the abbey church on May 23, 1627. Their union was blessed with three children in five years, beginning with John. A sister, named after her mother, was born in 1630; brother William, was born in 1633.

We know little about John Bunyan's mother, and we have no description, however fleeting, of her appearance. Of Thomas Bunyan we know little more. We are, however, certain of his trade. Though often portrayed as a tinker, he described himself in his will as a brazier.[8] The original edition of *The Dictionary of National Biography* states that Thomas Bunyan "was what we should now call a white-smith, a maker and mender of pots and kettles."[9]

Thomas Bunyan worked primarily in brass as he labored at his cottage-side forge and workshop. His days started early, perhaps before sunrise. The fire in his forge needed to be stoked or started anew each morning, and kept alight throughout the long, tiring day. There would have been a grimy aspect to his work, more than a little muck, muscle, and sweat as the bellows were worked and the hammer swung. Patience, perseverance, and a willingness to begin again should the tool being forged not look quite right, were needed along with strength and stamina. The brazier's trade was not easy.

Thomas was also a small freeholder, owning the cottage where his family lived as well as the furnace and workshop where he plied his trade.[10]

As children, John, little Margaret, and William were companions and rivals under the same thatched roof.[11] There were hours of play and chores under their parents' watchful eyes—churning butter and tending the forge fire among them.

The Bunyan cottage "stood in a field at the foot of a gentle slope, from which the tower of Elstow Church a mile away was plainly visible. In nearer distance," we learn from Bunyan's Pulitzer Prize–winning biographer Ola Winslow,

> were other thatched cottages similar to that of Thomas Bunyan. By walking to the end of the slope he could see the spire of St. Paul's Church in Bedford, scarcely further than a mile away also. Except for marginal glimpses such as these, however, . . . life was little wider than the immediate cottage neighborhood. Bunyan's End [where the family resided] was a dead-end street, and the village of Elstow, number[ed] no more than sixty families.[12]

"Clearly," Winslow wrote of Bunyan, "the imagination of this gifted boy had been nourished by country fact," such as the "sound of bells across the valley," and with them "wide spaces, secret dells, rocky slopes, fields stretching far away. There is dew on the grass, the music of brooks, a child's fear of dark places, the footprint of animals at dawn, . . . a robin with a spider in its mouth."[13]

Bunyan wrote almost nothing about his early education. That he attended school, though, is certain: "It pleased God," he wrote, to [prompt my parents] to put me to school, to learn me both to read and write."[14] We also know that he developed a lifelong love of reading that first manifested itself in a fondness for a kind of cheap pamphlet known as a *chapbook*,[15] an early form of popular literature. Most chapbooks were small paper-covered booklets, printed on a single sheet folded into books of eight, twelve, sixteen, and twenty-four pages. Often, they were illustrated with crude woodcuts.[16] Chapbooks varied widely in content: religious and political matter, nursery rhymes, poetry, folk tales, almanacs, history, and more.

Chapbooks were produced in astonishing numbers. In the 1660s, as many as 400,000 were printed annually, enough for one family in three in England.[17] Their very commonplace nature explains why so few survive today. Most who acquired the flimsy volumes had no thought of amassing formal libraries—certainly not with books of such indifferent quality. Consequently, they were put to other uses. Some became wrappers for baked goods; others became what contemporary sources called *bum fodder* (i.e., toilet paper).[18]

But some chapbooks ran to considerable length, were well produced, and in some cases were historically accurate. That Bunyan may have acquired one of these better-produced books seems plausible, for in his later writings he referenced Aristotle and Plato. Two particular chapbooks that he read, and referenced in one of his early works,[19] were *George on horseback* and *Bevis of Southampton*.[20] Thus Bunyan was familiar with two of the best-known legends of chivalric romance: the cycle of tales surrounding St. George and the dragon and the far-flung exploits of a knight named Bevis. There is no doubt that what John Bunyan read in chapbooks formed the first of two major literary streams flowing into the magnum opus that became *The Pilgrim's Progress*. Take away the influence of chapbooks upon Bunyan's literary imagination and his most popular book would never have been written.[21]

FEARFUL DREAMS

Bunyan's youth seems to have been somewhat idyllic. And in certain respects it was—else so many of the good things he had known and experienced during those years would not have lived on in the pages of *The Pilgrim's Progress*—faithfully rendered scenes of country life and the winsome folkways of the midlands among them.

But there was another and darker side to Bunyan's childhood. For a time during his preadolescent years, he was subject to what he called "fearful dreams" and "dreadful visions . . . apprehensions of Devils, and wicked spirits, who . . . laboured to draw me away with them." Day and night, he was "greatly troubled and afflicted" by fears of the day of judgment and thoughts of an eternity amid the torments of "fire, Devils and Hellish Fiends."[22]

What triggered such dreams? This much we know: Bunyan was a highly intelligent and impressionable child, with sensitivities that would later reveal themselves to be artistic in nature. He had a vivid, perhaps photographic memory, as his later recasting of chapbook legends in *The Pilgrim's Progress* attests. He may also have heard an apocalyptic message or two from an overzealous preacher, or read a particularly lurid religious broadside or printed sermon.[23] If so, horrific images conjured in his imagination could have imprinted themselves in deeply troubling and persistent ways. A boy deferential to and trusting of his elders could easily place too much credence in dire statements by an authority figure or the apocalyptic pronouncements of a broadside. A boy like Bunyan might well have believed that such things were *always* true and real.

Lord Macaulay (d. 1859) felt it a shame "that a lad to whom nature had given a powerful imagination and sensibility which amounted to a disease, should have been early haunted by religious terrors."[24] He was more right than he knew. Bunyan's "sensibility" did in fact amount to a disease. While terms such as "clinical depression" were not used in Macaulay's time, the condition known as melancholy was recognized and was often associated with a pervasive sense of religious anxiety. This appears to have been the condition to which Bunyan was periodically subject throughout his life, though we learn from Bunyan himself: "A while after [the first manifestations], these terrible dreams did leave me, which also I soon forgot, for my pleasures did quickly cut off the remembrance of them, as if they had never been."[25] In this way, Bunyan's childhood was not without a measure of grace.

❦

On August 22, 1642, right around John's fourteenth birthday, Charles I raised the royal standard at Nottingham and gathered several thousand loyalist soldiers to his banner. In opposition, forces loyal to Parliament, some ten thousand soldiers in all, rallied to the standard raised by Robert Devereux, 3rd Earl of Essex. On September 23, the two armies met for the battle of Powick Bridge. There a force of about one thousand royalist cavalry under the command of Prince Rupert defeated a Parliamentary cavalry detachment. So commenced a war that would last four long and tumultuous years, until Charles I's surrender to the Scottish army at Southwell on May 5, 1646.

In the meantime, John was becoming a man.

In June 1644, when Bunyan was just sixteen, he suffered the first great sorrow of his life: his mother died after a sudden onset of illness.

Only one month later, his father remarried.[26] Thomas Bunyan can be forgiven for this. He had two younger children to raise; necessity compelled him.

But John, too young to appreciate his father's plight, resented his father's decision.[27] He could only feel that his father had remarried with indecent haste and committed an indignity upon his mother's memory. To make matters worse, around the same time, his sister Margaret died, perhaps in her early teens.

How Bunyan weathered all of this we do not know. He never wrote of the loss of his mother and sister. We do know, however, that another great change would come within a matter of months.

A Soldier's Life

For Bunyan, the ravages of the first English civil war had remained the stuff of disturbing yet distant news—until the war came to his doorstep. Persuasive historical evidence suggests that he was drafted into the parliamentary army around November 30, 1644, just a few months after the deaths of his mother and sister.[28] He would remain in the army for the next three years.

He began his service under the command of Colonel Richard Cockayne and remained there until March 8, 1645. He then appears to have been transferred to the command of Major Robert Bolton, where he remained until September 1646.[29] Bunyan concluded his military service under Captain Charles O'Hara on July 21, 1647.[30]

According to the muster rolls, Bunyan was one of 128 "centinels" (or privates) in Cockayne's company.[31] Bunyan and his fellow centinels were in for a rude awakening as they entered the ranks. The conditions faced by Cockayne's troops, under the overall command of Sir Samuel Luke, were grim. Just a few weeks before Bunyan's arrival, Luke had written to his superiors saying that without the provision of much-needed funds, his soldiers faced starvation. His letter closed ominously, with a blunt statement of his concerns about a possible mutiny.[32]

Surviving records indicate that between October 12, 1644, and November 26 of the same year, the numbers under Luke's command were increased by the arrival of some two hundred foot soldiers, of whom Bunyan was almost certainly one. If so, he would have become instantly aware of the hardships Luke's men endured.[33] Low morale and insubordination were constant concerns. In January 1645 Colonel Cockayne reported to his superiors that his troops were losing respect for him and his fellow officers. It is easy to see why. The soldiers were owed three and a half months of back pay. Many were forced to pawn their clothes and other personal possessions to buy bread. And townsfolk had begun to refuse to house soldiers, because the soldiers had no money. For those who could find lodging, it was not unusual for soldiers to have to sleep "3 and 3 in a bed."[34] Beyond this, there was a serious shortage of boots, saddles, and horseshoes for the cavalry, as well as certain types of weapons, including muskets and pikes. The army in which Bunyan served was in dire straits.

In early February 1645 Luke's worst fears were realized. Food was so scarce for Luke's men that they could barely be supplied with the horsemeat and corn they had been reduced to eating, and a number of troops and dragoons mutinied. This uprising was, however, quelled quickly, and in the meantime, Bunyan was receiving his basic training.

Troops from the Newport garrison, which included Bunyan, took part in two major engagements in May and early June 1645: the parliamentary siege of Oxford and an attack by royalist troops upon the city of Leicester. Bunyan described a narrow brush with death during the Oxford siege:

> When I was a Souldier, I with others were drawn out to go to
> such a place to besiege it; but when I was just ready to go, one of

the company desired to go in my [place], to which, when I had consented he took my place, and coming to the siege, as he stood Sentinel, he was shot in the head with a Musket bullet and died.[35]

It was a mysterious providence—one Bunyan never forgot. His life had been spared in a remarkable way—though he did not yet know why. The awareness of this stayed with him far beyond the end of his military service in July 1647.

Spiritual Awakening

In January 1649, when Bunyan was twenty, Charles I was beheaded outside the palace of Whitehall. This regicide was followed by the establishment of the Commonwealth of England. A republic had replaced a monarchy. Sometime during this same year, Bunyan married. We do not know the exact date because no record of the ceremony exists. Worse, we have no record of his bride's name or birthplace. History has consigned this good lady to a sad oblivion.

Bunyan was himself partly to blame, since he never mentioned his wife's name in any published works or surviving manuscripts. *"This woman and I,"* he wrote, "came together as poor as poor might be, not having so much household stuff as a dish or spoon betwixt us both."[36]

"This woman" died young, so the most likely explanation for Bunyan's silence is that her death was too painful to speak of. But it is cheering to know that several years passed before Bunyan and his wife were parted. Based on such writings as have survived, there is every reason to think these were largely happy years,[37] in their little thatch-roofed cottage in Elstow.

Bunyan followed in his father's footsteps as a maker of pots, pans, and household utensils, and he was well known in and around Elstow and Bedford. Most area villagers worked on land owned by the local gentry. But as a tradesman, reddish-haired Bunyan worked for himself.

Despite Bunyan's slender inventory of possessions, his wife had brought something of a dowry with her: two books once owned by her father, a man who was "counted godly."[38] These books were to have a telling influence on Bunyan's life, even shaping its outlook. Their titles were *The Plain Mans Path-way to Heaven* and *The Practice of Piety*, and of them Bunyan wrote, "These books . . . though they did not reach my heart to awaken it . . . did beget within me some desires to Religion."[39] He had not been particularly religious early in life, but slowly, in ways of which he was only half-aware, he began to evaluate his heart and wrestle with the great questions about "the chief end of man."

❧

In his autobiography *Grace Abounding*, Bunyan referred to a time of spiritual awakening. It began in 1650, the year in which his first child, a blind daughter named Mary, was born. Prior to this, he wrote,

> [I would] go to Church twice a day, and . . . very devoutly both say and sing as others did; yet retaining my wicked life: but withal, I was so overrun with the spirit of superstition, that I adored, and that with great devotion, even all things (both the High-place, Priest, Clerk, Vestments, Service, and what else) belonging to the Church.[40]

This period of outward conformity lasted for about a year (from 1649 to 1650), until he heard a sermon on Sabbath observance that prompted a deep sense of reflection, tinged with feelings of guilt over the team sports he loved and the work he sometimes performed on the Sabbath. He recalled:

I fell in my conscience under his sermon, thinking and believing that [the minister] made that sermon on purpose to show me my evil doing . . . [A]t that time I felt what guilt was, though never before, that I can remember; [I] went home when the sermon was ended, with a great burden upon my spirit.[41]

But these feelings, however much Bunyan remembered them later, passed within a matter of hours. True, they had cast a pall over his "best delights,"[42] but "before I well dined," he wrote, "the trouble began to go off my minde . . . [M]y heart returned to its old course . . . I shook the Sermon out of my mind, and [returned] to my old custom of sports and gaming . . . with great delight."[43]

To the modern ear, it seems strange that any sense of guilt would attach itself to a habit of playing sports on Sunday (think American Sunday football). But in Bunyan's time religion dominated daily life in ways that are alien to us now. The Anglican faith was the state religion. Even if one was not particularly religious, attendance at Sunday services was compulsory. From baptism, schooling, and marriage to one's funeral and burial, week in and week out, from cradle to grave, the church's omnipresent influence was felt.

That very same day, Bunyan joined his friends for a game of tip-cat. But when his second turn to bat came, he suddenly had a vision of Christ "looking down upon me . . . very hotly displeased,"[44] and he felt his heart "sink in despair."[45] He felt himself to be damned.

He continued desperate and despairing for a month or more. Then one day, while standing before a neighbor's shop window, he found himself "cursing, swearing, and playing the Mad-man."[46] (After several years' service in the army, Bunyan could likely turn the air blue when the mood took him.)

The shopkeeper's wife overheard him, and she came outside and let loose a fusillade of scorn and reproach. "She told me," Bunyan recalled, "that I was the ungodliest fellow for swearing that ever she heard in all her life; and that I [would] spoil all the youth in a whole town, if they came . . . in my company. At this reproof I was silenced, and put to secret shame."[47]

Embarrassed and surprisingly repentant, Bunyan immediately ceased to curse and swear. In the days that followed, his neighbors were astonished by the marked alteration in his behavior. Not long afterward, he met a man "who . . . did talk pleasantly of the Scriptures." This appealed to him, and he "began to take great pleasure" in reading his Bible. He found himself drawn to the Ten Commandments, the careful observance of which, he thought, could furnish "my way to Heaven." For "about a twelve-month," he later recalled, "I thought I pleased God as well as any man in England."[48]

One day, in 1650, Bunyan's trade took him to Bedford, where he happened upon "three or four poor women sitting at a door in the sun, and talking about the things of God." Curious, he drew closer. "Their talk," he wrote,

> was about a new birth [and] the work of God on their hearts . . .
> they talked how God had visited their souls with His love in the
> Lord Jesus, and with what words and promises they had been
> refreshed, comforted, and supported against the temptations of
> the Devil . . . and how they were borne up under his assaults . . .
> they spake with such pleasantness of Scripture language, and
> with such appearance of grace in all they said, that they were to
> me as if they had found a new world.[49]

"[After] I had heard . . . [the women's discussion]," he wrote, "I left them, and went about my employment again: but . . . I was greatly affected with their words."[50]

Bunyan resolved to seek out others like these women. In a short time, this brought him to the congregation of John Gifford.

John Gifford was a remarkable man, and his story is fascinating.

A onetime major in the king's army, a fugitive from parliamentary forces, a drinker, and a heavy gambler, Gifford somehow acquired and read a book written by the Puritan Robert Bolton—a man once very much like himself, who had experienced a dramatic conversion. In time, Gifford was converted too, and in 1653 he became the unlikely pastor of the nonconformist church in Bedford where John Bunyan began attending.

Bunyan had served in the parliamentary army; Gifford was a royalist officer. As former soldiers on opposite sides of a war that had savaged Britain, both bore scars that were among the most difficult to heal, and the beguiling grace that had transformed Gifford's life contrived to bring them together. Gifford became Bunyan's mentor.

The year Bunyan began attending the Bedford church, 1653, was the same year Oliver Cromwell became Lord Protector of England. Sadly, Gifford died in early September 1655, leaving only about two years for Bunyan to benefit from his pastoral counsel. Nonetheless, Gifford's doctrine, Bunyan wrote later in *Grace Abounding*, "was much for my stability."

Bunyan did not gain a lasting stability, or peace, until some two years after Gifford's death. But that there was any stability at all during the stormy periods of his conversion owed much to the extraordinary man whom he would later immortalize in *Pilgrim's Progress* as Evangelist.

Between John Gifford's death in September 1655 and the resolution of Bunyan's spiritual turmoil in late 1657 or early 1658, Bunyan suffered greatly.[51] Hellish temptations beset him, and at times he was convinced he had committed the unpardonable sin and was irretrievably damned. During this time, he developed worrying symptoms of consumption[52] and thought he would not survive.[53]

How long Bunyan's symptoms lingered is not known. But near the end of his illness, his spiritual turmoil finally ended. One evening, as he sat by the fire, he had an epiphany: "I suddenly felt this word to sound in my heart, 'I must go to Jesus.' . . . At this my former darkness . . . fled away, and the blessed things of heaven were set within my view." His thoughts were drawn to Scripture, and as he opened his Bible and read, the words in each place to which he turned were words of comfort and tranquility, not of condemnation.

"That night," he remembered, "was a good night to me . . . I could scarce lie in my bed for joy, and peace, and triumph."[54] The memory of these feelings later formed the basis of one of the most cherished passages from *The Pilgrim's Progress*.[55]

IN THE PULPIT

For some time before he finally struggled free of his own slough of despond, Bunyan had been preaching. It had begun innocently enough, when in 1655 he was asked to "speak a word of exhortation" to the members of the Bedford church. Though he was hesitant, he and those who heard him soon discovered that he had a gift.

Bunyan's skills as a writer reveal that he had a ready wit and could tell a good story. He was also tall and good-looking, and so had an impressive "pulpit presence." His charm and genuine regard for people commended him to churchgoers, as surviving recollections of his ministry attest. These accounts reveal that people felt themselves to be "affected and comforted" when he spoke. And what an evangelist! When he first began attending the Bedford church, he wrote,

> Some of them [his townsfolk] would follow me . . . Yea, almost all
> the town at first at times would go out to hear at the place where
> I found good. Yea, young and old . . . Some of them perceiving
> that God had mercy on me, came crying to Him for mercy too.[56]

John Gifford must have wondered what he had on his hands when Bunyan and a small but dedicated entourage from Elstow started attending his services!

When Bunyan began preaching, his sermons were marked by clarity and freedom of speech. He used parables and homely illustrations to describe spiritual truths in a way that lingered in the memory. Then, too, there was a power to his address. At times Bunyan testified to the feeling that he spoke "as if an Angel were at his back."[57] No wonder those who heard him responded warmly.

Even so, the fledgling preacher was subject to intense and prolonged periods of depression and despair. This suggests that he suffered from a chronic psychiatric condition known as *dysthemia*[58]— a mood disorder marked by poor appetite, insomnia, listlessness, low self-esteem, and hopelessness.[59] All the same, he trudged on, and soon the Bedford church formally commissioned him for the task of public preaching, the same year he had preached his first "word of exhortation."[60]

In the summer of 1658, Bunyan published one of his early works, a volume with the ominous-sounding title *A Few Sighs from Hell, or the Groans of a Damned Soul, &c., by that poor and contemptible servant of Jesus Christ, John Bunyan*. This book, according to its title page, was printed in London "by Ralph Wood for M. Wright, at the King's Head in the Old Bailey."

In spite of its title, *A Few Sighs from Hell* was a plea with the reader to embrace the gracious and merciful offers of salvation in Christ presented in Scripture. Bunyan felt he had escaped the fate described in the book's title, and now he wished to rescue his readers from the fate he had so narrowly avoided. If his depictions of hellish torments were graphic (and they are), they were intended to underscore how precious a thing it was to be rescued.

That same year, at about the same time, Oliver Cromwell died and was succeeded by his son Richard. But closer to home, this was when Bunyan's dear, nameless wife also died. Now Bunyan would have to be both father and mother not only to little Mary, but also to three more children born after her.

Still grieving, in a matter of months he met and married a young woman named Elizabeth, whom he described in his will as his "well-beloved wife."[61] After all he had come through, she was an unlooked-for mercy. Elizabeth was a devoted, caring, and steadfast woman, willing to assume the daunting task of becoming a step-mother to four children who were not her own. Nine-year-old Mary, blind from birth, would require special care. This Elizabeth promised to give, as she would do her best to help raise Mary's siblings, Elizabeth, John, and Thomas.[62]

Bunyan's domestic happiness notwithstanding, storm clouds had gathered anew on the political horizon. On May 25, 1659, Richard Cromwell was forced to resign as Lord Protector of England, and George Monck, head of the army, briefly assumed power. Within a matter of months, he was deposed and the monarchy restored when in May 1660, Charles II became king, resuming the throne his father had lost. The period known as the Restoration had begun.

In September 1660, John Burton, Gifford's successor as pastor of the Bedford congregation, died. This faithful body of noncon-formists—dissenters against the established Anglican Church—was now without a minister. But worse yet, almost as soon as Charles resumed the throne, a crackdown on religious dissent began. In early November, Bunyan was arrested.[63]

According to biographer John Brown, on November 12, 1660, Bunyan saddled his horse and rode over to the little hamlet of Lower Samsell, about thirteen miles south of Bedford,[64] where he was to hold a religious service in a farmhouse belonging to a fellow dissenter.

He arrived to a subdued reception. Those already gathered told him that the neighboring magistrate, Francis Wingate, had issued a warrant for his arrest. The owner of the house then suggested that perhaps it would be best not to hold the meeting. Instead, he ought to make good his escape, for his apprehenders were on their way. Bunyan replied, "By no means I will not stir, neither will I have the meeting dismissed." Not only was he convinced that his cause, the preaching of God's Word, was good, but also, he wrote, "[It] came into my mind that . . . if I should now run, and make an escape, it [would] be of a very ill savour in the country. For what [would] my weak and newly converted brethren think?"[65] And what of people outside the dissenting community, or unbelievers? He feared that if he fled, they would take occasion to blaspheme the gospel.[66]

Soon after, he called the meeting to order, and then asked them to open their Bibles. Suddenly, the authorities burst in, ordering him to stop. They were going to take him away.

Bunyan must have asked them to wait a moment, for he recorded his parting words to the little congregation:

> I spake some few words of counsel and encouragement to the people, declaring to them, that . . . [though] we were prevented of our opportunity to speak and hear the Word of God, . . . they should not be discouraged, for it was a mercy to suffer upon so good account. For we might have been apprehended as thieves or murderers, or for other wickedness; but blessed be God it was not so, but we [were to] suffer as Christians for well doing.[67]

GOD WAS THERE

Bunyan was thirty-two when he was imprisoned. Elizabeth, his second wife, was expecting their first child. Mary was ten; Elizabeth, six; and John and Thomas, mere babies. We have scant record of Elizabeth's feelings when her husband was seized, only the sad fact that the shock of this news induced a miscarriage.

Bunyan was charged that he had "devilishly and perniciously abstained from coming to church to hear divine service"—in other words, he had refused to attend services of the Church of England—and further, that he was "a common upholder of several unlawful meetings and conventicles [secret, unauthorized religious meetings] . . ."[68] The indictment was based on a long-unenforced Elizabethan statute from 1593 that had been drawn up against "seditious sectaries and disloyal people."[69]

Initially, Sir John Kelynge, chairman of the Sessions, sentenced him to three months in prison.[70] Once this sentence was served, Bunyan would either agree to attend services in the Church of England or be banished from the country. If he were expelled but returned without the king's permission, he would be hung. Bunyan was taken to the Bedford County jail.[71] He would remain there for twelve years.

Early in his imprisonment Bunyan suffered greatly. "When but a young prisoner," he wrote, it "lay much upon my spirit . . . that my Imprisonment might end at the Gallows."[72] His greatest fear was not so much that he might thus meet his end, but that in dying, he might not show undaunted Christian courage, thus bringing reproach upon God. In the midst of his anguish he cried out to God, and when he did, he seemed to find a courage not his own. It occurred to him that he might even upon the scaffold give the message of life to the crowd who came to see him die. *"If God will but convert one soul by my . . . last words,"* he thought, *"I shall not count my Life thrown away nor lost."*[73]

The threat of the gallows was never to be realized. Instead, a lesson was learned. At Bunyan's point of greatest need, God was there to meet him. That thought would later infuse *The Pilgrim's Progress.*

~~~

The county jail (or "gaol" in British English) where Bunyan spent the next twelve years of his life stood on the corner of High Street and

Silver Street. Two dungeons lay underground, one situated in total darkness. Rooms above ground were eight and a half feet high, and prisoners slept on straw in unheated cells.[74]

Bunyan's prison possessions were few but precious. An account penned by a visitor whose name has not survived wrote that Brother Bunyan's library consisted of just two books, a Bible and *Foxe's Book of Martyrs*.[75] The Bedford church doubtless provided Bunyan what aid they could—probably food and such items of clothing as they could spare. But, as John Brown wrote, "they could not do all they would. For many of them were themselves at various times his fellow-prisoners in Bedford gaol; others had to flee from their homes, to avoid arrest; and many were stripped of their possessions to pay the ruinous fines imposed upon them as Nonconformists."[76]

Early on, there were some mitigations of Bunyan's confinement; his jailer granted him a substantial measure of liberty over a period of six months in 1661 and 1662, during which, said he, "I followed my wonted course of preaching, taking all occasions that was put into my hand to visit the people of God." On another occasion he wrote: "Having somewhat more liberty I did go to see Christians at London."[77]

Such extraordinary liberty could not last. The authorities who were so violently opposed to Bunyan got wind of what was going on. Thereafter, Bunyan was "under cruel and oppressive gaolers in an uncomfortable and close prison,"[78] where he suffered physically and mentally. He described some of his feelings during these years in his *Prison Meditations*, written during the winter of 1662–63.[79]

But there were still some concessions, perhaps the greatest being that he was granted permission to work to support his family. He was not allowed to leave prison, but within its walls he was permitted to make "many hundred gross of long Tagg'd laces" for shoes, and so provide much-needed income for his wife and children.

From the very beginning of Bunyan's confinement, he felt "like a man who at the bidding of conscience was pulling down his house upon the heads of those he loved best." This was the cruelest part of the suffering he endured. Perhaps no other passage from his writings was written with greater feeling than this:

> The parting with my wife and poor children hath often been to me, in this place, as the pulling the flesh from the bones; and [I] have often brought to my mind the many hardships, miseries, and wants that my poor family was like to meet with . . . especially my poor blind child, who lay nearer my heart than all besides. Oh, the thoughts of the hardships I thought my poor blind one might go under, would break my heart to pieces!—Poor child! . . . Thou must . . . beg, suffer hunger, cold, nakedness, and a thousand calamities, [and] I cannot endure [that even] the wind should blow upon thee.[80]

Yet somehow, separated from his family and confined within walls of thickset stone, John Bunyan discovered a grace that moved him to write. *The Pilgrim's Progress,* penned entirely in prison, was a work of art. Part knightly romance, part mystery play,[81] on the most basic level it was a quest story: recounting the journey of a pilgrim named Christian, amid great trials, to find the Celestial City.

A Timeless Masterpiece

The best scholarly research indicates that the bulk of the First Part of *The Pilgrim's Progress* was written during the final five years of Bunyan's first, twelve-year imprisonment, perhaps beginning sometime in 1667 and ending around March 1772, when he was released.[82] He then enjoyed four years of freedom, but was imprisoned again in 1676, for about six months. During this time, Bunyan may have made final revisions to the First Part—and perhaps wrote its Preface.[83]

The most reliable historical evidence indicates that around mid-December 1676 he was arrested by the sheriff of Bedfordshire.[84] Bunyan had neglected a summons to appear before the archdeacon's court in Bedfordshire, which, as a nonconformist, he was required by law to do. One of his old enemies, William Foster, obtained a writ against him calling for his arrest.

Once Bunyan was seized, several friends rallied to him. John Owen, the influential Puritan leader, appealed to the Bishop of Lincoln to secure Bunyan's release. Although it took six or seven months, at last Bunyan was set free.

In June, when Bunyan emerged from his cell, the manuscript for the First Part of The Pilgrim's Progress was complete. It was a book unlike any other he had written.[85]

⌒⌒⌒⌒

The Second Part of The Pilgrim's Progress is as beloved a story as there is in Western literature, and we owe its composition (at least in part) to a fraud, an unexpected rivalry, and a failed first attempt by Bunyan to craft a sequel.

Bunyan had not expected the striking success The Pilgrim's Progress had experienced, going through three editions in a year.[86] When the third edition was published in 1679, Bunyan began earnest work on The Life and Death of Mr. Badman, which he intended to be the sequel to The Pilgrim's Progress. He wrote quickly; the resulting manuscript was published in 1680. (He followed this work with The Holy War in 1682.)

Unlike Pilgrim's Progress, centered on "him that was going to Heaven," The Life and Death of Mr. Badman focused on "the Life and Death of the Ungodly and of their travel from this world to Hell."[87] But the public didn't like it. They wanted to revisit the world of The Pilgrim's Progress, not a world that marked the descent of a soul that was damned.

Not that *Badman* was a substandard book. Far from it. It has been hailed by subsequent critics as a precursor to the modern novel and was thus an important artistic achievement. But ultimately, so far as Bunyan's newfound audience was concerned, Badman's story was not acceptable. This was made painfully clear to Bunyan when several other writers who cheerfully ignored *Badman* took it upon themselves to complete *The Pilgrim's Progress* for him. In 1683 a writer who published under the initials T. S. stepped forward and wrote *The Second Part of the Pilgrim's Progress, from this present World of Wickedness and Misery to An Eternity of Holiness and Felicity: Exactly Described under the Similitude of a Dream*. It cannily mimicked Bunyan's work both in size and typeface.[88] Even so, T. S.'s fraudulent *Second Part* disappeared with scarcely a ripple.

But there were more unauthorized sequels, eventually leading Bunyan to make a second attempt at a sequel to the First Part of *The Pilgrim's Progress*. And this time, he would not write from prison. Working with his family gathered about him, Bunyan's fertile mind conjured up new elements for the Second Part, including a narrative device he had never used before,[89] even while reuniting characters and scenes readers had taken to heart from the First Part. If the First Part described a pilgrimage marked by danger, hardship, suffering, and final victory, the Second Part delved more deeply into the moments of joy and charity, sympathy and solace that also unfold amid a pilgrimage. It was a true tour de force!

BISHOP BUNYAN

In the last ten years of his life, John Bunyan became a great public figure. People took to calling him "Bishop Bunyan" and flocked to hear him preach. One sermon he delivered at a meetinghouse in London drew a thousand people at seven in the morning. Meanwhile, readers in the New England colonies knew *The Pilgrim's Progress* almost as well as readers in England.[90] Within Bunyan's lifetime, the book was translated into Welsh, French, and Dutch.[91] He also published sermons.

Still, the shadow of war or harassment was never far away. When James II ascended the throne in February 1685, it precipitated the violently suppressed Monmouth Rebellion and a last great wave of persecution for dissenters.[92]

Amid such pervasive violence and uncertainty, Bunyan feared imprisonment for a third time. So in a deed of gift drawn up in December 1685, he transferred all his property to his wife to protect his family from becoming homeless should he be imprisoned again and his property confiscated. (This deed was discovered in 1838, when workers were demolishing the celebrated cottage in which Bunyan had lived.)

In 1687, King James unexpectedly sought to conciliate dissenters that he might thereby generate popular support for the toleration of Catholics. Incredibly, an olive branch was extended from James to Bunyan. He was offered a government post. Bunyan declined.[93] He had seen enough of kings, war, and persecution.

In his final years, Bunyan gained a hard-won wisdom. The comings and goings of monarchs, civil wars, persecutions, and imprisonments—he had seen and known all of these. They seem to have been in his thoughts as he wrote his enigmatic 1684 work, *Seasonal Counsel or Suffering Saints in the Furnace—Advice to Persecuted Christians in Their Trials & Tribulations*. Now, near the end of his life, he had no desire to dabble in high politics. Instead he wished nothing more than "to show my loyalty to the king . . . my love to my fellow-subjects and my desire that all Christians should walk in ways of peace and truth."[94]

❧

In mid-August 1688, fifty-nine-year-old John Bunyan traveled to the town of Reading. His purpose was to preach, but he had another errand as well. A troubled young neighbor had approached him, confessing that he had deeply offended his father—so profoundly, in fact, that there seemed no hope of reconciliation.[95]

Bunyan's heart went out to his neighbor, and he agreed to intercede. He sought an interview with the young man's father and they talked for a long while, Bunyan speaking of the evils of anger. "Can you not," he asked his host, "forgive your son?"

Moved by this entreaty, the father agreed, and Bunyan left the interview knowing he had done a good service. He mounted his horse and continued on to London, to preach.

At some point on the road, a chilling rain began, thoroughly drenching him. He rode on for many dreary miles before reaching the home of his friend, John Strudwick, with whom he was to stay.

Bunyan gratefully entered Strudwick's house and changed his wet clothes. He was doubtless taken to sit by a fire and provided with food, perhaps a stew, that would help to warm him. Before long, he would have gone to his room, grateful for rest and a good bed.

The Sunday sermon Bunyan delivered at Whitechapel on August 19 was a memorable one. He spoke of escape from "the Dark Dungeon of Sin," and the glory of Christ's resurrection from the grave. He described how the righteousness of God enveloped those who had come to faith.[96] It was his story, he said to those who heard him. It could be theirs too.

It is possible that even as he was speaking, Bunyan knew he was not well. Returning to Strudwick's home, he soon became gravely ill. He may have contracted influenza—a flu epidemic had been recently reported—but it was just as likely he had been stricken with pneumonia.

Soon a "violent fever" and "sweating distemper" racked his body. For ten days he lingered, even as every effort was made to save his life. Whether word ever reached his wife and children in time for them to be by his side is not known. Such news would have taken several days to reach them, and several days more for them to get to him.[97]

On Friday, August 31, 1688, John Bunyan died peacefully in a house that was not his own. But then, for so many years, he had been a pilgrim. Now he had passed over. All struggles and conflict had ceased. He would know, at last, a peace without end.

But John Bunyan lives on through *The Pilgrim's Progress*, his matchless alloy of imagery, plot, and language. More than three hundred years after its publication, the influence of this improbable masterwork is not yet spent. It still endures, and will endure, so long as people are drawn to the music of the written word and the triumph of the human spirit.

To learn more about John Bunyan, read Kevin Belmonte's *John Bunyan* (Nashville: Thomas Nelson, 2010) from the Christian Encounters Series.

5 | JOHANN SEBASTIAN BACH
(1685–1750)

by Rick Marschall

Music has been mandated by God's Spirit.

—JOHANN SEBASTIAN BACH

It would not have been illogical to knock on the door of Johann Ambrosius Bach in the little German town of Eisenach just after March 21, 1685, and predict that *his* newborn son was destined to be the greatest music maker of the human race. That is, it might not have surprised the *Stadtpfeiffer* (town musician), because the Bachs could trace many musicians and composers in their family, going back a century and spread across four crowded branches of the family tree. The family was so associated with music that, in one area, town musicians were nicknamed "bachs" even after no Bachs remained among them. Many of these, including Johann Sebastian's uncles and older cousins, held respectable places in musical history without his eventual luster casting a glow upon their names. Music was what the Bachs *did*. They wrote music, made music, transcribed music, performed music, taught music, *breathed* music. Little Johann Sebastian would grow up to command the world's attention with his music? *Warum nicht?* (Why not?)

The most profound composer of his age, Johann Sebastian Bach, of the area now comprising provincial northern Germany, was a product of his times. Just one generation before his birth, the Thirty Years' War had ended, leaving devastation in its wake.

The war had resulted, partly, from the death throes of the Holy Roman Empire and the clear, widespread establishment of Protestantism. There had been rivalries between Catholics and Protestants, the Reformation and Counter-Reformation and, yes, the Counter-Counter-Reformation. It had also been a fight over trade routes, rich farming and mining lands, access to seaports, and more. Spain wanted some territories. Denmark and Sweden wanted others. France and Britain got involved too. Battles had been fought in many places, but none so fiercely as on German soil, specifically, Thuringia and Saxony. The male population in the German states, by some estimates, was reduced by half. Armed conflict, looting, mercenaries, expropriation, and expulsion of entire communities contributed to the death tolls in persecuted Germany.

Exacerbating these horrors were starvation and disease: the bubonic plague, dysentery, the bizarre "Hungarian disease," and a "spotted" ailment now thought to be typhus.

This was the world into which the generation preceding Bach had been born. By the time little Bach was growing up, the culture was returning to "normal."

The postwar era, with its new freedom, became a time of faith. Deeply held Christian beliefs, and specifically the tenets of Martin Luther, were the foundation stones of a spiritual revival among the peoples of Thuringia and Saxony. As everywhere in Christian Europe, towns and cities of Bach's regions were built around the church. Chapels, churches, basilicas, and cathedrals were the centers of every community, not just where people worshiped but where they convened for meetings, concerts, festivals, and more.

The eighteenth century—and nowhere more than in Bach's vicinity—also gave rise to the nuclear family as a social entity. Family units embraced extremely strong expressions of faith, around each hearth as well as between neighbors. The Lutheran church served as a social unifier.

Lutheranism emphasized the individual's relationship with God, recognizing no intermediary but Christ. And the "priesthood of all believers" not only removed barriers between individuals and God but also encouraged people to evangelize others and participate corporately in worship, contrasting sharply with the seventeenth-century Catholic Church, where simple appearance at Mass was enough.[1]

Bach's inheritance of these Lutheranisms fully informed his faith. Knowledge of his "personal" Savior would result in modesty in the exercise of the exceptional musical talents he was to manifest. Music, dedicated to God, would be more important than Bach's own celebrity.

Between the times of Luther and the French Revolution, music played a major role in making everyday life bearable, pleasant, even joyful. As with iPods today, it was possible for many Europeans, specifically in Germany, to enjoy music almost all their waking hours.

Many villages had *Stadtpfeiffers* on the municipal payrolls—town musicians who roamed the streets, and played in parks, atop towers in town squares, or at the city gates. Also prevalent at the time was *Tafelmusik*—literally "table music"—performed in the background during meals.

Musical instruction at the time—even for women, otherwise second-class citizens in many ways—was so ubiquitous that when people gathered for social visits, everyone participated in the performance of some music. (Bach was a strong proponent of women singing, if not always in churches, then at other gatherings.)

And church music was *everywhere*.

FAITH AND FAMILY

Albert Schweitzer, the noted theologian, medical missionary, and master church organist, stressed Bach's spiritual side in his biography of the composer written one hundred years ago.[2] Indeed Protestantism, specifically Lutheran theology and worship traditions, was central to Bach's preoccupations, his composing, his life. Corporate worship and praise—congregational singing and a heightened role for music as a means of exhortation and exposition of the gospel—were Lutheran hallmarks that Bach was to intensify and standardize.

When combined with Bach's astonishing mastery of musical form, his profound Christian faith, grounded in deep scholarship (his library boasted as many theology texts as musical treatises), made him unique not just in *his* time, but for *all* time. One church music historian noted: "There are those who argue for Bach's exclusive Lutheran orthodoxy, others who claim he was a Pietist, and still others who state that he was influenced by mystic theologians. In some sense, they are all correct, for Bach was a confessional Lutheran with great personal piety who was influenced by the mystics."[3]

Bach definitely devoted himself to more than music. One interesting piece of evidence is his famous copy of the *Calov Commentary* on Luther's translation of the Bible. Incredibly, this mammoth work—the ownership of which reveals so much about Bach's Christian scholarship—was discovered in an old trunk in Frankenmuth, Michigan, a rural German community, in 1938. The insights gained from it have put to rest any doubts concerning the reality of Bach's faith. In the markings are four comments in Bach's hand that directly relate music to worship. He even filled in some of Luther's commentary that was missing from the *Calov* Bible, demonstrating his familiarity with and careful study of both Luther's writings and the Bible.

Bach also marked, in some cases with unusual emphasis, eight passages of commentary concerning one's office and calling.[4] This marginalia and other evidence of his earnest study of the Word reveal Bach's conviction "that his office claimed the whole man and the whole artist as one indivisible unit." Further, they "must be taken seriously as the expression of a mature person conscious of his responsibility, as a Christian and an artist."[5]

Bach was writing for an audience of one: God. In the providence of passing time, Luther and Bach both would be surprised to hear their music—especially *"Ein Feste Burg"* ("A Mighty Fortress"), Luther's martial anthem upon which Bach wrote several variations—sung in Catholic churches today.

⌘

Just as we cannot understand Bach's music apart from his faith, neither can we understand his life without visiting his family.[6]

In the late 1500s, Veit (Vitus) Bach, a "baker of white bread," settled in Thuringia, evidently from Hungary. According to family legend, Veit's "greatest pleasure [was] playing a little cittern," an instrument of the guitar family. Veit's son Johannes ("Hans," d. 1626) turned an avocation into a profession when he became a piper, nicknamed *der Spielmann*, "the player," and the Bachs were off to the races, or to the music fests. In all, fifty-three musical Bachs are on the family tree.

The father of Johann Sebastian was Johann Ambrosius. As noted, he was a *Stadtpfeiffer*, an official town musician, court trumpeter, and freelance musician. His cousins Johann Michael and Johann Christoph were remarkable composers in nearby towns. (By the way, if it seems that every Tom, Dick, and Harry in the Bach family bore the name Johann, it is because its use as a first name for every son is a longstanding tradition, extending even into the early twentieth century. In most cases it was not the name of common address. Family and friends invariably addressed *our* Johann as "Sebastian.") Bach's mother, Elizabeth, also came from a musical family. Ambrosius's twin brother, another Johann Christoph, had similar musical talent.

Ambrosius and Elizabeth died when Johann Sebastian, their eighth child, was nine. He and his brother Johann Jacob were taken to the household of their eldest brother, Johann Christoph, a church organist, in nearby Ohrdruf. Bach scarcely knew his brother Christoph, who was fifteen years his senior and had left home early to study with Johann Pachelbel—a family friend, organist, and composer of the famous *Canon*, so often played today at weddings.

Bach likely received his earliest training in composition and keyboard in his brother's house. Here arose a story that might be only legend, but its flavor confirms his musical affinity. Young Bach was forbidden access to a musical score from which he wished to play. But the cabinet where it was locked away had a lattice door with openings allowing a boy's hand to slip through. Every night while the house slept, young Sebastian quietly secured the musical manuscript and copied it by moonlight. When almost completed, however, the elder brother discovered the game and destroyed the copy as punishment for disobedience. This story led some people to conclude that the eyestrain resulted in Bach's blindness at the end of his life.

Despite this account, young Bach received his first serious, and evidently intense, musical training from his elder brother. His lifelong affection for playing the lute likely began in Christoph's home. The youngster absorbed keyboard instruction on both harpsichord and organ there as well. (Eisenach also had one of the grandest organs in Europe, so no doubt, Sebastian was already preconditioned by listening to its regal sound to master the organ.)

Bach reportedly began writing his first compositions—variations on Pachelbel's music—at the age of ten, the same as did another young music lover, born the same year as Bach in nearby Halle: Georg Friedrich Händel. Bach's precocity was evident from the start. His compositions were not mere variations but extensions of Pachelbel's tunes.

After five years Christoph secured a position for his fifteen-year-old brother in the choir of St. Michael's Church in Lüneburg, in exchange for Bach's schooling, principally theology, Latin, Greek, and French. He was reputed to have had a beautiful soprano voice, which soon cracked as he matured. He remained in the program, however, thanks to his proficiency on various instruments. While he could, he immersed himself in the church's musical library—one of the finest in Europe—of more than eleven hundred musical manuscripts by approximately 175 composers. He likely also received instruction from Dietrich Buxtehude of the north German school of organ playing during this time. Bach was always at the head of his classes, often advanced as many as four years over his classmates.[7]

Within three years, Bach was accomplished enough to be hired at age eighteen as organist at the "New Church" of Arnstadt. Later, when it was suggested that he might also lend a hand directing the choir or occasionally teaching extra classes (he was younger than many of his pupils), Bach refused. For a time, he practically lived with his organ, all the time learning its sonorities and possibilities, and experimenting.

Even when Bach allowed himself time for romance, it was in the shadow of the church organ. Once, he allegedly brought a young woman to the choir's balcony and was reprimanded. Bach claimed that he was instructing the girl (a distant cousin, Maria Barbara, whom he was to marry) in music.

There are other reports of friction during his service at Arnstadt. He was once attacked on the street by a music student who resented Bach's insulting assessment of his abilities. The student wielded a club and Bach drew a knife in self-defense before they were separated. When called before the consistory to defend himself, Bach repeated his opinion. Justified or not, again he was admonished.

In 1705, two years into his employment, he asked permission to travel to Lübeck to listen again to the influential organist Buxtehude. He was granted four weeks.

Mesmerized by the north German/Danish style of church organ music performed there, Bach attended every service. He evidently established a relationship with the legendary Buxtehude and learned all he could. When he returned to Arnstadt—four *months* later—he calmly responded to his consistory's displeasure by reminding them that he had left his duties in good hands, namely, his Bach cousin's. Then, beginning with his very first service, he began to play the organ in different styles, to the consternation of the music committee. Bach praised God in a new way that worshipers in Arnstadt had never heard using organ chorales: grand, multilayered, lengthy, with sounds produced by unorthodox combinations of organ-stops and counterpoint-melodies. Bach's feet virtually danced over the pedalboard, and his hands flew across the manuals (keyboards), leaving his listeners, or at least his music committee, impressed but very confused. There were more scoldings.

The Grand Tour

In 1707 Bach left Arnstadt for a post as organist at St. Blasius Church in Mühlhausen, bequeathing his old position to his cousin Ernst Bach. His new duties required more composition, which inspired him to write larger-scale organ works including secular pieces like the stunning *Toccata and Fugue in D minor*. It was during his short Mühlhausen year—a fire decimated the church—that he first addressed the musical genre known as the *cantata*. Bach subsequently codified elements of this form so definitively that no composers after him altered it further.

Deriving its name from the Latin root word for *sing*, the church cantata usually employed a full choir and soloists, plus instruments playing in various combinations as well as *tutti*, or all together. Sometimes movements were broken up and performed throughout the service, to introduce readings, echo the sermon message, or emphasize other important moments. Otherwise they served as a solid "second sermon" on the day's text. Cantatas added to the Lutheran service in a variety of ways. As Bach made the cantata a musical and worship *experience*, church services became magnets that attracted and inspired awestruck worshipers.

Soon after the fire that devastated Mühlhausen, Bach moved on. He had received an offer of tremendous honor and prestige as court organist, concertmaster, and chief chamber musician at the court of Duke Wilhelm Ernst of Sachsen-Weimar. This royal appointment allowed for both Christian and secular music to be composed and performed, and placed twenty members of the court band under Bach's direction. In 1708 he assumed his duties in Weimar (really his second "tour" there; in 1703 he had served as a musician and court "lackey"—the actual title!—for a few months).

At Weimar, Bach was charged with propagating the new forms of concert music sweeping Europe. He was to write at least one cantata every month—a stupendous achievement, even without his other output. It was there that he also began the famed *Brandenburg Concertos*, written in an unsuccessful bid for a position with Margrave Christian Ludwig of Brandenburg-Schwedt. In addition, he experimented with new instruments, including the clavichord, solo violin, and flute.

As he had earlier incorporated some French, Danish, and Dutch styles, Bach feasted upon Italian fare at the Weimar court. The prince had acquired many musical scores by Antonio Vivaldi, who composed hundreds of concerti. Impressed and mightily influenced by Vivaldi's technical style, Bach transcribed some of Vivaldi's works, preserving the melodies but always making them his own. Soon he was writing his own concertos for two, three, and four harpsichords, and for other solo instruments or combinations of solo instruments.

Bach's steady path to greatness saw an uptick during his service in Weimar. His performances were welcomed in other churches, not just in the court chapel, and his secular works were performed at salons, in public houses, in gardens, and in concert halls. His fame was spreading. When composers and musicians traveled anywhere near Saxony, many endeavored to visit Bach and hear him play.

Bach was to father twenty children, and almost symbolic of his fecundity during the Weimar years, two sons born there—Wilhelm Friedemann (1710) and Carl Philipp Emanuel (1714)—went on to become distinguished and famous composers themselves.

ᘓᘓᘓ

In time, criticism and bureaucratic friction caused Bach to scan the horizon, not just for a new position, but for a position with authority: *Kapellmeister*—the master or conductor of a chamber orchestra.

There was an opening for a *Kapellmeister* in Cöthen, under Prince Leopold von Anhalt-Cöthen, and Bach was invited to fill the appointment; he accepted. But when he announced his intentions to his employer in Weimar, Bach was promptly tossed into jail. For a month in 1717, he lived behind bars as the Ducal court tried all means to dissuade the composer from taking up the new position. Eventually, though, Bach was declared free to move to his next post.

Prince Leopold of Cöthen, just twenty-three, loved music with all his soul. Bach became the personal composer to the prince and was free to do as he pleased as a musician.

During five short years Bach produced a freshet of astounding works, including the six memorable *Brandenburg Concertos* begun in Weimar; the *Well-Tempered Clavier* (Book One), which became a standard component of music theory and the performance repertoire; the suites for violoncello; the French and English suites for harpsichord; the suites for lute; sonatas and partitas for solo violin; and many other solo and chamber masterpieces.

Bach's life was touched by tragedy when his wife, Maria Barbara, fell ill and died in 1720. Bach, then thirty-five, was devastated; theirs had been a happy marriage, and seven children were now his to rear alone.

117

Within a year of Maria Barbara's death, Bach remarried. Twenty-year-old Anna Magdalena Wülcken, seventeen years his junior, proved to be another inspired and joyful match. A gifted soprano who performed at the court in Cöthen, she was the daughter of a noted trumpeter. The new Frau Bach was a worthy successor to Maria in providing professional support and household leadership, and was also a mature partner to Bach the music maker. Anna continued to sing at concerts and gatherings, and she played several instruments well. She frequently transcribed or copied her husband's scores as needed. For her instruction, and as a token of his love and respect, Bach later composed a series of keyboard pieces known as "The Notebook for Anna Magdalena Bach," today a part of the standard keyboard repertoire.

CANTOR IN LEIPZIG

By 1722, Bach had grown restive in the court of Prince Leopold. He missed the church duties—liturgical music, organ playing, organizing services, teaching—he had enjoyed in previous posts. Without a doubt, he longed to write music again for Lutheran worship. So he began to inquire about openings in Hamburg, Berlin, and Leipzig, and in 1723 received a commission in Leipzig, the largest city yet for him and his large family to call home.

Leipzig was to be Bach's last earthly posting. For twenty-seven years the city would be his home and his platform. His initial appointment was to be as cantor (chiefly, choir director) of St. Thomas Church. But before his hiring, Bach "had to undergo, as was the custom of the time, an examination of his religious belief . . . He also had to sign the [Lutheran] Concordia Formula, for without signing this no one could hold an appointment in Saxony."[8]

The Formula of Concord was an edict delivered by the Elector of

Saxony in 1580, a confession intended to particularize the differences from the Roman Church, condemn liberal Lutheran tendencies, oppose Calvinism, and unite the Lutheran factions. It addressed, among other things, free will, predestination, justification, works, the Law and the gospel, the person of Christ, and church customs. It eventually became the handbook of Lutheran orthodoxy. Bach passed the examination concerning the Formula of Concord.

In German ecclesiastical tradition the cantor was not just a singer, as an English speaker hearing the word might assume, but the director of all music programs, akin to a dean of music in a scholastic setting and covering, as one might say, a multitude of dins. As one source observed, "the Cantor had the second position within the pecking order of [St. Thomas's entire] ministry."[9]

Religious and civic authorities heralded Bach's appointment. In addition to serving the church, the new cantor was obliged to teach, manage, and oversee both Latin instruction and music at St. Thomas's school. (Eventually he devolved some of his responsibilities, like Latin instruction, to subordinates.) Over nearly three decades, his duties were expanded to include three more churches and several other venues in the city.

Yet Bach found time to do even more. To his composing, performing, administrative, and teaching duties, he added freelance consulting to instrument makers; including vital suggestions for designing and building the first pianos, though he didn't care for their sound. He endorsed and sold various keyboard instruments, and invented one that sounded like a lute. Then there were his musical score sales, composing for weddings and funerals, private music lessons, and directorship at the Collegium Musicum, a private association that met weekly in Zimmermann's Coffee Shop.

Every Friday evening there were public performances—many written and performed by Bach—of music both secular and religious, including short mini-operas, generally called "secular cantatas."

Bach's Leipzig period produced some of the most awe-inspiring music ever lifted to God. Most of his 250 cantatas were composed and performed there. Whereas he once composed a cantata a month, at Leipzig he composed one a week over several periods. The mighty Passions—two of which, the *St. John* and *St. Matthew*, survive today— were written for the St. Thomas Church. The majestic *B minor Mass* was written during Bach's Leipzig period, which also produced the instrumental *Goldberg Variations*, named after a court musician charged with playing music so his sovereign could sleep; the second book of the *Well-Tempered Clavier*, which along with the first volume revolutionized keyboard composition by requiring new "tempered" tuning that allowed easier transition through all twenty-four musical scales; *The Musical Offering*; and the *Art of the Fugue*. As always, the quality was as impressive as the quantity. Bach routinely wrote one masterpiece after another.

During his years at St. Thomas Church, Bach managed an estimated fifteen hundred–plus performances—writing the music and performing at the vast majority—to an average audience of two thousand.[10] Other works composed then include the *Magnificat* and the *Christmas Oratorio* with its electrifying opening, *Jauchzet, Frohlocket!*

In all his work, Bach seamlessly fused two overarching functions, discussed by Bach scholars in a 2000 radio roundtable:

JOHN KLEINIG: The Gospel, if you like, is proclaimed by Bach as a cantor as much as by the preacher from the pulpit.

MICHAEL MARISSEN: [Bach] is a very good preacher— what a good preacher should be nowadays: comforting the afflicted and afflicting the comfortable. Bach is very good at doing both of those things.

ROBIN LEAVER: So this is Gospel music, folks![11]

And so it was.

☙❧

As Bach's service in Leipzig progressed, he also received, in 1736, a "side" appointment as honorary composer to the court of the Elector of Saxony in Dresden, which allowed him extra opportunities for composition. This brought greater honor to St. Thomas and Leipzig, because their own composer was so honored by a major sovereign. Royal Court *Compositeur* was Bach's title—honor of honors. He was like a composer laureate, an occasional guest conductor, in Dresden.

A House Filled with Music

But for all his musical and professional success, the greatest joy of Bach's life during his time at St. Thomas Church in Leipzig was his family. He was exceedingly proud of his children, most of whom inherited the Bachs' musical talent. Barbara had given birth to seven children and Anna Magdalena bore him thirteen.

The Bach household in Leipzig exuded activity: children coming and going, students practicing, visitors of all stripes, voluble dinner conversations, family reunions, and daily Bible studies and prayer, all interspersed with music, music, music. In the Bachs' humble but spacious apartments Johann Sebastian kept several keyboard instruments, including a harpsichord, a clavichord, and a now obsolete type of spinet of Bach's design that played very quietly. He was particularly fond of the lute, the violin, and the viola.

Bach practiced every day, and so did most of his children. Nights were set aside for composition, when Anna Magdalena and various children assisted by copying and transcribing Johann Sebastian's work. Bach also organized performances of his *Coffee Cantata*, other secular cantatas, small-scale church cantatas, and music recitals at a rate that would have exhausted many composers. His family assisted, performed, or—to Papa's delight—starred in virtually everything.[12] He loved and encouraged all his children equally, even wayward son Johann Gottfried Bernhard, who left home and incurred debts, and Gottfried Heinrich, a troubled child who might have had the greatest musical ability of all the siblings but suffered some sort of mental disability.

Of the prominent musical children, two were from his first marriage. Wilhelm Friedemann became a prominent composer and performer. Carl Philipp Emmanuel (C.P.E.) Bach likewise made a successful career for himself.

Johann Christoph Friedrich Bach, whom Friedemann considered the best keyboard performer of his siblings, was concertmaster of Bückeburg's court. Johann Christian Bach, first called "Bach of Milan" and afterward the "London Bach," was only fifteen when his father died and was therefore the least influenced musically by his father. Still, he became extremely popular in his day and exerted a major influence on the boy Mozart, whom he bounced on his knee. Some of Mozart's very earliest compositions, written when he was only a small boy, were transcriptions of J. C. Bach pieces.

Two daughters—Catharina Dorothea, Bach's firstborn, and Elisabeth Juliana Friederica ("Liesgen") of the second marriage— were also accomplished singers and musicians. It is remarkable that in a family with so many music makers, history has recorded no fallouts, jealousy, or bitter rivalries.[13] Surely a shared devotion to the Lord and a common and profound faith at least partially explains this.

With help from his two wives in succession, Bach managed what was by all accounts a busy, friendly, and spiritual household that sometimes included students boarding with them. Their home and hearth–centered lifestyle provides a key to understanding Bach's music, its appeal, and even its purpose. Among his many masterpieces are works written for friends, family, and precocious young musicians.

To affirm the kinder and gentler personality of the Bach who otherwise stares at us rather sternly from two surviving portraits, we can look to accounts of Bach family reunions. These were at least annual affairs and were jolly, sometimes raucous, and always musical.[14]

Every festivity invariably began with songs of praise thanking God for blessings past, and asking His further blessing for the future. Then there was food; yes, there was beer. There was fellowship and gossip. But the highlight of the day was a good-natured competition between various branches of the clan. Each group prepared and rehearsed for what became a "Can you top this set?" sing-off. The only consistent aspect was variety, but usually the music and words, sometimes presented as staged performances, were humorous, filled with silliness, sarcasm, non-sense—and sometimes bawdiness.

Similar to these family *"sing-offs,"* the "Coffee Cantata" provides a glimpse of Bach with his hair down. The fact that it was likely first performed at Zimmermann's Coffee Shop, and that the beverage was sweeping Europe like today's Starbucks mania, obscures the fact that Bach composed it as an inside joke for his family. It was a humorous commentary on courtship more than coffee, and while never naughty—Bach never went there—it doubtless made some singers and auditors blush with its good-natured in-jokes about dating, marriage, and the dynamics of the Bach household. So though he was always serious *about* music, Bach clearly enjoyed being funny *through* music.

There is further evidence of Bach the sentimental family man, composer of music meant for other than church or concert hall. In 1704, Bach's older brother Johann Jakob decided to serve as oboist in King Karl XII of Sweden's military band. Several of the family, evidently including Johann Sebastian, dissented from this choice, but when Jakob was set to travel north and take the assignment, his younger brother wrote the heartfelt *Capriccio on the Departure of My Beloved Brother*. An amazing testament to familial attachments, it opens with a representation of Jakob's friends and family pleading that he remain among them. The following *andante* and *adagio* warn of possible dangers and melancholia. A fugue then represents the several arguments of the coachman who agrees with the family's viewpoint, to no avail—a musical portrait of family ties and deepest concern.

The second Frau Bach, Anna Magdalena, a superb copyist and a skilled musician and singer, is one of the reasons we have inherited so much of Bach's music. In 1722 Bach wrote one of his French suites for harpsichord, perhaps the most difficult of the series, in her notebook. Three years later he dedicated a collection of intricate and masterful keyboard instructional pieces to her. The *Clavierbüchlein* [Little Notebook] *für Anna Magdalena Bach* still challenges, pleases, and amazes listeners and performers today, almost three hundred years later.

MASTER OF HIS CRAFT

The spiritual instruction of the Bach children was as strong at home as in schools, usually overseen by Frau Bach. The quality of the schools in town always played a role in Bach's decisions to seek or accept postings. His children's education—spiritual first, then educational, then musical—was important to the father of this very large household.

Bach read daily from the Bible and from Luther's works. Once he won a major collection of theological texts at an auction and jubilantly reported the purchase to a friend. He neither boasted nor complained about the auction price, but its receipt has survived;

Bach paid the equivalent of a tenth of his annual salary for the books. Christoph Wolff noted that for Bach, "theological and musical scholarship were two sides of the same coin: the search for divine revelation, or the quest for God."[15]

Bach was responsible for supporting a larger household than most. In a letter to his boyhood friend Georg Erdmann, Bach reported that his annual salary at St. Thomas, likely his best-paid position, was approximately 700 Thalers (about $50,000), yet technically, only about a hundred Thalers was fixed.[16]

Most of the cantor's extra income derived from weddings and funerals. The highest payment for weddings, he told Erdmann, was two Thalers; for funerals one Thaler, 15 Groschen (approximately $200 and $150, respectively).

Bach closed his letter to Erdmann with a remark either sarcastic or humorous, perhaps unconscious: he complained that on account of the "clear [healthy] air," fewer people were dying, and therefore his income was off a hundred Thalers!

⌘

Bach worked at St. Thomas Church in Leipzig nearly half his life—twenty-seven of his sixty-five years.

In his last years he grew increasingly reclusive but certainly was not a hermit. Though he still had duties as a worship leader, he did reduce his travel to learn from masters. *He* was now one whom musical pilgrims sought. Bach clearly enjoyed the company of other musicians. It is supposed that during his last years he wrestled with theoretical music problems few others at that time could understand.[17] And yet, in many of his compositions, he *solved* music problems that had plagued composers for generations and left posterity with masterpieces that will live, in the words of H. L. Mencken, "as long as men have ears."

The three musical tools most closely associated with Bach,

honed during his time at St. Thomas Church in Leipzig, happen to be a "trinity" of Cs: *counterpoint*, *cantata*, and *chorale*.

COUNTERPOINT

Music is built, Bach insisted to his students, on a foundation of the bass line. Over this melody it should be possible to build another melody, or several, based on the harmonies going up the musical staves. In so doing, the composer can construct several tunes to stand alone or harmonize.

CANTATA

Under Bach, the cantata became the central music of the church service, taking on a role complementary to the sermon. Broadly speaking, the cantata *provided* the message, and the sermon *explained* the message. Bach wrote five cycles of cantatas, each comprised of a different cantata for every Sunday of the year. Unfortunately, only the equivalent of three cycles are extant. Counting cantatas written for special events and a few secular cantatas, that totals about 215 surviving from an estimated 300.

CHORALE

Chorales were an important aspect of the Lutheran service. Briefly, a chorale is a brief strain of music, usually "borrowed" from a hymn or other music. It can stand alone, but its main function is as a musical interlude or introduction to parts of the service (liturgy, offering, etc.). The chorale can be vocal, instrumental, or both. Some of Bach's most profound and beautiful music was in simple chorales. And he wrote hundreds of them.

Oddly, Bach's catalog is almost bereft of love songs, despite a few *Lieder* that prefigured those of Mozart and Schubert. And yet in a way, everything Bach composed was a love song—to God.

MUSIC NOT *ABOUT*
GOD BUT *TO* HIM

By some reports, Bach filled twenty pages of music a day, seldom using an instrument for testing or experimenting but going straight to paper—and rarely making corrections on the score. Of his eighteen hundred to two thousand separate works, approximately twelve hundred have survived.

Bach began virtually every composition, even his secular music, by writing the words *Jesu, juva* (Jesus, help me), then penned *Soli Deo Gloria* (To God alone the glory) at the bottom of the completed score. His output was almost exclusively Christian or instrumental music—no opera or ballet. He occasionally incorporated folk music but shunned popular tunes and never based music on drinking songs, despite legends claiming otherwise.

◈

Bach produced two works in his final years that, far from betraying any evidence of an aging composer's diminished powers, are stunning in their scope and mastery of form. The first was the *Mass in B minor*,[18] his highest achievement, written in the fashion of the traditional Catholic Mass. Bach prepared it most earnestly in 1748 and 1749.

Then there was *Die Kunst der Fuge* (*The Art of the Fugue*). Contrary to traditional assumptions, this was not a deathbed composition, though Bach was preparing its publication when he died. He had actually begun work on it in the early 1740s. He never quite finished the work and he never indicated the scoring. Nevertheless, *The Art of the Fugue* is not just a pinnacle of Bach's career, it is a highpoint in the sweep of Western culture.

◈

In the closing years of his life, Bach received an honor unique in his time. Bach's son Carl Philipp Emanuel was prominently employed as a musician by Friedrich der Grosse—Frederick the Great of Prussia—whose glittering French-style court, Sanssouci in Potsdam, was becoming a cultural hub of Europe. Frederick, a respectable composer and accomplished flautist, had long pressed his court composer, C.P.E. Bach, to bring his legendary father to the court's music chambers. At length, the arrangements were made.

Old Bach and son Wilhelm arrived at the king's residence, and before he could change from his traveling clothes, Bach was rushed into the music hall, a flattering welcome accorded by the monarch. Bach played the piano to the astonishment of everyone.

Then Frederick presented Bach with a random but challenging musical phrase, upon which Bach improvised a three-voice fugue. Frederick raised the creative ante by requesting that Bach devise a six-voice fugue. Bach gladly accepted the challenge but asked to go home to realize it properly.

Two months later Frederick the Great was significantly impressed to receive an incredibly complex set of fugues (properly, canons), a four-movement trio sonata for flute in honor of the king, and "musical riddles" over whose scores Bach wrote how rising notes, ascending modulatio, and so forth made specific allusions to the king's fortunes—all based on the simple musical phrase the king had provided. Bach not only wrote this astounding series of compositions, but also had them engraved and printed. Today we know the set as *The Musical Offering*.

In Bach's final days, he composed one last piece, a grand fugue based on the letters of his name—B A C H—"as unto the Lord." In German musical notation, B indicates B-flat, and the letter H stands for B-natural. More than a clever conceit or musical pun, it is clear that Bach knew he was writing his last earthly music—not *about* God, but *to* God.

In Leipzig, old Bach's eyesight steadily deteriorated in his last years. From written descriptions of his symptoms, some believe cataracts were the culprit. Ironically, Händel, in London, was also losing his sight.

These two great composers, born within months and miles of each other, never did meet. However, they were united in having to confront blindness in their final years—and being mistreated by the same doctor.[19] Händel was visited a year after Bach's death in Leipzig by the itinerant English eye surgeon whose questionable efforts relieved neither composer's affliction and who may have hastened Bach's demise.

In early 1750 a one-man medicine show, "Chevalier" John Taylor, appeared in Leipzig. A surgeon of dubious skill, he ultimately confessed to blinding hundreds of patients. (By then, ironically, he was sightless himself.) He rode across the continent in a wagon painted with eyes and the legend "Giving Eyes Is Giving Life." Taylor usually ordered bandages, infused with baked apples, to remain over patients' eyes for many days, by which time he frequently had ridden out of town. Yet he talked a good game, cited endorsements of celebrities from England to Persia, and occasionally attained happy results. Amid his chicanery he developed some legitimate procedures, for instance, the surgical approach to strabismus—which causes a person's eyes to look in two different directions—by means of cutting an eye muscle.[20]

It is not recorded whether Bach freely or reluctantly went under the Chevalier's knife for cataract surgery. Operations took place in March and April. A follow-up was deemed necessary because of an apparent reappearance of the cataract; Bach sat nearly upright in Taylor's chair and was constrained by an assistant. There were no anesthetics and, obviously, any movement by the patient was dangerous.

Cataracts and knives were possibly the least of Bach's worries under this medical incompetent. Taylor practiced bloodletting, the prescription of laxatives, and eyedrops custom-made from pigeons' blood, sugar, and salt. Family members later spoke of Bach's severe pain after the operations and of "complete blindness" in both eyes. Bach's four final months of life were racked with ocular pain and fevers. A few days before his death on July 28, his family reported that his sight returned for a few hours; then a stroke eased his departure from this life.

Johann Sebastian Bach was mourned both for his musical work and for his Christian faith. But the two were not just intertwined, they were *one*. That is the testimony of Bach's work and his life.

THE FIFTH EVANGELIST

For a generation following his death, Bach was virtually unknown outside of his musical offspring and students. New musical forms, a new direction in his church's liturgical fashions, and a near-universal societal desire for change relegated him to obscurity. The age of the American and French revolutions was dawning. Gradually, however, through the nineteenth century people discovered and embraced his music anew. His hymns were added to hymnbooks of various denominations, and composers of all styles were awestruck by Bach's mastery of the "science of music."

In 1781 the Gewandhaus of Leipzig had Bach's portrait painted on the ceiling of its new concert hall. For whatever reason, Bach's star was rising by the end of the century. Or, his "sun" was rising. An illustration in the influential periodical *Allgemeine musicalische Zeitung (General Musical Newspaper)* in 1799 depicted a sun with many rays emanating from it. Some of the German musical names it displays are forgotten today (Seidelmann, Stölzel, Graun); others are great (Händel, Mozart, Haydn) . . . but at the center of the sun is the name "Joh. Sebastian Bach."[21]

In 1799, Nikolaus Forkel wrote a landmark biography of Bach. Then the floodgates were opened. The great German writer Johann Wolfgang von Goethe discovered Bach's music and described it. The composer Felix Mendelssohn Bartholdy, a Lutheran converted from Judaism, was awestruck by the *St. Matthew Passion* and staged a legendary performance on Good Friday 1829. Bach's music was also a model for Mendelssohn's early church music.

Music historian Clemens Romijn has traced just some of the major figures in music whom Bach influenced in the years since his death:

> Without Bach, Haydn's late string quartets and Mozart's latest symphonies and *Requiem* would have sounded quite different. Beethoven, Mendelssohn, Schumann, Chopin, Liszt, Brahms, Debussy . . . too played . . . Bach's works, . . . feeling very small next to Bach. Carl Maria von Weber considered Bach's music to be so new and perfect that everything before him lost its significance. . . . And Debussy said: "Bach is Our Dear Lord of music. Every composer would do well to pray to him before commencing work."[22]

The Bach *Gesellschaft* (Bach Society) was founded in 1850 to celebrate the master, and it has been chief among scholarly sources that have continually analyzed Bach's work and updated the catalog. Today, there are hundreds of Bach societies and Bach festivals around the world.

In the 1870s the monumental biography by Philipp Spitta was published, three volumes of analysis, musicology, and history, setting the standard for appreciation and further scholarship. Andre Pirro's *L'esthetique de Jean Sebastian Bach* (1907) and Albert Schweitzer's *Johann Sebastian Bach* (1905–1911), extended the study of Bach, emphasizing his vocal and organ works.

In 1940 Walt Disney's *Fantasia*, a brilliant, avant-garde animated feature cartoon, opened with an explosive display of cascading colors to accompany the musical tour de force of Bach's *Toccata and Fugue in D minor* arranged for symphony orchestra.

By the 1960s, Johann Sebastian Bach seemed to be everywhere. Walter Carlos, using the Moog synthesizer, scored a tremendous hit with the album *Switched-On Bach*. The Swingle Singers, from France, likewise sold many albums, starting with *Bach's Greatest Hits*, *Going Baroque*, and *Back to Bach*. Another Frenchman, Jacques Loussier, merged Bach with cool jazz in a series of innovative albums, *Play Bach*.

Nonesuch Records released an album of Bach translations played on electric guitar by Andre Benichou and His Well-Tempered Three, *Jazz Guitar Bach*. Joshua Rifkin's *The Baroque Beatles Book*, songs of the Fab Four as Bach would have scored them, achieved great acclaim.

Actor Brian Blessed portrayed old Bach in *The Joy of Bach*, a 1978 motion picture enhanced by clips of choirs from, among other places, Bach's own St. Thomas Church in Leipzig. Also shown was pop concert organist E. Power Biggs, playing Bach under a light show and leading his audience in a college-style cheer, B! A! C! H!

Johann Sebastian Bach fully arrived as a cultural icon when in 1977 the *Voyager* spacecraft was launched in search of some alien civilization in a remote part of the universe. Perhaps aliens would discover and understand something of mankind from the spacecraft's unique payload—a copper and gold alloy disk. Among its playlist of global music, Bach was the only composer represented three times. When asked what he would have nominated for the message to unknown civilizations, biologist Lewis Thomas replied, "The complete works of J. S. Bach . . . But that would be boasting."

In its 1968 Christmas-season issue, *Time* magazine placed a portrait of Johann Sebastian Bach on its cover and ran a major essay on him, "The Fifth Evangelist." And evangelist he was. Fully half of the music he wrote was Christian. He managed church musical staffs and taught Christian education. He was not an ordained pastor, yet he knew the Bible so well that the examinations he was obliged to pass proved him the peer of clergy. Johann Sebastian Bach was indeed one of the most equipped and effective "preachers" of his age.

Soli Deo Gloria.

To learn more about Bach, read Rick Marschall's *Johann Sebastian Bach* (Nashville: Thomas Nelson, 2011) from the **Christian Encounters Series.**

6 | JANE AUSTEN
(1775–1817)

by Peter Leithart

[Jane] had no other hope of mercy, pardon, and peace, but through the merits and suffers of her Redeemer.

—HENRY AUSTEN, JANE'S BROTHER

Jane Austen's world was a world in upheaval. She was born nine months after the beginning of the American War of Independence, and during her girlhood French revolutionaries stormed the Bastille and later unleashed the Terror. As a young adult she heard accounts of the Napoleonic Wars from her brothers, and watched as the entire British nation mobilized for war.[1] Britain was at war again in America when she was in her thirties; and two years before she died, the Napoleonic era ended with the Treaty of Vienna.

A literary revolution matched the political one. The 1784 death of poet, Christian moralist, and novelist Samuel Johnson marked the end of an era. By the end of the next decade William Wordsworth and Samuel Taylor Coleridge had launched the Romantic movement in British poetry. The lives of the younger Romantic poets are almost contained within Austen's. Byron was born in 1788; Shelley lived from 1792 to 1822, and Keats from 1795 to 1821.

Jenny Austen was born on December 16, 1775, in the parish rectory at Steventon, a small village in the Hampshire Downs. Steventon lay in an angle formed by two roads, one running from London to the West Countries and the other from London to Winchester. Austen's world was one of chalk hills dotted with sheep, of wheat fields, of green meadows, and of forests. When Austen was born, there were some thirty families in the parish,[2] but her closest neighbors were her immediate family. Fortunately for little Jenny, that family was enchanting indeed.

A Scholar and a Poet

Few families could have been more suited to encouraging Jane's particular talents than the Austens. A comfortable though not wealthy middle gentry family, they shared the patriotic Tory inclinations of their class, with one notable difference: they were an exceptionally literate, clever, witty, jovial, affectionate, and accomplished family. They were amused by the world around them and often laughed at it. Early on, Jenny learned to do the same. It was a family Jenny could love and admire.

George Austen (1731–1805), Jane's father, was ordained to the Anglican ministry in 1754.[3] Prior to the eighteenth century, many Church of England clergymen were little more than peasants, with slight education and slighter inclination to elevate culture in the English countryside. As the parish minister in Steventon, Rev. Austen was one of a new breed. With his intense eyes and a shock of thick hair that earned him the nickname "the Handsome Proctor," George looked like the cultivated, well-read gentleman scholar that he was.[4]

Though a classicist, George was not bound to his studies. Church of England clergymen lived off the combined income of tithes and glebes—a portion of land donated by parishioners for the support of their rector.[5] George began pig breeding and by 1801 had acquired three sows and twenty-two pigs,[6] and had enough glebe land not only to fill his own table but also to produce a surplus for sale, even while remaining a faithful pastor.

George Austen was the perfect father for a young writer. Possessing a library of some five hundred volumes, he enjoyed reading and writing and passed on these amusements to his children. He read romances and poetry to the family, and the one book that still survives with his signature and bookplate is *Reliques of Irish Poetry* by Charlotte Brooke.[7]

Rev. Austen taught his children that prayer, morning and night, was an absolute "[d]uty which nothing can excuse the omission of." Though he was a man of the *Prayer Book*, he encouraged his son to recall that "a short Ejaculation to the Almighty, when it comes from the heart will be as acceptable to him as the most elegant and studied form of Words."[8] In his own mind, George Austen's most important contribution to his children's education was to direct them to the highest end of man, that "first & most important of all considerations to a human Being," which is "Religion."[9] Jenny learned this lesson alongside her siblings.

Jane's mother, Cassandra (née Leigh; 1739–1827), by the age of six, was considered the "poet of the family,"[10] and she wrote verse throughout her life.

Despite an august ancestry, Cassandra was a practical woman and an energetic housekeeper. She devoted her time to cooking, overseeing the garden and farm work, managing the house, sewing clothing for her large family, and maintaining discipline of her own children and later of her husband's students.

Jane did not get along very well with her mother. Though she outlived her famous daughter by more than a decade, Mrs. Austen was a hypochrondriac, and Jane often found her complaints exasperating.

The Austens

The Austens were a lively, spirited family, unified by common interests, tastes, and enthusiasms.

It was a predominantly masculine family. Jenny was the seventh of eight children, mostly boys. Her oldest brother, James, left home when Jane was only four but visited Steventon regularly during Jenny's childhood. Born in 1765, he began training at his father's alma mater, St. John's in Oxford, in 1779 at age fourteen, then accepted a call as a curate and later as a vicar. He was an aspiring poet (though he never published a poem in his lifetime) in the waning tradition of Thomas Gray and William Cowper; and even after Jane began publishing her books, Mrs. Austen, and perhaps others, thought of James as the writer of the family.

While at University, James edited a literary magazine, *The Loiterer*, modeled on the great eighteenth-century literary magazines of Addison and Steele, which ran for sixty issues during 1789–90 and for which he wrote many of the articles.

The Austens' second son, George, is almost never mentioned in family records. He lived apart from the family, suffered from some debilitating disease that was likely epilepsy, and was probably deaf and dumb. Jane learned to speak "with [her] fingers," perhaps to communicate with him.[11]

The third son, Edward, was born in 1767. Though he lacked James's intellectual sparkle, he was a natural leader. When Napoleon threatened England, Edward distinguished himself by leading the East Kent Volunteers in patrolling the Kentish coast.[12]

Two of Jane's other brothers, Francis and Charles, entered the navy and served with distinction. A year and a half older than Jenny, Francis—known to his family as Frank—eventually became commander in chief of the North America and West India Station, though this happened decades after his sister's death. He had listened to his father's advice and was known for his upright moral and religious principles. In a time when most naval officers stood during worship, he was known as "*the* officer who knelt in church."[13] He married Mary Gibson in 1806, and they had eleven children.

Being Jenny's only younger sibling, Charles was her "particular little brother." He married Fanny Palmer in 1807, while serving with the British navy in Bermuda; and during the 1850s, he became commander in chief of the East India and China Station.

Of all her brothers, Jane was closest to the Austens' fourth son, Henry, who early on showed promise of being the most accomplished of the Austen brothers. He never quite lived up to the promise, as his life shifted regularly from one path to another. He attended Oxford, spent time in the Oxfordshire militia, and managed a bank. As a young man he considered following his father and older brother into the ministry, but after his bank failed he entered the church and finished his life as a clergyman.

Though "Jane was a very affectionate sister to all her Brothers,"[14] there was little doubt that Jenny was closest to her only sister, Cassandra, elder by two and a half years. Their niece Anna Lefroy later remembered Jane and Cassandra walking together "in wintry weather through the sloppy lane between Steventon & Dean in pattens [overshoes], usually worn at that time even by Gentlewomen," wearing bonnets "precisely alike in colour, shape & material" so that Anna had to guess which was which. Rev. Austen took to calling them, no doubt with complete accuracy, "the Formidables."

A HOUSE OF CHARITY

Austen's home was a Christian home, and Jane Austen shared the faith of her parents. Her father led the family in prayer each morning in the parlor, and they all attended church every week.[15]

Jenny was baptized soon after her birth and went through a full christening ceremony in early April 1776.[16] In his biographical sketch of his sister, Henry described her piety: "Jane Austen's hopes of immortality were built upon the Rock of ages. . . . She had no other hope of mercy, pardon, and peace, but through the merits and suffers of her Redeemer."[17] Jane never used such evangelical language, preferring the more formal cadences of prayer-book Anglicanism, but that doesn't falsify the substance of Henry's characterization.

The Austens' Christianity was not the excitable Christianity of Bunyan or John Newton, but a cooler, more rational and ethically focused Christianity, which expressed itself chiefly in acts of charity. The Austens were not rich, but what they had they shared freely.

As Jane grew up, she noted that her two favorite women in the world demonstrated charity to the people of the parish. Jane followed suit. But charity did not come naturally to her. She had a childish, selfish streak and was too amused, appalled, and provoked by human folly to be entirely gentle or sympathetic. Still, her prayers show that she saw this as a fault, and she prayed for a gentler, kinder heart.

In at least one way her prayers were answered: Jane eventually penned one of the great English novels about charity, *Emma*.

EDUCATING JENNY

Jane Austen, for all her talent, had limited formal education and little exposure to the world. Despite all that was happening about her—the American and French Revolutions, the Napoleonic Wars, the Romantic movement in poetry and other arts, the evangelical revival in the Church of England—she chose to focus on a few families in the rural backwaters of southern England. The world she depicted was rapidly being overtaken by a very different one, the urbanized and industrialized England painted so vividly by Charles Dickens during the mid-nineteenth century, but readers find few signs that Jane even noticed it was happening.

Glimmers of interest in the wider world shine through here and there, but they are just enough to prove the contrary. Sir Thomas in *Mansfield Park* has plantations in Antigua, and there are some passing references to the slave trade, greatly expanded in the 1999 film adaptation. *Persuasion* focuses on officers of the British navy, and *Pride and Prejudice* teems with soldiers, though their main job in that novel is to dance and look delicious enough in their cherry-red coats to set young female hearts aflutter at balls.

Twice, the Austens sent the girls away to school. In 1783, when Cassandra was ten and Jane seven, they went to Oxford to be students of Mrs. Cawley, the widow of a relative of Mrs. Austen's whose husband had been principal of Brasenose College, Oxford. Within a few months, Mrs. Cawley unexpectedly moved the school to Southampton, where much of the student body contracted typhus. Jenny nearly died. The Austens brought their daughters home.

In spring 1785, the Austens placed the girls in the Reading Ladies Boarding School, known as the Abbey School because it was built on the ruins of an old monastery. Jenny and Cassandra learned sewing, dancing, writing, arithmetic, French, history, and music.[18] They stayed at the Reading School until the end of 1786 and then came home for good.

Coming home was hardly a blow to the girls' education; by now the Steventon rectory was a school. Since 1770, Rev. Austen's finances had been dwindling, so he did what many of his fellow clergy did in similar circumstances: he took in boys and turned his home into a school.

A MIND IMPROVED BY EXTENSIVE READING

Jenny and Cassy didn't get the attention the boys received, but they breathed the literary atmosphere. Mrs. Austen had taught her girls to read, and Jenny learned history from children's history books and read moralistic tales like *The History of Little Goody Two-Shoes*, then published by John Newbery.[19] She studied French from *Fables choisis*, and learned Italian.[20]

Jenny studied piano with Mr. Chard, a future organist at Winchester Cathedral,[21] and she continued to play into adulthood. Her niece Caroline remembered that "Aunt Jane began her day with music" and "she practised regularly every morning."[22]

As an adult, Jane was a reader of sermons, though a discriminating one. She enjoyed Henry's sermons,[23] but disliked the best-selling evangelical sermons of her cousin, Rev. Edward Cooper, because he was "fuller of Regeneration & Conversion than ever—with the addition of his zeal in the cause of the Bible Society."[24]

In Jenny's estimation, William Cowper ranked above all other poets of her time. Born in 1731, Cowper combined intense, occasionally terrifying, religiosity with a deep, conservative appreciation of natural beauty. Lines from Cowper slip into Austen's prose.

Though Austen never mentioned the great Romantics as among her favorite poets, she was familiar with them. As one scholar said, "[Sir Walter] Scott and [the poet Lord] Byron . . . are alluded to prominently in *Persuasion*," and in *Sense and Sensibility* "Scott is mentioned . . . as among the favorite authors of Marianne Dashwood." In *Mansfield Park* they are "quoted admiringly by Fanny Price; and both poets are referred to in the letters, Scott several times, Byron once."[25]

Most of all, Jenny read novels. The late eighteenth century was awash with novels of sentiment, which depicted the rapturous feelings of the heroes and heroines, and with Gothic novels, picturesque tales of horror set in exotically haunting locations. Austen devoured these novels, but not because she wanted to imitate them. Many of her earliest forays into writing were actually burlesques of these popular genres; she mercilessly satirized some of them in *Juvenalia* and *Northanger Abbey*.

Samuel Richardson's *Sir Charles Grandison* left a deeper impression. Jane is reputed to have read Richardson's cumbersome volume so often that she nearly memorized the thing and based some of her characters on his.[26]

Jenny did receive some informal literary education from Anne (Brydges) Lefroy, known in the neighborhood as "Madam Lefroy." This beautiful woman with lively eyes and copious conversation, who had published in the *Poetical Register*, captured the interest of the precocious Jenny Austen. The two, separated by twenty-five years in age, became fast friends.[27]

JUVENALIA

On December 5, 1794, George Austen paid twelve shillings for "a Small Mahogany Writing Desk with a Long Drawer and Glass Ink Stand Compleat," probably as a birthday gift to his daughter, soon to turn nine.[28] He knew how much she would appreciate it. Sometime in her preteens, Jenny was beginning to try her hand at writing.

Between eleven and eighteen, Jenny produced a collection of tales, essays, and plays, both finished and unfinished, for her family's entertainment. She later collected her writings into three "high-quality quarto notebooks" to be passed around the family.[29] Among this collection of twenty-nine works, Jenny included a short epistolary novel, *Love and Friendship*, in which she mocked the popular "novels of sensibility." She made fun of biased historical writers in her *History of England*, which Cassandra illustrated for her, and Jane added a number of plays and other stories. This early collection is known as Austen's *Juvenalia*, and these works are essential for getting to know Jane Austen, "for in them, and for the first time, we hear her voice."[30] It is, above all, a comic voice: "She hardly writes a paragraph unlit by the glint of a smile.[31]

Jane's imagination was robust and slightly bawdy. She was, remember, raised in a houseful of boys, and her early stories are full of scandal, drunkenness, and gory deaths. Through it all, Austen maintained a tone of lightness and glee: "there is nothing heavy-handed or 'sick' about it, only an impish infectious gaiety."[32] There is an absurdist streak as well, especially in the drama "The Mystery," which includes a scene where a character standing alone onstage says, "But Hush! I am interrupted" and another in which the characters find that the scene is already over and leave the stage. In another age, Austen might have written for *Saturday Night Live*.

A keen reader of histories, Jenny also attempted to write her own. In her *History of England*, she described Henry VI's reign. But much of Jenny's early writing is pure nonsense. One evening Laura is sitting with her parents when there is a knock at the door:

> My Father started—"What noise is that," (said he). "It sounds like a loud rapping at the door"—(replied my Mother). "It does indeed," (cried I). "I am of your opinion; (said my Father) it certainly does appear to proceed from some uncommon violence exerted against our unoffending door." "Yes (exclaimed I) I cannot help thinking it must be somebody who knocks for admittance." "That is another point (replied he); We must not pretend to determine on what motive the person may knock—tho' that someone does rap at the door, I am partly convinced."[33]

Jane's physical appearance is impossible to recover. Family members describe her as tall, more than "middle height," with a graceful and firm walk, "bright hazel eyes," and "mottled skin," or as having a "bright, but not a pink colour—a clear brown complexion." Her hair is described as everything from "darkish brown" to "light brunette." A remaining lock of her hair is too faded to be of help.

Cassandra, the family artist, painted her sister twice. One painting shows Jane sitting with her back to the painter, her hair invisible beneath her ubiquitous bonnet. The dowdy figure is awkwardly drawn, so it is impossible to get any sense of her body. Cassandra also painted a miniature portrait, but Jane's face looks so sourly screwed that we can hardly believe it is an accurate portrayal, or at least a flattering one. When Austen's nephew James Edward Austen-Leigh published his memoir in 1870, he used a softened, Victorianized version of the miniature. No other visual evidence exists.

JANE'S MEN

Jane may have been no "husband-hunting butterfly,"[34] but she did notice men and often talked about them. She referred to a Harry Digweed as "dear Harry,"[35] and she playfully told Cassandra that middle-aged bachelor James Holder intended to seduce her.[36] At eighteen Jenny returned from a visit to her brother Edward infatuated with Edward Taylor's "beautiful dark eyes."[37] Several men found her attractive enough to consider her a potential wife.

One Christmas, Jane met Tom Lefroy, a year her senior, at a public ball and again at the Harwoods' home at Deane House. A recent graduate of Trinity College, Dublin, Tom shared Jane's passions, including reading, and so impressed Jane that she bequeathed all her other suitors to a friend.[38] However, no long-term relationship formed.

Incidentally, Tom was not the boxing, drinking, whoring rebel depicted in the 2007 film *Becoming Jane*. He later studied law at Lincoln's Inn, then practiced in Ireland until his death at age ninety-three, a full fifty years after Austen died. Late in life, he confessed to a boyish crush on the famous novelist Jane Austen, whom he met during a visit to his uncle and aunt at Ashe, two miles from Stevenson, in 1796.

LOSSES, REALIZATIONS, AND FRUSTRATIONS

Jenny's early twenties were marked by some tragic losses. In 1795 Cassandra had become engaged to the Reverend Thomas Fowle, a former pupil of Rev. Austen's. The engagement was kept secret while Tom went to the West Indies to serve as a chaplain. In February 1797 the Austens received news from San Domingo that Tom had contracted yellow fever and died. Cassandra never seriously contemplated marriage again and entered almost immediately into a premature spinsterhood.

James's first wife, Anne, also died, suddenly and inexplicably, in May 1795. James's two-year-old daughter, Anna, wandered the house, calling for her mother, prompting James to send her off to her aunts for feminine attention. James remarried, to Mary Lloyd, less than two years later. Mary had been a friend to Jane and Cassandra, but once she entered the family, things fell off. Mary was inconsiderate toward her stepdaughter Anna, and simply could not forget that James had once had another wife.[39] Jane thought Mary domineered over her husband, and the effect on James was frustrating: "I am sorry and angry that [James's] visits should give more pleasure . . . His chat seems all forced, his opinion on many points too much copied from his wife."[40]

Throughout these events Jane continued writing, and during the late 1790s, her output far surpassed her already impressive body of juvenile work. She wrote *Lady Susan*, an epistolary novella about a beautiful, conniving widow who manipulates all the dolts—male and female—to achieve her will. During 1795, before she was twenty, Jenny wrote the first version of *Elinor and Marianne*, an epistolary novel that was later rewritten into *Sense and Sensibility*. From October 1796 to August 1797, she wrote *First Impressions*, which later became *Pride and Prejudice*. *Susan*—published posthumously as *Northanger Abbey*—was likely begun in the summer of 1798, and she finished it by early the following summer.

Pride and Prejudice has proven the most enduring and popular of the three early works. It focuses on the romance of the haughty, aristocratic Mr. Fitzwilliam Darcy and the witty, strong-willed, but socially inferior Elizabeth Bennet. Elizabeth forms an early prejudice against Mr. Darcy because of reports she receives from a handsome young soldier, Mr. Wickham, who grew up on the Darcy estate. Meanwhile, Darcy is falling in love with the sparkling young Elizabeth. Elizabeth severely rebuffs his first, awkward proposal, but when Darcy gives his side of the story of Wickham, she begins to revise her estimate of the man. When Darcy intervenes to save the Bennet family from a scandal involving Elizabeth's younger sister, Lydia, Elizabeth comes to admire him deeply. Despite the objections of Mr. Darcy's overbearing aunt, Lady Catherine de Bourgh, Elizabeth and Darcy marry.

Austen's original title for *Sense and Sensibility* named the two principal characters Elinor and Marianne Dashwood. When their father dies and they receive little assistance from their half brother, John, they are left to eke out a life with their mother in a cottage provided by the generous John Middleton. Young, romantic Marianne falls wildly in love with the dashing John Willoughby when he rescues her after a fall. When Willoughby suddenly leaves Marianne to pursue a socially advantageous marriage, she is crushed, and only gradually recovers her liveliness. Sobered by her loss, she falls into a quiet love with the older Colonel Brandon. Elinor, meanwhile, is attracted to the diffident Edward Ferrars, who is training for the ministry. Standing in the way of her romance is Lucy Steele, a manipulative young woman who is already secretly engaged to Edward. In the end, of course, Elinor, too, gets her man.

Northanger Abbey is a very different sort of book, written to poke fun at the gothic romances and novels of sensibility that were so popular in Austen's day. These novels were set in old and frightening castles, followed macabre plots, and were populated by characters whose every emotion was openly expressed. Catherine Morland, Austen's female protagonist, has been reading too many of these novels when she visits the spooky Northanger Abbey near

Bath, the estate of the Tilney family. She frightens herself into believing that Henry's father is a monstrous murderer, but Henry slowly weans her away from her fantasies and they are, of course, eventually married.

By the middle of 1799, Austen had completed these three novels, all of which are classics in their way—*Pride and Prejudice* and *Sense and Sensibility*, now canonical romances and comedies of manners, and *Northanger Abbey*, that rare satire that continues to entertain when the object of its satire is long out of fashion. She was twenty-four.

George Austen knew his daughter had extraordinary talent, and in November 1797 had sent a letter to the London publisher Cadell offering the novel that would later become *Pride and Prejudice*. Cadell wasn't interested. They returned the letter without comment.

In 1803, Henry Austen's attorney, William Seymour, was able to sell an early version of *Northanger Abbey*, then known as *Susan*, to the London publisher Benjamin Crosby & Sons,[41] but it remained unpublished until after her death.

JANE, ON MARRIAGE

From what we know of the final products, Jenny arrived early at her characteristic views on marriage, romance, love, women, and morality. They were views taught by her father, shared by her siblings, and confirmed by her critical reading of romance novels. Austen was not an enemy of passion or wealth, but she was an enemy of marriages founded entirely on passion or contracted for material advantage. The best marriages in Austen's novels are marriages of minds and temperament, that make both husband and wife more fully themselves. Compare Austen to the latest "chick flick," and the difference is apparent in an instant.

Austen has often been viewed as an advocate for women. But she is too subtle to fit easily into a spectrum whose poles are "feminist" and "antifeminist." On the one hand she created immensely capable and appealing women. (Elizabeth Bennet can match wits with anyone, and even when pressured by the imperious and the great, she holds fast to her own views and hopes.) On the other hand, Austen's novels all end with a strong, independent woman seeking and finding the man of her dreams. (Elizabeth eventually puts her wit and vivacity into service as Mrs. Fitzwilliam Darcy.)

Her most mature meditation on femininity comes in her final complete novel, *Persuasion*, where the opposition between male and female characters is sharper and more stereotyped than in other novels. The book's Captain Wentworth was the manliest man Austen ever created. Its Anne Elliot, by the same token, is Austen's most stereotypically female heroine.

JANE, ON RELIGION

The central importance of Austen's piety has been underemphasized by most biographers and critics, in part because her reticent, Anglican piety is so drastically understated. Austen refrains from religious passion and speaks of Christian truths in a balanced, matter-of-fact manner that lacks existential power and is completely free of the spiritual terrors of a Luther or Bunyan. This can appear to be indifference or rationalism, but it is simply eighteenth-century Christianity.

One early reader got her right, commending Austen as a "Christian writer" whose merit is "enhanced . . . by her religion being not at all obtrusive." Religion is "alluded to, and that incidentally, than studiously brought forward and dwelt upon. . . . She probably introduced it as far as she thought would be generally profitable."[42] Perhaps Jenny had half-listened to too many mediocre, uninspiring sermons to think that sermonizing would be effective in a novel.

Despite her comparative reticence and her careful avoidance of moralizing, Austen's faith was sincere and deep. "On Sunday we went to Church twice," she wrote.[43] Austen also composed prayers, one of which includes these petitions:

> Look with Mercy on the Sins we have this day committed, and in Mercy make us feel them deeply, that our Repentance may be sincere, & our resolutions stedfast of endeavouring against the commission of such in future. Teach us to understand the sinfulness of our own Hearts, and bring to our knowledge every fault of Temper and every evil Habit in which we have indulged to the discomfort of our fellow-creatures, and the danger of our own Souls.[44]

The woman who wrote this had the rhythms of the Anglican prayer book in her blood, a deep sense of her own sinfulness, and a desire to live with more humility.

DISRUPTIONS

Despite her satiric mockery of Romantic excesses, she was a lover of nature, and her letters are full of observations about changing weather and the effect of thunder and snow upon her moods. When Cassandra was away, Jane kept her abreast of the condition of the vegetable and flower gardens: "Some of the Flower seeds are coming up very well. . . . The whole of the Shrubbery Border will soon be very gay with Pinks & Sweet Williams, in addition to the Columbines already in bloom."[45]

The orchard sent Jane into Marianne-like ecstasies: "It is not in Human nature to imagine what a nice walk we have round the Orchard . . . I hear today that an Apricot has been detected on one of the trees."[46]

In 1800, suddenly, she was cut off from her beloved landscape. After visiting the Lloyds at Ibthorpe, Rev. Austen's "daughters came home to be met by their mother. 'Well girls!' she said abruptly, 'it is all settled; we have decided to leave Steventon and go to Bath.' Overcome by shock, Jane fainted dead away."[47] Mrs. Austen believed herself to be in poor health, and Bath promised abundant remedies and a physician on every corner. So George Austen rapidly settled his affairs and moved the family into the city.[48]

Bath was one of the places to be in eighteenth-century England, the baths a destination for the ailing and the whole city a tourist trap boasting England's most ostentatious display of Georgian taste in architecture, consumerism, and city planning. Jane rapidly decided to make the best of it. Later she even set two novels—*Northanger Abbey* and *Persuasion*—partly in that city.

Change of location was not the only disruption in Austen's life at this time. During a holiday at a seaside resort of Sidmouth, Devonshire, she met a young man who fancied her and caught her attention as well. Nothing is known of him for certain, though family lore determined he was a clergyman. He was called away from Sidmouth, promising to return and rejoin the Austens, but they soon received news of his death. No letters from the following months remain, and one can only speculate on the real relation between Austen and this mysterious maybe-lover.

In 1802, a twenty-one-year-old named Harris Bigg-Wither proposed to Jane, who was six years older. Jane had known and loved his family for many years and considered Harris a decent man. She accepted his proposal, but by the following morning, she thought the better of it and reversed her decision. Perhaps she was reluctant to part with the freedom to write that singleness offered. (Or maybe she just wanted to spare future generations of English literature students from having to read the works of "Jane Bigg-Wither.")

MORE LOSSES

The ups and downs of Austen's romantic life were slight compared to the double tragedy of the winter of 1804–1805. On December 16, 1804—Jane's birthday—Madam Lefroy died when a horse bolted and threw her to the ground.[49]

Less than a month later, more devastating, Jane's father died on January 2, 1805, from an illness that lasted only forty-eight hours. "It has been very sudden!" she wrote to brother Frank, serving at his post as a naval captain aboard the HMS *Leopard*.[50]

With the death of Rev. Austen, Mrs. Austen and her daughters were instantly deprived of most of their livelihood. But worse, Jane was deprived of a *father* and of her most enthusiastic literary advocate.

It is commonly thought that these disruptions interrupted Austen's literary career for the better part of a decade, creating a break between the early novels of her twenties and the published work of her midthirties. Cassandra's catalog of the dates of her sister's work contributes to this impression, with its gap between the beginning of *Sense and Sensibility* in November 1797 and the beginning of *Mansfield Park* in February 1811. Austen ended the eighteenth century with three manuscripts and a collection of comic *Juvenalia*. None of it had been published. Her work over the following decade is obscure; we know she wrote *The Watsons* in 1804, but laid it aside unfinished. Even so, that she ceased writing for a decade is scarcely conceivable.

❦

In the years after Rev. Austen's death, the Austen women moved several times within Bath. In July 1806 they moved from Bath for good, settling in Southampton,[51] and placing them within easy reach of James and Edward.

Still, life was not easy, and though Jane had always been conscious of money, at times, she went beyond carefulness to anxiety.[52]

Particularly when visiting Bath or other cities, she noted prices for meat, butter, cheese, and fish, as well as silk, cotton, and clothing.[53] Later she carefully tracked her income.[54]

STILL JENNY

The Austens' residence at Southampton was not permanent. After Edward's wife, Elizabeth, died in 1808, the Austen women moved into the Chawton Cottage on his Hampshire property in July 1809. Jane spent her time doing household chores, and writing when she could. Caroline remembered that Aunt Jane "was fond of work—and she was . . . adept at overcast and satin stich—the peculiar delight of that day."[55]

Austen was also fond of children. This may seem surprising, since she never married and had no children of her own. (It is also surprising because her books contain some of the most brutally funny portraits of bratty children in English literature.) But James had three children by two wives; Edward had eleven; and Francis had eleven. Austen became particularly close to James's eldest, Anna, and Edward's eldest, Fanny.

Anna remembered Jane as a "general favorite with children." And Caroline remembered: "She would tell us the most delightful stories chiefly of Fairyland, and her Fairies had all characters of their own—The tale was invented, I am sure, at the moment, and was sometimes continued for 2 or 3 days, if occasion served."[56]

PUBLISHED AUTHOR

Only a woman of more than ordinary determination could have finished six novels, started two more, and left behind three volumes of juvenile writing in forty-one years. We get a rare glimpse of Jane's determination, which borders on competitiveness, in a letter to Cassandra written shortly after Jane's move to Bath. She took a walk with one Mrs. Chamberlayne, with whom she was becoming acquainted: "It would have amused you to see our progress;—we went up by Sion Hill . . . in climbing a hill Mrs. Chamberlayne is very capital; I could with difficulty keep pace with her—yet would not flinch for the World."[57]

"Would not flinch for the World." That is the voice of a woman who continued writing even after all her efforts at publication were frustrated and kept writing until she had written herself a place in every literary canon in the world.

The delays in publication must have rankled. Books by lawyer, genealogist, and aspiring novelist Samuel Egerton Brydges got published and sold briskly. Austen was confident enough of her own gifts to know that her work was vastly better than his.

But delay had its advantages. "The longer Austen remained unpublished," Claire Harman observed, "the more experimental she became, and the more license she assumed with bold, brilliant moves."[58]

Advantageous or not, remaining unpublished did not appeal to Austen. And so it was, at the Chawton Cottage, from the mahogany desk purchased by her father, that the thirty-something Jane Austen launched a literary career.

How it happened is, characteristically, obscure. There are no surviving letters from 1810, and when Jenny reemerged in the sources in the spring of 1811, she was sending off the manuscript of *Sense and Sensibility* to the London publisher Thomas Egerton, a publishing deal already made. It was published at the end of October 1811. The following year, she finished revising *Pride and Prejudice*, and it was published in January 1813.

She hid her authorship from all but her closest relatives, for the title page of *Sense and Sensibility* said the book was "By a Lady" and *Pride and Prejudice* "By the Author of *Sense and Sensibility*."

By the time *Pride and Prejudice* was released, Jane had already started *Mansfield Park*, which she finished by summer 1813 and published the following year. She began writing *Emma* in late 1813 and finished it by the early months of 1814. Between 1809 and 1814, she rewrote or finished rewriting two novels, wrote two more—apparently from scratch—and published all four.

Mansfield Park has been regarded as Austen's most complex and profound novel. Its main character, Fanny Price, is mousy, retiring, shy, and badly out of place, having been displaced from her poor and crowded family home to Mansfield Park, where her aunt is the lady of the house. Edmund Bertram, the heir of Mansfield Park, is kind to Fanny, but she is bullied by Edmund's sisters and by another aunt, Mrs. Norris. Two visitors from London, the brother-sister pair Henry and Mary Crawford, bring a dazzling and seductive new force into the Park, and Mary tries to entice Edmund away from his plans to seek ordination. Despite her apparent weakness, Fanny shows moral strength that ultimately wins Edmund's admiration and love. Faced with a choice between the seductive Mary Crawford and the upright and pious Fanny Price, Edmund chooses Fanny.

Sense and Sensibility went to a second edition, and Austen surprised herself by earning £140 from it.[59] The first edition of *Mansfield Park* sold out within a year of its publication. Soon Jane's cover of anonymity was slipping.

⊱⊰

Though in another time Jane might have become a CEO of a publishing house, by later standards she never achieved literary celebrity during her lifetime. Her books sold well, and she earned what to her was a considerable sum of money from them. *Emma* turned out to be Austen's most popular and profitable novel, and it alone brought in £450.[60] But by the end of the century, a literary celebrity like Dickens was selling hundreds of thousands of copies of his serialized novels and getting rich.

It is ironic that *Emma*, published in December 1815, should bring Austen closest to literary celebrity, for she feared that book, even lighter in tone than *Pride and Prejudice*, would be panned by people who liked her earlier work. She joked to Cassandra that her books decreased in sense in inverse proportion to the price the publisher paid for them. *Emma*, she theorized, must be her "stupidest" book, because it was the most profitable.

Nonetheless, Austen's work was clearly beginning to be noticed. *Emma* brought Austen recognition from a most discerning quarter when, in March 1816, the *Quarterly Review* devoted an article, written by Walter Scott, to her work. Austen had risen to literary heights that few achieve. To be approved by the giant of the literary world was no small achievement.

Austen did not live to enjoy her moment of modest celebrity for long. A year later, she was mortally ill, and by July 1817 she was dead.

DEATH

Austen was, as she would have said, "stout" throughout her life. But during 1816–1817, her health collapsed. It was only one of the collapses of that year. Henry's bank failed, putting the family, especially the women, at financial risk and leaving Henry permanently deflated. A ship Charles commanded wrecked, and though Charles was exonerated, he was anxious about getting future commissions. And a Chawton family sued Edward. He eventually paid them off, but the suit left his possession on his Hampshire properties—including Chawton Cottage—uncertain for some time.

Jane was suffering too. As early as spring 1816, she began showing symptoms of what would later be known as Addison's disease, a disorder in the endocrine system that causes fatigue, muscle weakness, joint pains, and darkening of the skin. Austen also suffered back pains.

Yet, her illness did not dampen her creativity, and she continued writing for publication. By August 1816 she had finished her last complete novel, published as *Persuasion* the following autumn. *Persuasion*, whose conclusion she rewrote because she found the original "tame and flat," contains one of the most famous endings in English literature.

Early in 1817, Jane began *Sanditon*, but within a few months she was too exhausted to continue. She never returned to her novels after March, but what we have of *Sanditon* shows that she had lost none of her literary powers.

By May her symptoms had gotten worse, and her family moved her to Winchester, under the nurture of the respected Dr. Lyford. Cassandra cared for Jane day and night, Henry and James visited to administer the sacrament, and Edward was regularly at her side. Nieces visited too. Jane's life was ending as it began, surrounded by family.

On July 17, Cassandra went to town on an errand. She returned to find her sister recovering from a faint. "When I asked her if there was any thing she wanted, her answer was she wanted nothing but death & some of her words were 'God grant me patience, Pray for me Oh Pray for me.'"[61]

They were Jane's last words. The next day, July 18, 1817, she died at age forty-one and was buried at Winchester Cathedral.

FROM DIVINE JANE
BACK TO JENNY

Critics of her day did not quite know what to do with Jenny Austen. One can hardly blame them. They were used to sensational Gothic romances and tales of passion, but suddenly, Austen had invented a new genre—the modern novel. All English novelists since Austen have had to work within, or renounce, the genre she made her own.

In themselves, critical reviews were respectful enough. A "very pleasing and entertaining" work said one of *Sense and Sensibility*, and another added that it was "well written; . . . the conclusion such as the reader must wish it should be."[62] *Pride and Prejudice* was greeted with somewhat more enthusiasm,[63] but *Emma* brought Austen's reputation to its highest point during her lifetime, along with the help of a reviewer who understood what she was up to. Sir Walter recognized that her talents were, in her field, superior to his own:

> That young lady has a talent for describing the involvements and feelings and characters of ordinary life, which is to me the most wonderful I ever met with. The big Bow-Wow strain I can do myself like any now going; but the exquisite touch which renders ordinary common-place things and characters interesting . . . is denied to me.[64]

Several years after Austen's death, Richard Whately published a perceptive review of her work in the *Quarterly Review* that set the terms for much of later Austen criticism. For the first time, Austen was set alongside the greatest writers of the Western tradition, Homer and Shakespeare. Whately recognized that Austen aimed to instruct, but that she instructed obliquely rather than directly. Unlike Evangelicals such as Hannah More and Maria Edgewood, Austen left the reader to "collect" moral lessons from the narrative, which Whately found more effective.[65]

But the times were changing. A different sensibility—passionate, romantic, Gothic, everything that Austen found so amusingly improbable—was taking form in the Romantic movement. Austen's books went out of print for a time, and when in print did not sell particularly well.

After mid-century, James Edward's work reawakened interest in Austen. Thomas Babington Macaulay described Austen as second only to Shakespeare as a "truthful drawer of character";[66] Oxford's A. C. Bradley delivered a lecture that marked the beginning of serious critical attention to Austen; and by the beginning of the twentieth century, Henry James could see a commercialized cult of Austen in the making.[67]

But the Victorians had created an imaginary Austen, sanitized, civilized, and bowdlerized. Even her physical appearance was adjusted to Victorian sensibilities.

Literary critic Roger Sales has argued that the family embarked on a reinvention of Austen soon after her death, blunting the satiric strain of her novels and turning her into a quaintly domestic figure. He makes his case persuasively by comparing the edited letters that James Edward included in his memoir with the full text. One of Austen's letters closes with "Give my love to little Cassandra! I hope she found my Bed comfortable last night and has not filled it with fleas." Austen's nephew obligingly left out the part about the fleas, one of the best bits in the letter.

Another of James Edward's letters leaves out Austen's reference to the elegant "naked Cupids over the Mantlepiece" in the drawing room at a London school, and her observation that these "must be a fine study for Girls." Apparently, he could not bear the thought of his dear aunt contemplating naked cupids.

Stripped of her punchy humor, the Victorian Austen was transfigured, bizarrely, into a celebrant of home and hearth, of feminine decorum and private domesticity.

JENNY RECOVERED

It was not until the twentieth century that Jenny reemerged from behind the fictitious Jane Austen that had been concocted by her family and their Victorian collaborators. Only then did critics and readers begin to hear again the impish, satiric laughter that is Austen's characteristic tone. It is fitting that, since Austen invented the modern novel, the recovery of the full Austen occurred with the rise of modernist fiction.

Rudyard Kipling recovered Jane as a writer for men. In his 1924 story "The Janeites," Kipling puts Austen in the trenches, where British soldiers have found consolation in her while enduring the terrors of trench warfare. They even form a secret society of Janeites.[68]

It was Virginia Woolf, however, who recaptured the original feel of Austen's work. Importantly, she turned to the *Juvenalia* and found a highly sophisticated, laughing fifteen-year-old writing for an audience bigger than her schoolroom.[69]

Jesus told His disciples to become like children. This has often been misunderstood, but simply, to "become as a child" meant not to take the world as seriously as it takes itself—as did, perhaps, Dante, Shakespeare, and Dickens. Dante wrote out of frustrated love; Shakespeare, to give something to his actors to perform; and Dickens, to express his anger at the world. But at her best, Jane Austen wrote out of laughter. Her art came from the mischievous glee of a precocious teenager amused by the follies of the world around her, wanting to get us in on the joke.

Jane's final voice, though deepened and matured by life's losses, is still the playful voice of the *Juvenalia*—the voice of the supremely talented writer who lived and died as Jenny. Her greatness as an artist is that of one who became, and remained, a little child.

To learn more about Jane Austen, read Peter Leithart's *Jane Austen* (Nashville: Thomas Nelson, 2009) from the Christian Encounters Series.

7 | D. L. MOODY
(1837–1899)

by Kevin Belmonte

Love is the lever with which Christ lifts the world.

—D. L. MOODY

F our-year-old Dwight Moody had just begun to attend school when, on May 28, 1841, a neighbor poked his head in at the window of the schoolhouse in Northfield, Massachusetts, and asked if any of Ed Moody's children were there. Their father, the man said, had just died. Coming home, complaining of a great pain in his side, the rugged stonemason had staggered to his bedside and collapsed.

We know nothing of the scene that met Ed Moody's children when reunited with their grief-stricken mother, Betsy, but later in life, Moody wrote: The shock made such an impression on me . . . that I shall never forget it.[1] . . . My father died bankrupt, and the creditors came and swept away about everything we had."[2]

"My mother," Dwight remembered, "was left with . . . [seven] children. One calamity after another swept over the entire household. [A month after my father's death] twins were added to the family, and my mother was . . . taken sick."[3]

Counseled by some to break up her family and let others rear them, she refused, saying: "Not as long as I have these two hands."[4]

An unlooked-for grace entered her life in the person of the Reverend Oliver Everett of the Northfield Unitarian Church. He urged her not to part with her children, but to keep them together. What is more, he promised to help.

W. H. Daniels wrote: "True to his promise, Pastor Everett used to help the widow [Moody] in the care of her children. He would visit them betimes, cheer them up with some pleasant words, settle quarrels among the boys, give the little ones a bright piece of silver all round, and bid the mother keep on praying, telling her God would never forget her labour of love."[5]

Betsy Moody warmed to this compassionate man. Several weeks after Edwin Moody's funeral, Everett baptized her and all her children.

Young Dwight Moody was little less fond of Everett than his mother was, and the depth of the affection he bore for the old pastor was revealed in the days following the appointment of a successor. The new pastor undid much, if not all, of the good work Everett had invested in the Moody family, especially where Dwight was concerned. He now began "to look upon Sunday with a kind of dread,"[6] and soon ceased to have any interest in church at all.

SEEKING HIS FORTUNE

When Dwight Moody's years of formal schooling were done, he had gained the equivalent of a fifth-grade education.[7] His friend J. Wilbur Chapman commented: "His reading is described as outlandish beyond description . . . He never stopped to spell out an unfamiliar word, but mouthed his sense of it without full dependence upon his training, or made up a new word which sounded to his ear as suitable as the original."[8]

Other elements were a part of the unbroken and coltish aspects of young Dwight's personality. J. C. Pollock, one of Moody's ablest biographers, wrote: "Farm work was irksome . . . Dwight loved to be free on the hills. He loved to run, . . . to fight other boys; to swim."[9]

Young Moody's love of swimming appears to have led to a

brush with death. The event left a lingering impression: "Once I was drowning, and as I was about to sink the third time I was rescued. In the twinkling of an eye it seemed as though everything I had said, done, or thought of flashed across my mind."[10]

Sobering as this experience may have been, it was soon after subsumed by a wish to strike out on his own. His son Will Moody wrote: "While cutting and hauling logs on the mountain side with his brother Edwin one day in the early spring of 1854, [seventeen-year-old Dwight] exclaimed, in his characteristically abrupt manner: 'I'm tired of this! I'm not going to stay around here any longer. I'm going to the city.'"[11]

❦

Moody stepped off a train in Boston in early April 1854. After arriving, Dwight, or "D. L.," as he now preferred to be called, wasted little time in getting to the prosperous shoe store owned by his mother's brother Samuel Holton.[12] It soon became apparent that the young man harbored hopes his uncle did not share. D. L.'s plan seems to have been to present himself at his uncle's store, whereupon he fully expected to be offered a position.

Such thinking had little basis in fact. When D. L. walked through the door, Uncle Samuel took his nephew to the shoe store office, where they chatted pleasantly for a few moments about family doings. He then abruptly indicated he had no more time to visit. A few moments later D. L. was back out on the street, not knowing quite what had just happened.[13]

Kindness then intervened in the person of Uncle Samuel's younger brother Lemuel, a partner in the shoe store. He approached the boy and suggested he lodge with him and his family in their suburban Winchester home until he found work.[14]

After days of efforts and meeting nothing but failures, Dwight grew discouraged with Boston and told his uncle Lemuel he was going to New York. The uncle strongly advised against this and urged him to speak to his uncle Samuel again about the matter.

So D. L. asked his uncle Samuel for a place in his store.

His uncle replied, "I am afraid if you come in here you will want to run the store yourself. . . . If you want to come in here and do the best you can, and do it right, . . . and if you are willing to go to church and Sunday school when you are able . . . you may come [and] we'll see how we can get along."

And so it was that a chastened young man began to work in his uncle's shoe store.[15]

The Call of God

Dwight began to attend church services at the Mount Vernon Congregational Church, which his uncle Samuel attended. It was here that he met one of the most important people he would ever meet in his life: his Sunday school teacher, Edward Kimball.

Though Moody was untutored in the basics of the Christian faith, Kimball soon sensed that his young friend, for all of his rough edges, might be hearing the call of God to his heart. The more he thought and prayed about it, the more settled this conviction became. And so, on April 21, 1855, he decided to seek Moody out at his uncle's store.

I found Moody in the back part of the store wrapping up shoes in paper and putting them on shelves. I went up to him and put my hand on his shoulder . . . Then I told [D. L.] of Christ's love for him. . . . It seemed that [he] was just ready for the light that then broke upon him, for there . . . in the back of that shoe store in Boston [he] gave himself and his life to Christ.[16]

It was the watershed moment of D. L. Moody's young life. The God and Savior of whom Kimball spoke seemed to answer all of the most important questions D. L. had ever asked within the deep places of his heart. An eternal moment kindled within him, and he embraced the Christian faith.

❦

Grateful for his nephew's conversion, Uncle Samuel had nonetheless become increasingly frustrated with Moody. By 1856, D. L.'s success as a salesman was beyond dispute; but little else about their relationship seemed to be. "When a crisis finally came in [their] relations, and there seemed little opportunity for advancement, he decided to go to Chicago."[17]

Soon after his arrival in Chicago, D. L. "joined the Young Men's Mission Band of the First Methodist Episcopal Church, whose purpose was to visit hotels and boarding houses on Sunday mornings, distributing tracts and inviting people to church services."[18]

On Sunday afternoons he attended "a little mission Sabbath-school on the corner of Chicago Avenue and Wells Street." He soon offered to teach a class. The school superintendent told Moody that he had twelve teachers already and only sixteen students. "But," he said, "if you can work up a class of your own, you would be welcome."[19]

The following Sunday, Moody arrived with eighteen ragged and dirty children taken straight from the streets of the city.

As he looked back on that first Sunday, he felt a tremendous sense of satisfaction and fulfillment. "That was the happiest Sunday I have ever known," he said.[20]

❦

In the fall of 1858, when he was twenty-one, Moody concluded that not enough children were being helped. And so, rather than continue to ask children to come with him to the school on Chicago Avenue, he would go to them.

Years later, one of Moody's "boys," Jimmy Sexton, described his first impressions of the man he came to know as a friend. Sexton and the other boys found him very much like themselves—rough, rowdy, and down to earth.[21] Moody invited Sexton and the other ragged boys to help him start a mission Sunday school.

From the start, Moody threw convention to the winds. His first task was to commandeer an abandoned freight car on North State Street and start holding classes there.

Jimmy Sexton and the other members of the gang rounded up more boys until the old freight car was full to the bursting. One of Moody's church friends, Lawyer King, heard about the stir Moody's school had created and told D. L. that he knew of an abandoned saloon on Michigan Street. Rotting and ratty, it was nonetheless roomier than the freight car.[22]

A Chicago minister named G. S. F. Savage recalled: "In this tumble-down old house he began to gather in the children. He went out into the streets with candy and knickknacks and got the good will of the children."[23] King remembered: "All loved [Moody], because he took such an interest in their welfare. No one [forgot his] pleasant smile."[24]

Sunday events proved so successful that Moody opened the saloon for the first weeknights it had seen in years. Savage visited one evening and never forgot what he saw: "I found him with . . . a child on his knee who he was trying to teach. There were twenty-five or thirty children in all, and they were as sorry a lot of little ragamuffins as could have been found in Chicago."[25]

Lyle Dorsett, one of Moody's finest biographers, has described their plight better than anyone: "These children were emotionally and physically wounded. Often beaten, sexually abused, malnourished, and exposed [to] drinking, [drug addiction], gambling, and prostitution, these youngsters were discarded and treated like rats and other vermin that roamed their wooden shanties and tenement hovels."[26]

Moody's Chicago friend W. H. Daniels described Little Hell, where they came from: "This was a section on the Lake shore, north of the river . . . It was a moral lazaretto.[27] . . . It was . . . dangerous for any decent person to walk those streets after nightfall. Thither went Moody to recruit his Sunday-school."[28]

THE CRUCIBLE OF WAR

President-elect Abraham Lincoln visited D. L. Moody's Sunday school in November 1860. The man soon to be inaugurated as America's sixteenth president spoke poignantly. It was an event rich in symbolism, a harbinger of events that would change America forever.

"I was once as poor as any boy in this school," he said, looking out over the small sea of dirty faces before him, "but I am now President of the United States, and if you attend to what is taught you here, some of you may yet be President of the United States."

But what neither he nor Moody knew was how quickly the dread specter of civil war would overtake them—and, indeed, so many of the young people Lincoln saw that day. When the Civil War commenced in 1861, approximately seventy-five of the boys to whom Lincoln had spoken would take up arms to defend the Union. Some would give their lives for it.

The Civil War was a crucible for D. L. Moody, but not in the way one might expect. For reasons of conscience, he did not enlist in the Union army, but along with John Farwell and another Chicago friend, B. F. Jacobs, he organized an army and navy committee of the Chicago YMCA, which later became a branch of the United States Christian Commission.[29]

But he was not solely an organizer. He actively took part as a volunteer in the Commission's mission of promoting "the spiritual good, intellectual improvement, and social and physical comfort" of the soldiers. On nine occasions he traveled to the front with the Union army during the war.[30]

At the outset of hostilities, however, Moody's work as a relief worker centered on Camp Douglas, a military outpost located just a few miles south of Chicago. Moody's role developed over time into a position that was one part chaplain-at-large, one part relief worker.

What lingered long after Moody's wartime service were the scenes and people he encountered. They became the subject of stories he told time and again from the pulpit.

The following story, concerning the Battle of Shiloh, is taken from a stenographer's transcript of one of Moody's later sermons.

On the morning of April 6, 1862, Confederate forces attacked General Ulysses S. Grant's encampment near Pittsburg Landing, beginning the bloodiest engagement of the war.[31] The fighting lasted for two days, resulting in a narrow victory for Union forces; but one secured at a horrific cost. Shiloh was a battle in which more than 13,047 Union soldiers had been killed—nearly 24,000 men in all when Confederate casualties (10,699) were taken into account.[32] Moody was with Grant and an eyewitness to it all—the carnage, the desperate heroism, and heart-rending visits to offer what comfort could be given to the dying. It's little wonder that he never forgot what he saw.

Moody later recounted in a sermon:

One night . . . after the terrible battle of Pittsburgh Landing I was in a hospital at Murfreesboro looking after the wounded and dying. . . . Just as I had fallen asleep in the middle of the night a soldier woke me up and said that a man in a certain ward wanted to see me.

. . . So I went with him, and he led me to the wounded man's cot. The dying soldier said: "Chaplain, I want you to help me die."

. . . I told him about Jesus Christ; but he shook his head and said: "He won't help me, because I have been fighting against Him all my life."

. . . Then I turned to the third chapter of John, and said: "I am going to read a conversation that Christ had with a man who went to Him in your state of mind."

. . . The dying man's eyes were riveted upon me, as he eagerly listened to every word that fell from my lips, and when I got to the fourteenth verse and read, "And as Moses lifted up the serpent in the wilderness, even so must the Son of man be lifted up: That whosoever believeth in Him should not perish, but have eternal life" . . . a radiant smile came over his face, and it seemed as if a new life had dawned upon him. When I had finished the chapter, I sat quietly beside him for some time. I noticed that his lips were moving, and I thought perhaps he was trying to pray. I bent over him and I could hear him faintly whisper, "That whosoever believeth in Him should not perish, but have eternal life."

Then he opened his eyes, fixed a calm, resigned look upon me and said: "Chaplain, you needn't read to me any more; it is enough; Jesus Christ was lifted up in my place. I am not alone now."

After I had prayed with him and made him as comfortable as possible, I left him for the night. The next morning I hastened back to the ward. The cot was empty. I asked the nurse . . . "Tell me how he died?"

"Why," said she, "he kept repeating those verses over and over again, and just as he breathed his last I heard him say, 'As Moses lifted up the serpent in the wilderness, even so must the Son of man be lifted up!'"[33]

C. F. Goss, who had hired the stenographer to take down the Moody sermon in which this story appeared, summarized Moody's wartime service. "The effect of this terrible experience upon [Mr. Moody's] mind can be traced through all the rest of his life in many of his sermons and addresses. The immense activities which he beheld, . . . the blood, the tears, the carnage . . . lent a new color, deep, somber, [and] solemn—to all he did and said."[34]

But not all was devastation for D. L. Moody during the Civil War. He married Emma Charlotte Revell on Thursday, August 28, 1862.

They had first gotten to know one another in Chicago in 1858 when Moody noticed her as a fifteen-year-old new teacher for girls in a Sunday school he sometimes attended on Wells Street.[35] He soon began calling at the Washington Street home where Emma and her English émigré family lived.

Moody was bowled over by this pretty girl with her "quiet maturity and happy laugh."[36] Still, he would have to bide his time. No thought of engagement could be entertained until she turned seventeen—two years hence.[37] Even then, he would have to wait two more years before they could marry.

Straightaway, it seems, she began to smooth his rough edges. Though she was only fifteen, and he a very independent-minded young man of twenty, he assented. He was too deeply in love to kick at the traces over much. Their son Paul described his father's high regard and love for his mother: "My father's admiration for [my mother] was as boundless as his love. To the day of his death, I believe, he never ceased to wonder at . . . the miracle of having won the love of a woman he considered so completely his superior."[38]

Following a brief honeymoon, the Moodys took up residence in a tiny house in the then slummy north side of Chicago. Emma's pluck and gentle courage may have been more understated than her husband's, but they were no less strong than the faith-based devotion each bore for the untouchables of that great city. They would serve God and those children together.

And they grew together—over a marriage of almost forty years.

GOD LOVES SINNERS

Moody once shared a story of how he had been spectacularly wrong. His coming to terms with that fact changed the course of his life and ministry. Had this transformation not taken place, he would never have become the herald of God's grace, mercy, and love so many remembered him to be.

He told a large audience one memorable evening: "There was a time when I preached that God hated the sinner, and that God was after every poor sinner with a double-edged sword.

But I have changed my ideas upon this point. I will tell you how."[39]

In 1867, when I was preaching in Dublin, in a large hall, at the close of the service, a young man . . . came up to me and said he would like to go back to America with me and preach the gospel.[40] . . . He asked me if I would write to him when I went, and he would come with me. When I went I thought I would not write to him, as I did not know whether I wanted him or not.

After I arrived at Chicago, I got a letter . . . stating he would be in Chicago next Thursday. . . . I said to the officers of the church: "There is a man coming from England, and he wants to preach. I am going to be absent on Thursday and Friday. If you will let him preach on those days, I will be back on Saturday . . ."

[And so,] at my request, they let him preach.

On my return on Saturday I was anxious to hear how the people liked him, and I asked my wife. . . .

She said, "They liked him very much. *He preaches a little different from what you do. He tells people God loves them.* I think you will like him."

. . . I went down Saturday night to hear him, but I had made up my mind not to like him because he preached different from me.

[That evening] he took his text . . . the third chapter of John and the sixteenth verse . . . He preached a wonderful sermon from that text. "For God so loved the world that he gave his only begotten Son, that whosoever believeth in him should not perish, but have everlasting life."

My wife had told me he had preached the two previous sermons from that text, and I noticed there was a smile over the house when he took the same text. Instead of preaching that God was behind them with a double-edged sword to hew them down, he told them God wanted every sinner to be saved, and He loved them.

I could not keep back the tears. I didn't know God thought so much of me. . . .

On Sunday night, . . . he preached his fourth sermon from that wonderful text, . . . and he went from Genesis to Revelation to show that it was love, love, love, that brought Christ from Heaven, that made Him step from the throne to lift up this poor, fallen world. He struck a higher chord that night, and it was glorious.

The next night he preached his fifth sermon from that wonderful text. . . .

The whole church was on fire before the week was over. Tuesday night came, and there was a greater crowd than ever. . . . He preached his sixth sermon from that wonderful text . . . It seemed as if every heart was on fire, and sinners came pressing into the kingdom of God.

On Wednesday night . . . he preached his seventh sermon from that wonderful text.

I have never forgotten those nights. I have preached a different gospel since, and I have had more power with God and man since.[41]

Love, as expressed in John 3:16, now became the hallmark of Moody's preaching. "Love is the lever," he declared, "with which

Christ lifts the world."[15] Moody held to this truth with an ardor that only increased with time.

❧

When the city bell first rang the alarm for what would come to be known as the "Great Chicago Fire," Moody was in the midst of preaching a sermon at Farwell Hall in midtown.

Like most who heard him that night, Moody thought nothing of the alarm at first. Fires—always tragic events to be sure—were commonplace in 1870s America.[42] Hopefully, this fire could be quickly contained. But it wasn't. As Moody's service drew to a close, the bell began to ring out a general alarm. Many people quickly departed following the last hymn.

In his sermon he had asked his audience to go home and ponder the question, "What shall I do with Jesus, who is called Christ?" and to return the following Sunday, when he would unfold the answer that had transformed his life—and he hoped, would transform theirs.

Almost immediately after Moody exited Farwell Hall, an apocalyptic scene met his eyes. Off in the distance, fire was breaking out all around.

By midnight, much of Chicago was caught up in a horrific bedlam: Buildings fell in upon themselves. Terrified people and horses screamed amid the roar of the flames. The streets were thronged with firefighters trying to do what they could, as well as an ever-increasing crowd of refugees.

Moody saw no immediate need to flee his home on State Street, the flames as yet somewhat distant from the district in which he lived. But in the early morning hours, a policeman's knock at the door roused the entire household. "We're telling people to leave," he said.

Hastily, the Moodys began to gather what little belongings they could carry. He and Emma then made for her sister's home.[43]

Moody's recollections of this disaster would forever remain vivid. Moody had seen "people rush through the streets crazed with fear" and he would learn something that filled him with an abiding grief. "Some of those," he said, "who were at the [Farwell Hall] meeting were burned to death."[44]

Years later, when preaching at the Chicago World's Fair, the memory of that tragedy still haunted him:

> Twenty-two years have passed away, and I have not seen [the Farwell Hall] congregation since, and I never will meet those people again until I meet them in another world.
>
> But I want to tell you of one lesson I learned that night, which I have never forgotten, and that is, when I preach, to press Christ upon the people then and there, and try to bring them to a decision on the spot. . . . I have asked God many times to forgive me for telling people that night to take a week to think it over . . . I will never do it again.[45]

TRIUMPH IN BRITAIN

The greatest preaching tour Moody ever undertook nearly came to grief before it had begun. In June 1873, at the invitation of friends in Britain, he took ship with his friend Ira Sankey and their wives for what would be his third visit to that country. Both cherished the hope of conducting an extensive series of evangelistic meetings throughout the British Isles.

The Moodys and Sankeys arrived in Liverpool, England, on June 17, 1873. Only when they disembarked did they learn of the deaths of three men—William Pennefather, Henry Bewley, and Cuthbert Bainbridge—who had pledged to pay the expenses of their evangelistic tour.[46]

Dumbstruck and dismayed, the Moodys and Sankeys parted to find temporary lodgings. D. L. and Emma traveled to stay with her family in London, while Ira Sankey and his wife, Fanny, went to stay with Henry Morehouse and his family in the city of Manchester. All they knew to do was to pray.

A glimmer of hope emerged a short time later when Moody remembered an invitation he had received from George Bennett, a chemist in the great Cathedral city of York who was a leading organizer of that city's YMCA. Moody sent word to Sankey: "Here is a door which is partly open, and we will go there and begin our work."[47]

The first public report of the meetings in York appeared in the form of a letter from George Bennett printed in the July 10 issue of a periodical called *The Christian*. Bennett wrote:

On Sunday morning, June 22d, Mr. Moody preached in Salem Congregational Chapel to Christian workers; in the afternoon, in the Corn Exchange, to about a thousand persons, and in the evening in Wesley Chapel. . . .[48]

During the past week the Lord has greatly blessed us in the ingathering of souls. On Sabbath day, June 29th, Mr. Moody preached in two other chapels, and also twice in the Corn Exchange, to audiences numbering about a thousand each. . . . [49]

. . . From the first the Lord has greatly blessed our brothers' labors in the strengthening and stimulating of Christians and in the bringing of many out of darkness into light; their visit will long be remembered in this city. The congregations have from the first been increasingly large.

P.S.—Sunday evening, 11pm. . . . I have just come from the evening service, where every aisle and standing place, the vestries and lobbies, even the pulpit stairs, were crowded nearly half an hour before the evening service commenced. The Holy Spirit worked mightily, sinners in all positions in life sought the Lord earnestly . . . Over fifty gave their hearts to Christ.[50]

After five weeks of meetings in York, several hundred people had been converted. Many others testified to a deepening of their spiritual life that left them forever changed. Moody and Sankey were now at the eve of departing for a series of meetings scheduled for Sunderland.[51] The whole of Great Britain, it seemed, lay open to the work they had come to do.

⬥

The preaching tour that commenced at York grew in time to become a two-year crusade that fostered a nationwide spiritual renewal in Great Britain. No one had ever seen anything quite like it. Many marveled that a rough-hewn American was at the heart of it—not least D. L. Moody himself.

After a five-week campaign in Sunderland, and additional preaching tours before ever-increasing crowds throughout Yorkshire and Northumberland, Moody and Sankey moved on to Scotland to what was later called "the awakening in Edinburgh."

Along with the Edinburgh meetings, services were also held in Leith. The meetings in Leith proved crucial, for due to the large shipping interests of the city, they attracted people from almost every part of the world. Many seafaring men attended the services, and in consequence, the message of the meetings Moody and Sankey held not only extended throughout the great population of Scotland but was carried in ships around the world.[52] Thousands may have heard the gospel in Edinburgh and Leith. But the ripple effect was international in scope. Something extraordinary was beginning to take shape.

⬥

Moody and Sankey moved on to Glasgow after the Edinburgh mission closed. Will Moody wrote:

> One of the most impressive gatherings during this mission was a meeting held . . . especially for warehouse girls, of whom there are probably more than twelve thousand in the city . . . While five thousand were seated in the building and several hundred standing, outside was a crowd of more than a thousand girls.[53]
>
> On the following evening the meeting was for young men, when nearly six thousand were brought together. A service was held for children also, and another for young women. The final meeting was held in the Botanical Gardens on the following Sunday. . . .
>
> Mr. Moody preached for an hour on "Immediate Salvation."[54]

After the sermon when Moody asked those who wished to place their faith in Christ to stand, two thousand people rose to their feet.[55]

⁐

The capstone of Moody and Sankey's mission to Britain was the four months of the London mission of 1875. Some 285 meetings were attended by 2,530,000 people.[56]

Ireland, Scotland, and England—all had been deeply stirred by spiritual renewal. Moody and Sankey had been much blessed of God. Nothing like the tour they had undertaken had been seen since the days of the Wesleys and Whitefield, and perhaps not even then.

CHRISTIAN EDUCATION
FOR ALL

After returning to America, Moody went to his hometown of Northfield, Massachusetts, for a rest. One day, sometime prior to

1876, Moody was on his way back to Northfield from travels else-where. Driving with his brother Samuel over one of the mountain roads near the village, they passed an isolated cottage, far from town or any neighbor. Sitting in the doorway were a mother and two daughters braiding straw hats.

Moody decided to stop for a few moments to visit. As he and Samuel talked with the two daughters, they learned that their father was bedridden with paralysis and could do nothing to support his family. The burden of providing for the family had fallen to the two girls. They were able to make ends meet but had no time left to pur-sue their schooling—something they ardently wished to do, since their ailing father was well educated and had stirred a deep desire within them to learn.

Both Moodys were greatly moved by this story. Because they had been reared in Northfield themselves amid poverty, and without a father, they knew only too well that for every family like this with daughters who wished to learn, there were many others similarly circumstanced. It moved them to see these young women consigned to lonely lives of toil with no hope of something better.

Samuel felt particularly burdened. In subsequent discussions with his elder brother, he spoke often of the idea of doing something to change things for the girls they had met, and others like them.

Moody resolved to do as his younger brother had suggested. He would found a school "to put such educational advantages within reach of girls living among the New England hills as would fit them for a broader sphere in life than they could otherwise hope for."[57]

Things got going in 1878, though not in a way that Moody could have foreseen. In the autumn of that year, Moody was at his home in Northfield, discussing the ideas of a school for girls with H. N. F. Marshall, of Boston. As they talked, Moody saw that the owner of sixteen acres of adjoining land to his own was passing by. Moody approached his neighbor and asked him if he would sell his land. The neighbor said he was willing and named a price, whereupon Moody and Marshall invited the man into Moody's home, "made out the papers, and before the owner had recovered from his surprise, the land had passed out of his hands."[58]

In the spring of 1879, construction of a recitation hall commenced. Will Moody fondly remembered how it all began: "[Father] could not wait for a dormitory to be built, but altered his own house to accommodate the students. . . . The Northfield Seminary for Young Women was formally opened on November 3, 1879, classes being held in the dining-room of [our] home until the recitation hall was completed the following December."[59]

Among the first students who met together in the dining room were the two girls Moody had seen braiding straw hats outside their mountain home. They excelled as students and were models of all that the Northfield Seminary sought to be and perpetuate.

As the campus grew, a copy of the Scriptures was placed in the cornerstone of each of the school buildings as they were built. This was, Will Moody wrote, "symbolic of the place that God's Word holds in the life of the schools. It [was] indeed, foundation, cornerstone, and capstone of [Father's] whole system."[60]

In June 1899 the Northfield Seminary celebrated its twentieth anniversary. By this time, its enrollment had risen to nearly four hundred students, with a staff of teachers and matrons numbering thirty-nine. The campus had also grown considerably, now consisting of "five hundred acres of land, nine dormitories, a gymnasium, library, recitation hall, auditorium, and farm buildings."[61]

It was all a sight that gladdened D. L. Moody's heart. His faith had been the source of all that was good in his life. Now a vibrant school existed that could commend that faith to young women and give them the education he never had.

No sooner," Will Moody wrote, "was the [Northfield] Seminary under way than a corresponding school for boys suggested itself. [The] Mount Hermon School for Young Men was therefore started on similar principles. The first purchase of property was made in November 1879."[62]

Will Moody recalled, "In both [of the] Northfield schools, the end in view [was] to impart knowledge, not so much as an accomplishment [in and of itself,] but as a means of making men and women more serviceable to society."[63] In short, the gifts and talents each student possessed were to be carefully cultivated and nurtured—that in the future these young men and women would enter spheres of service fully recognizing they were among those "to whom much had been given."[64] It was devoutly hoped that their lives and future endeavors would be guided by the desire to make a grateful return in service to God and others for all they had been given. To foster this good end, every course of study at the Northfield schools included what was then called "Bible training." By 1900, eight hundred students at the Northfield Seminary and the Mount Hermon School were receiving instruction in the Scriptures twice a week.[65]

Will Moody described the results: "In the twenty years that have elapsed since these two schools were first established, nearly six thousand students have felt the influence of the work, and hundreds have given their time and talent to the proclamation of the Gospel."[66]

A former student, the Reverend Alexander McGaffin of Brooklyn wrote, "I went to Mount Hermon as a mere boy—without any particular aim in life or any serious religious convictions. . . .

"Mount Hermon was the gateway of Heaven for me . . . It helped me to cherish every lofty desire. It inspired me with courage . . . It placed before me a holy ambition, and when it launched my little craft out into deep water, there were a compass and pilot aboard—and I have not yet run aground."[67]

In 1886 Moody decided to do something for Chicago, the city that lay close to his heart. He would establish a school for the nations in the heart of the city.

The Chicago Evangelization Society, later renamed the Moody Bible Institute, was born.[68] Its mission statement was a realization of D. L. Moody's vision. It would foster the "education and training of Christian workers, including teachers, ministers, missionaries . . . who may completely and effectively proclaim the gospel of Jesus Christ."[69] One hundred and twenty-six years on, the Moody Bible Institute (MBI) endures and continues its commitment to this mission.

Young men and women from every corner of the globe can now receive a first-rate education in the heart of America's third-largest city. Undergraduates can pursue a diverse array of studies, including biblical languages, communications, electronic media, youth ministry, pastoral studies, women's ministries, sacred music, theology, apologetics, world missions and evangelism, urban ministries, and applied linguistics. Graduate students can earn advanced degrees in biblical studies, intercultural studies, urban studies and spiritual formation, as well as the more traditional master of divinity.

A Story, Not a Sermon

Billy Graham, it has been said, always sought "to put the cookies on the lower shelf" when preaching—that is, he spoke in ways readily understood, even by those who were unchurched. Long years before, Moody had begun weaving the rustic proverbs he learned as a boy into his sermons. Over time, he took to coining phrases of his own with the ease of a born raconteur. Both were techniques that came naturally to him and are reminiscent of the gilded age's most celebrated speaker, Mark Twain.

Moody could be bracing in his use of word pictures, as in this challenge to the cold and lifeless conformity that characterized so much nineteenth-century spirituality—a recurring theme of his preaching: "There are too many religious meetings which are sadder than a funeral. They are hindrance to the cause. They breed people with faces bearing an expression as chilling as an east blast from the lake."[70]

Dry, censorious, turgid, and often brimstonish homilies were a staple of nineteenth-century preaching and a reason why many stayed away from church. Moody's sermons were nothing like this, and they stood out.

Because he was never ordained and had no formal training for the ministry, Moody never became steeped in the hoary traditions of a church that in many respects had become stagnant with them.[71] Using Christ's parables as a model, he interspersed his sermons repeatedly with stories. "Men will listen to a story," he said, "when they won't listen to Scripture, and the moral of a story remains with them a long time, and often sets them thinking along the lines they refuse to consider in sermon form."[72]

Storytelling is a staple of preaching now. But in Moody's time, it was a novel and appealing innovation, especially in the extent to which he used it. And the proof was in the response—hundreds of thousands heeded his call to embrace the Christian faith.

Heaven Opens Before Me

In the morning and evening of Tuesday, February 13, 1898, D. L. Moody addressed overflow gatherings of students at Yale University. A third meeting, described by the *New York Times* as a "monster meeting," was held in the Hyperion Theatre. There, the *Times* continued, "2,000 were turned away for lack of room."

In 1899, Moody accepted an invitation to conduct a series of meetings in Kansas City in the autumn of that year. Departing

Northfield, he started for the west by train on Thursday, November 8.[73] Stopping over in Philadelphia, he was met by his friend John Wanamaker, who "coaxed him very hard to defer his journey as I thought he wasn't very well." But Moody could not be dissuaded.[74] He pushed on to Kansas City.

Arriving in Kansas City on Saturday, November 11, Moody was joined by C. C. Case, a gifted musician who had agreed to conduct the choir during the mission.

Upon arriving at his lodgings at the Coates House, Moody was visited by his old friend Charley Vining. Later that day Vining noted, "I noticed that he was not himself."[75]

At the Convention Hall on Sunday night, November 12, Moody seemed back in step and "preached with his old fire and spirit."[76] The building was filled to its capacity of fifteen thousand, and several thousand people had to be turned away.[77] J. Wilbur Chapman recalled: "The meetings on Monday fulfilled the expectations aroused by Sunday's services. . . . Mr. Moody . . . presented the truth, just as though he were sitting by the side of each one before him."[78]

At breakfast on Tuesday, November 14, Moody looked decidedly unwell. On Friday, November 17,

> Mr. Moody went out driving. He came back thoroughly exhausted. Not until then did he relinquish the hope of preaching that day. He sent for one of the ministers of the committee . . . to preach that afternoon. . . .
>
> It was decided, upon consultation with his physician, Dr. Schauffler, that he should go home at once. Mr. Moody was sitting in his armchair. He was breathing heavily, and his face seemed puffy and bloated. He said his limbs were swelling, and he had a feeling of oppression about his heart.

"Under the imperative order of his physician," Will Moody wrote,

"[Father] reluctantly consented to cease work." It was then agreed that he would leave Kansas City that very night on the evening train.[79]

Alighting at the train station, Moody was met and driven twelve miles to his home. "He went upstairs with little difficulty to prepare for tea," Will Moody wrote, "but never descended again."[80]

His beloved wife, Emma, and children, Will, Emma, and Paul, along with Will's wife, May, and Emma's husband, A. P. Fitt, stayed close to his bedside and kept a sad vigil. By Thursday, December 21, Moody's health had declined precipitously. His heart was failing.

Within a few hours of the end, Moody "fell into a natural sleep," from which, as Will Moody recalled,

> he awoke in about an hour. Suddenly he was heard . . . saying: "Earth recedes; Heaven opens before me."
>
> The first impulse was to try to arouse him from what appeared to be a dream.
>
> "No, this is no dream, Will," he replied. "It is beautiful . . . If this is death, it is sweet. There is no valley here. God is calling me, and I must go."[81]

Then, for a time, it "seemed as though he saw beyond the veil." Suddenly, with a strength that belied his condition, he exclaimed: "This is my triumph; this is my coronation day! I have been looking forward to it for years." Joy overtook him. "Dwight! Irene!" he said, calling out the names of the two beloved grandchildren who had died earlier in the year. "I see the children's faces!" Then, thinking he was about to lose consciousness, he spoke again: "Give my love to them all."

It was not long after, Will Moody wrote, "that he 'fell on sleep'— quietly and peacefully."[82]

Following Moody's death, the *New York Times* hailed him as a man who "did more to convert people to the profession of the Christian faith than any clergyman of his time."[83] And he preached what he believed. Not long before his final illness, Moody said in a sermon, "Death may change my position but not my condition, not my standing with Jesus Christ. . . . I wish you all felt as young as I do here to-night. Why, I am only sixty-two years old! If you meet me ten million years hence, then I will be young."

To learn more about D. L. Moody, read Kevin Belmonte's *D. L. Moody* (Nashville: Thomas Nelson, 2010) from the Christian Encounters Series.

8 | GEORGE WASHINGTON CARVER

(ca. 1864—1943)

by John Perry

I love to think of nature as an unlimited broadcasting station, through which God speaks to us every hour, if we will only tune in.

—GEORGE WASHINGTON CARVER

One of the five slaveholders listed in the 1860 Marion Township, Missouri, census was Moses Carver. He and his wife, Susan, were relatively prosperous farmers. Carver was also a successful stock trader and horse trainer.

Like many Americans, Carver was against the idea of one human being owning another but saw slavery as an economic necessity. He owned two slaves, a woman named Mary and her mulatto (half white) infant son, Jim, born the previous October.

By late 1863 Mary had another son, George. As with most children born in the countryside, especially slaves, there was no record of his birth. It is possible that a baby recorded as born in Marion Township on July 12, 1860, was George. A birth date so soon after his brother's indicated he arrived prematurely. That would account for his being small, frail, and hampered by severe breathing problems, which he dealt with all his life. George never knew his father.

Mary and her boys lived in what had once been Moses and Susan's cabin, a one-room log building with a fireplace, one window opening with shutters but no glass, and an earth floor.

During the Civil War, some slaveholders in southwestern Missouri abandoned their homesteads in the face of threats, raids, and destruction, but Moses would not be frightened off his property.

Stories vary as to how many times the Carver farm was raided. During one incident, Moses was working in the field with Jim while Mary was in her cabin with George. Seeing the attackers ride up, Moses and Jim hid, but Mary and George were kidnapped.

As soon as the men left, Moses started planning to rescue Mary and her boy, but he had no idea where to look first. His neighbor, Sergeant John Bentley, a Union scout, agreed to help. Riding through the night, Sergeant Bentley and his search party found George alone in an abandoned cabin. The next day Bentley returned George to the Carvers, but George's mother was never heard from again. Susan and Moses moved the two motherless slave boys into their house to raise as their own. Technically they remained slaves until a new state constitution was enacted on July 4, 1865, since the Emancipation Proclamation covered only the Confederacy. Yet the Carvers loved and cared for George and Jim as blood kin. The brothers even assumed the Carver family name.

After the end of the war, the newly constituted Carver family settled down to life on the farm. Jim grew tall and strong, but George remained a slight, sickly boy who fought off one respiratory illness after another.

Moses Carver was known in the community as a man who understood animals. He raised and traded horses, mules, hogs, and other livestock. Added to his experience with crops, fruit trees, and bees, his animal knowledge made Moses something of an expert on the natural world in general. As George grew older, he became attracted to nature as well, spending hours in the orchard and in the vegetable garden near the house. He planted a flower garden of his own and had what later generations would call a green thumb. He could make things grow, and could even coax sick plants back to health.

George loved learning and was as eager to go to school as he was to know about plants. The Locust Grove School was only a mile or so away, but it didn't allow black children to attend. The same building hosted church services on Sunday and Wednesday. George was welcome there then, even though he couldn't attend school within the same four walls. The Carvers didn't go to church, but George was so interested in Christianity that he walked the mile by himself every Sunday morning.

George Carver developed into a shy older boy who was consumed with the desire to know about everything. Susan Carver taught George to read and write, but he longed to know more. On his frequent walks through the woods he began praying for a chance to learn more about the plants he so enjoyed, and that God would direct his life.

Eventually, Moses found a school in the county seat of Neosho that would take "colored" students. George moved there, boarding with a black couple named Andrew and Mariah Watkins.

Mariah was a midwife with a wealth of knowledge about the medicinal uses for plants. George absorbed everything she would tell him about them. Mariah was also a devout Christian who took George to church and encouraged him to read the Bible. That Christmas she gave George a Bible of his own, which he kept for the rest of his life.

George received his graduation certificate on December 22, 1876, and immediately began looking for a way to continue his education. When he heard that a family from Neosho was traveling to Fort Scott, Kansas, where there was a school open to blacks, he convinced them to take him along. Within a few days, George bid the Watkinses good-bye and headed west for "Sunny Kansas," where emancipated slaves were streaming for the offer of free land and a fresh start.

THE LONG ROAD TO LEARNING

The first order of business for young George in Fort Scott was to find a job and a place to live. Carver applied for a job cooking and doing housework for Felix Payne and his wife. Payne, a blacksmith, decided to give the teenager a chance.

The moment he could afford it, George enrolled in school and spent two happy years in Fort Scott. Under normal circumstances he might have settled in town indefinitely.

But Carver's future was redirected on the night of March 26, 1879, when a black man was accused of raping a twelve-year-old white girl and thrown in the county jail. Wearing masks, a mob of thirty men swarmed the jail, grabbed the suspect, and hanged him from a lamppost as a huge crowd watched. Then they dragged the body through the streets, stopping in front of the Payne house to beat his brains out on the curb as George watched in terror from his window. Later the corpse was doused with kerosene and set on fire. Though he had seen and experienced discrimination all his life, George had lived mostly with white families who treated him as an equal. A savage lynching before a cheering crowd of a thousand or more was unimaginable to him. "As young as I was," Carver remembered a lifetime later, "the horror haunted me and does even now."[1]

He left Fort Scott immediately.

In time, Carver decided to pursue a professional career. He moved east to Kansas City and enrolled in business school. Carver quickly mastered typing and shorthand and found a job as a stenographer at the telegraph office in the railroad terminal. Against all odds, he now had a marketable skill, a steady job, and money in the bank. Yet his desire for education was as strong as ever.

Carver applied for admission to Highland College, a Presbyterian school north of Kansas City, and was accepted. Brimming with anticipation, Carver took the train to Highland and went straight to the president's office to get his class assignments. The college president looked him up and down with an expression of surprise. "You didn't tell me you were a Negro. Highland College does not take Negroes."[2] Stunned, then devastated, Carver silently turned around and left the room.

George resumed his familiar role as housekeeper for a John Beeler, who owned an apple orchard south of town. He spent a year or so working for John, still studying plants on his own, marveling at how beautiful and varied God's creation was. Soon George began looking for other opportunities.

The Homestead Act of 1862 was to encourage settlers to move to western Kansas. Anyone willing to live there five years got 160 acres of land for only a twenty-four-dollar filing fee, paid at the end of the five years. In the summer of 1886, George moved west to Ness County and staked his homestead claim. He planted seventeen acres of crops and three dozen fruit trees using tools borrowed from county commissioner George Steeley, who had hired him as a housekeeper. He also bought ten chickens.

Until his first crop came in, Carver continued working for the commissioner, who recognized his obvious gift for growing things, an especially valuable skill in so arid and barren a place. With Steeley's permission he built a small addition onto the side of the Steeley hut and filled it with horticultural samples. George and his employer both enjoyed taking visitors into this "greenhouse" to see plants that appeared healthier and more lush than elsewhere in the county.

George would have owned his acreage if he'd lived there till 1891. However, by the summer of 1888 he had had enough of the frontier. He mortgaged his homestead for three hundred dollars and moved east, to Winterset, Iowa.

About a year later, still determined to improve himself, George applied to Simpson College, a few miles away in Indianola, and was accepted. When he started the semester on September 9, 1890, he was the only black student on campus. Even so, Simpson College must have seemed a taste of heaven on earth to George. He was soon excelling at a "real" college, making friends, painting pictures of the flowers and plants that so interested him, and throwing himself into church services and revivals.

George's art teacher at Simpson was one of the most important figures in his life. Etta Budd recognized Carver's incredible natural skill as a painter, and sensed that it stemmed from a genuine love of plants and all of nature. Yet she was afraid that no matter how good his paintings were, people would not buy works from a black artist. Therefore Miss Budd encouraged George to study plants instead of painting them. Her father was a professor of agriculture at Iowa State College in Ames. When she left Simpson at the end of the school year to care for her mother at home, she told George he should come to Iowa State and turn his attention to science.

George eagerly took her advice.

❦

As he had been at Simpson, George Carver was the only black student at Iowa State in the fall of 1891. As such, he had to pick his way along an uneasy trail of social and practical challenges. Fortunately he found a staunch ally in Professor James Wilson, director of the agricultural experiment station, who quickly recognized Carver's intellect and his natural skill and interest in horticulture. In time, Carver and Professor Wilson started a Wednesday night prayer group that was so successful they started a second, then a third.

George threw himself wholeheartedly into every aspect of college life. He entered the college cadet corps, rising in time to captain. He joined the football team as a trainer and masseuse. He played the guitar and gave guitar lessons. He became a star member of the Welsh Eccentric Society, devoted to "development in science, literature, and the art of speaking." Carver spoke at the organizational meeting of the Iowa State College Agricultural Society in March 1892. For two years he was a delegate to a national YMCA summer program at Lake Geneva, Wisconsin. Four of his paintings were accepted for a statewide exhibition in Cedar Rapids. At least one of his pictures was chosen for display at the 1894 Chicago World's Fair. Carver got to go to Chicago as a member of the Iowa Cadet Honor Guard, escorting the governor on his official visit to the fair.

At one point, though, in spite of his artistic success and rank as a cadet officer, he endured shouts of "Nigger!" as he marched in his uniform.

If these slurs bothered him, he kept it to himself, choosing to focus on his studies and earn consistently high grades. In 1894 Carver received his degree from Iowa State.

Immediately he enrolled in a graduate program, where he worked as assistant director of the agricultural experiment station under his mentor Professor Wilson, who later became U.S. Secretary of Agriculture.

During the fall of 1895, Carver received an offer to teach at Tuskegee Institute in Tuskegee, Alabama. Part of the appeal to Carver from Tuskegee's president, Booker T. Washington, was that up to that time Tuskegee had filled all its faculty positions with black men and women. The institute had received money to start an agricultural station and needed someone to work there. If he couldn't find a qualified black applicant, Washington would be forced to hire a white teacher.

Carver decided to accept the job. It was agreed that he would finish his master's work, then take up his teaching duties in the fall of 1896.

PROFESSOR CARVER

Classes had already begun when Carver arrived at Tuskegee. His first assignment was to take charge of the campus dairy. This in-house operation had the twofold benefit of teaching students how to be dairy farmers and supplying the dining hall with milk, butter, and cream. This was not the sort of academic pursuit Carver had expected, but Washington required all the instructors to have hands-on participation in making the school and its students as self-sufficient as possible.

One of Carver's shining successes early on was a series of agricultural bulletins funded by a small state grant. The idea was to conduct agricultural research, then present the results as practical advice to local farmers in simple language. The first bulletin he produced, "Feeding Acorns," advised farmers to mix wild acorns with the corn they fed to livestock in order to stretch expensive corn and to make use of acorns that would otherwise go to waste. His research showed that chickens laid more eggs and cows produced more milk when fed the cheaper mixture.

The second bulletin, "Experiments with Sweet Potatoes," advised farmers to fertilize their sweet potato patches with a certain combination of phosphate and potash. A one-tenth acre test plot with no fertilizer produced small potatoes worth 25¢ a bushel at a yield of 40 bushels per acre. The phosphate/potash plot produced potatoes worth 50¢ a bushel at a yield of 266 bushels per acre. The potatoes from the first test plot netted $2.50; those from the second plot, after deducting costs, netted $121.00.

The agricultural bulletins won high praise from black and white farmers alike. Iowa State praised the bulletins in print, as did Auburn University and Mississippi State.

Not long after he arrived at Tuskegee, Professor Carver was out collecting plant specimens when a white woman stopped him and asked if he was a peddler. He explained he was looking for plant diseases and insects harmful to plants in order to study ways to prevent them. She asked him to come look at her failing roses. "I showed her just what to do for them," he told Booker T. Washington later, "in fact, sat down and wrote it out for her."[3] Carver's reputation as a plant doctor grew rapidly. Before long he welcomed a steady stream of amateur gardeners asking for advice.

By 1902 Carver had settled into a familiar routine. He spent part of every day teaching agriculture and chemistry classes, oversaw 170 acres of experimental crop fields, ran the dairy, and also supervised a poultry farm Washington had started.

The next decade for George Washington Carver would be filled with growing scientific and educational success with a reputation to match.

⌒⌒◦⌒⌒

What Carver loved most, as he had since he was a boy, was studying plants. He spent long hours ambling through the woods around campus collecting specimens, then cataloging, preserving, and experimenting with them in his office. He sometimes carried colored pencils with him and would make sketches along the way on whatever stray pages he happened to have with him. At the university he tended a huge collection of living plants, his "plant museum" or "herbarium," stuffed with specimens.

Most days Carver also visited the agricultural experimental station, where he monitored assorted strains of crops. One departmental report listed a hundred acres of sweet potatoes and forty acres of black-eyed peas under cultivation, plus smaller plots of onions, collard greens, turnips, beets, beans, squash, lettuce, and radishes. Professor Carver determined what combinations of fertilizer and other additives produced the best yield, and developed as many uses for the crop as possible so nothing would be wasted and the farmer would get the maximum benefit from his labor and investment.

Carver also enjoyed sharing what he learned with as wide an audience as he could, in order to help blacks live more fulfilling and independent lives. Many of them struggled as sharecroppers or as tenants farming rented acreage. Carver wanted to improve their crop yield enough so they could afford their own farms, decent homes for their families, and modern equipment to make their lives less wearisome while improving production even more.

Professor Carver's research produced a wealth of practical information that could help the family farmer of modest means, including soil conservation techniques. He showed farmers how to reduce erosion of fertile topsoil by plowing their crop rows in a way that kept rain from washing it away. He taught them to plant peanuts and beans in rotation to add nitrogen to the soil that other crops took out.

Another goal Carver set was to find a substitute for "king cotton," the most important cash crop in the South and, in many communities, the foundation of the entire economy. Cotton is hard on the soil and, until automated equipment became widespread in the 1950s, required endless, diligent, backbreaking labor.

Carver wanted to offer small farmers an alternative to cotton that was easier on the soil and required less relentless physical labor. Adding to Carver's sense of urgency was that in 1894 the boll weevil had crossed the Rio Grande from Mexico and was creeping northward, evidently unstoppable. Carver and other scientists knew the small beetle, which could destroy a field and a year's work within days, would arrive in eastern Alabama eventually. George wanted to have an alternative crop ready to propose.

Carver believed sweet potatoes would be the best cash crop replacement for cotton, and the more uses he could find for them, the likelier farmers would be to plant them. From the sweet potato or its vine he developed a range of food items including candy, molasses, and breakfast cereal, plus substitutes for flour, sugar, coconut, tapioca, ginger, chocolate, yeast, coffee, and vinegar. He also produced sweet potato dyes, paints, library paste, ink, shoe polish, paper, and much more.

In the meantime, Carver's agricultural bulletins led to other beneficial programs. Tuskegee had been hosting its Farmer's Conferences since 1892. Attendance grew steadily, especially after Carver arrived and his reputation grew. In time both black and white farmers, some traveling long distances from the North, flocked to the annual gatherings. One farmer wrote to the school, "I thank God on my knees for these Conferences. They are giving us homes."[4]

In 1898 Tuskegee added a Farmer's Institute Fair, giving farmers a forum for displaying their crops, livestock, and homemade products from cross stitching to canned goods. The event was such a success that in 1911 it was combined with the Macon County Fair.

One of Carver's most popular and enduring outreach efforts was a portable display and demonstration setup known as the Jessup Wagon. The idea started with a suggestion from Booker Washington that Carver design a wagon that could be equipped as a traveling agricultural school.

The professor sketched a design for a wagon that student carpenters and wheelwrights could build, with fold-up sides that opened to display charts on soil improvement, stock raising, and other farm work, plus samples of farm equipment for demonstration. It was a classroom on wheels a teacher could transport directly to working farmers in the field. In 1906 the first Jessup Wagon took to the road, traveling to whatever crossroads or country store, farm or field its audience could reach. The first summer, more than two thousand people a month attended Jessup Wagon presentations.

For all the effort Carver made to get practical information into the hands of farmers who needed it, that work never overshadowed his love for teaching. He felt a special calling to the field.

Carver was a tenderhearted mentor who took a sincere personal interest in his desperately poor, homesick students. Word spread through each new class that Professor Carver was a kind, approachable man, a good listener who gave wise advice. Generations of students would say he transformed their lives.

Carver believed that direct observation and hands-on experience were essential to learning. He often brought plant samples or results of his experiments into the classroom. Rather than using textbooks, he emphasized seeing and examining plants. This may have been in part because botany had been so important to him from so young an age. He observed and experimented with plants long before he knew anything about formal procedures.

CREATION AND THE CREATOR

Thanks to his adopted parents, his friends, and to his own pursuit of faith, George became a devout Christian as a young man. He knew that some scientists and others scoffed at the idea of a supreme being creating the physical world out of nothing. It had to evolve, they said. Carver believed just the opposite: the more he learned about the beauty, complexity, and interconnectedness of the world, the more convinced he was that it could only have been formed supernaturally, by the hand of God.

Carver often talked about the Creator in the classroom. He told his students that the more they knew about plants and the rest of the natural world, the more they could know about the Creator who made those things—and made the students as well. Some days his botany lectures were more impromptu sermon than science lesson. His sincerity and conviction carried over to his students, who responded excitedly. Religion suddenly had a new relevance, a new immediacy.

In 1907 Carver was asked to teach a Bible study on Sunday night after supper. The professor agreed, and was pleased to see about fifty boys come to his first session. Within three months, attendance averaged more than a hundred. In these classes, as in his weekday classroom lectures, Carver returned time and again to the connection between the natural world and its Creator.

Professor Carver was by now one of the most popular professors on campus. His teaching style nurtured a sense of discovery and excitement. Rather than a dry recitation of facts, Carver continually encouraged his students to learn for themselves and to appreciate the beautiful, useful world the Creator had made for them.

In 1913, Professor Carver was in his seventeenth year at the school. Having taught thousands of students by now, he remained as enthusiastic and compassionate as ever. He reached out to new students more as a friend than as a professor, asking them where they were from and learning about their families. He was a sympathetic sounding board for the catalog of problems that students carried to school with them.

After his students graduated or left the campus, Carver wrote to many of them, some for years afterward, following their careers, admonishing them to remember what they'd learned at school, and instructing them to be kind to others. Almost invariably his letters began, "My Dear Boy," and adopted a fatherly tone. For the three decades that followed, generations of students shared stories of Carver's kindness, teaching ability, generosity, and personal interest in them, and they treasured the letters he wrote by the hundreds.

Along with teaching new farming techniques and inspiring his students, Professor Carver had a keen interest in developing and marketing profitable products made from simple natural ingredients. As early as 1902 he had identified a clay sample sent by the

National Building and Loan Company of Montgomery, Alabama, as a potential source of valuable paint pigment. He produced a Prussian blue color that seemed at least equal to any other pigment available. Carver mixed batches of paint himself and tested them side by side. But when Carver sent samples to paint and pigment manufacturers, they pronounced them inferior to the pigments they were already using, adding that they had considered them only because they came from "Professor George W. Carver, the Chemist and Commissioner of Agriculture of the famous Tuskegee Normal and Industrial School [colored] of which Mr. Booker T. Washington is Principal."[5]

The prospect of commercial production resurfaced again in 1911, when Carver started working with some of his chemistry students to make whitewash, paint, and wood stain out of clay near the Tuskegee campus. The school began using these products on their buildings rather than buying paint. A white Episcopal congregation in Tuskegee ordered Carver's stain for the interior of their new church building. They were elated with the results, at a price of one-tenth of what commercially manufactured stain would have cost. Carver reported the results in one of his continuing series of Experiment Station Bulletins. He also experimented with making dyes from a list of other plants including tomatoes, radishes, maple bark, and onions.

Binding all the threads of his life into one cord was Carver's overarching belief in a Creator who had made everything he studied so intently, and gave him and his students the insights to understand and appreciate them. Since Tuskegee students came from the Caribbean and Central America as well as the American South, there were generally non-Christians in his classes. Carver explained that the Creator God tied all creation and all learning together. As a student named Alvin D. Smith later explained, Carver told his students that his faith was "the key to all that he had been able to do."[6]

A NATIONAL FIGURE

Busy and popular with the students as Professor Carver was, his star shown brightly in a relatively narrow world. He was almost unknown outside Tuskegee and the scientific community after nineteen years on the faculty.

During those same years, Booker T. Washington became the most renowned black man in America and arguably the most famous black individual in the world. But in 1911, powerful presence though he was, Washington was assaulted in a New York apartment building, requiring sixteen stitches to close wounds in his head and ear. By that time the articulate, immaculately dressed college president was already suffering from a string of ailments and had undergone treatment for severe indigestion. By 1915 he was buying stomach pills by the hundreds, had kidney stones, and registered blood pressure of 215.

On a fund raising trip to New York that fall, Washington became gravely ill. He made it back to Tuskegee just in time to die in his own bed on November 14.[7]

George Washington Carver was shattered by Washington's death even though, as long as the gifted orator was alive, Carver always stood in his gigantic shadow. Washington wrote the books, hobnobbed with presidents, and took tea with the Queen at Windsor Castle. Carver remained in his classroom, his laboratory, and his woods, nurturing his plants and the young minds that came to him for guidance. When Washington died, the stage was set for Carver to emerge from the sidelines and blossom in the sun.

By 1916, Carver's reputation began to gather critical mass and the mainstream white establishment was paying new attention to him. Carver accepted an invitation to join the advisory board of the National Agricultural Society and was elected a Fellow of the Royal Society for the Encouragement of Arts, Manufactures, and Commerce in London.

Impressive as they were, these honors were still limited to the scientific field. Carver's first taste of sustained popular attention came after America entered World War I in April 1917. With overseas trade suddenly halted, the United States had to find substitutes for common items or do without them. Carver was filled to overflowing with ideas about how to substitute homegrown raw materials for formerly imported goods, saying he was working on making rubber from sweet potatoes and rope from peanut hulls. The best pigments, many of which came from Germany, could be replaced by substitutes made of local clay or native plants. In interviews, Carver assured America that bread flour to feed its soldiers could come from sweet potatoes as well.

After the Allied victory in 1918, America found itself emerging as a center of economic power and heavily invested in overseas trade. Foreign growers could produce goods cheaper than their American counterparts; the Americans ran the risk of being priced out of business. To protect the domestic farm economy, growers and traders lobbied Congress for protective tariffs on a variety of foods. One lobbying group, appearing in a mundane hearing, inadvertently completed the transformation of George Washington Carver from obscure botany professor to international celebrity.

⁓

The United Peanut Growers Association mounted a full-court press in Congress to protect its members from the economic consequences of competition from cheap imports. A bill in the House of Representatives looked promising, proposing a substantial import duty on peanuts, but its progress was slow and tenuous.

The peanut tariff legislation originated in the House Ways and Means Committee. Day after day, representatives assembled on Capitol Hill to listen to a parade of witnesses explain why the farmers they represented needed trade protection from foreign growers. Each witness was allowed ten minutes.

On January 20, 1921, Republican chairman Joseph W. Fordney gaveled the committee to order for another day of testimony on the importance of domestic peanuts to the American economy, which promised to be much like the days before. That assumption changed when the next witness was called and a nattily dressed black man entered the large, elegant room with a big box under his arm. He was introduced to the committee as George Washington Carver, from Tuskegee Institute in Alabama.

United Peanut Growers knew Carver by reputation and had retained him as an expert on peanuts. Outside the South and outside the study of agriculture, no one had any notion who he was. Very likely not a single member of the committee had ever heard Carver's name. The small figure settled himself in his seat at the witness table and asked if he could make room for some of the exhibits he had brought. As the previously bored committee members leaned forward in their chairs, Professor Carver began unpacking his box. He set out blocks of crushed peanut meats that he called "crushed cake," explaining that it made a tasty breakfast cereal and many other products.[8] He showed the committee ground peanut hulls, which he said were good for burnishing tin.

The chairman asked slyly if Carver had brought anything to drink—a reference to Prohibition, which had been in effect a little more than a year. When Carver answered that liquid examples might "come later if my ten minutes are extended," the committee broke out in laughter. The professor then showed his audience chocolate covered peanuts and a sample of breakfast food made from peanuts and sweet potatoes. "I am very sorry that you can not taste this, so I will taste it for you," he said, taking a bite. Once more laughter rippled through the committee.

Every minute or two Carver reached into what he called his "Pandora's box" to pull out another example: peanut hay for livestock, dyes, a quinine substitute. When his ten minutes were up, Chairman Fordney offered him more time.

Carver moved on to discuss peanut milk, which he displayed beside a bottle of cow's milk. The two looked almost identical, complete with "cream" floating on top. He said peanut milk could be used to make buttermilk, instant coffee, Worcestershire sauce, cheese, salad oil, ink, fruit punch, and much more.

When his time ran out again, Chairman Fordney exclaimed, "Go ahead, brother. Your time is unlimited." Carver closed his testimony by saying that peanuts were part of a "natural diet" given as a great gift from the Creator.

Eventually the committee approved the highest tariff ever on peanuts up to that time, three cents a pound shelled and four cents unshelled.

Carver's appearance was a rare event in that it showed the public an intelligent, articulate black person who made an important contribution to all society, including white society. Blacks were generally considered lazy, uneducated, untrustworthy, slow-witted, and thought of mostly as janitors, dishwashers, and other menial workers. Yet here was a professor, a scientist, a recognized expert with a graduate degree, teaching congressmen in Washington what they needed to know to consider national legislation.

⁓⁓⁓

Carver became the new public face of the notion that blacks deserved respectful treatment. He believed that the way to equality was through patience, humility, and a level of excellence too great to be ignored. For more than a year after his Ways and Means Committee appearance, Carver saw his story retold time and again in newspapers across the country. The tale of a slave boy kidnapped by marauders and raised by his former owners made tremendous copy. The press acclaimed Carver as a "great specialist in foods and food values," "God's Ebony Scientist," and the "wizard chemist."

An Intuitive Approach

Scientist and master's graduate that he was, Carver never embraced the generally accepted scientific method, whereby a researcher meticulously compared one experiment with another that was different in only one detail; if the outcome was different, that detail was the cause. Instead, Carver took a subjective, intuitive approach to research, skirting the empirical, rational, logical process. And in his public lectures, as in the classroom, Carver explained that God the Creator revealed the miracles of His creation to anybody willing to look for them. As Carver became a national figure during the early 1920s, his methods were subject to more intense scrutiny.

In November 1924 Carver spoke at the landmark Marble Collegiate Church on Fifth Avenue in New York. There he repeated his belief that scientific discoveries were a product of divine revelation, not the scientific method.

A reporter with the *New York Times* challenged Carver's position. Two days after his speech, on November 20, the paper ran an editorial titled "Men of Science Never Talk That Way," declaring the professor displayed a "complete lack of scientific spirit" that reflected poorly on him, his race, and Tuskegee. Bona fide researchers in Carver's field "do not ascribe their successes, when they have any, to 'inspiration.'"[9]

The *Times* was inundated with letters supporting Carver and criticizing their editorial stance. Prominent among them was a letter to the editor from Carver himself. His reply leaves behind one of the most detailed explanations in his own words of his approach to science.

I regret exceedingly that such a gross misunderstanding should arise as to what is meant by "Divine inspiration." Inspiration is never at variance with information; in fact, the more information one has, the greater will be the inspiration.

Paul, the great Scholar, says, Second Timothy 2:15, "Study to show thyself approved unto God, a Workman that needeth not to be ashamed, rightly dividing the word of truth." . . .

I receive the leading scientific publications. . . .

[But] while in your beautiful city, I was struck with the large number of Taros and Yautias [vegetables typically grown in tropical climates] displayed in many of your markets; they are edible roots imported to this country. Just as soon as I saw them, I marveled at the wonderful possibilities for their expansion. Dozens of things came to me while standing there looking at them. I would follow the same or similar lines I have pursued in developing products from the white potato. I know of no one who has ever worked with these roots in this way. I know of no book from which I can get this information, yet I will have no trouble in doing it.

If this is not inspiration and information from a source greater than myself, . . . kindly tell me what it is.[10]

❧

In 1925, the animal feed and cereal manufacturing giant Ralston-Purina approached Professor Carver about developing a new breakfast cereal for them. Carver declined the offer, but soon warmed to the idea of heading his own company.

A wealthy white Tuskegee man, Ernest Thompson, had long been an admirer of Carver and had given him money and equipment over the years for research and experiments. The two of them shared a vision for a nonprofit company that would identify worthwhile products, refine them for commercial applications, then manufacture and market them at rock-bottom prices. They called their enterprise the Carver Products Company and set up operations in downtown Atlanta.

As exciting and innovative as Carver's ideas were for making products out of peanuts and sweet potatoes, they turned out not to be practical for manufacturing on a commercial level. Carver filed three patents over the next two years, the only patents he ever applied for in his life, but none of them ever produced a marketable product. Thompson and Carver discovered that other patents similar to theirs protected competitive products that were already well established. The Carver Products Company faded away to nothing in 1927.

But in 1928, Carver realized a long-held dream. Simpson College, where Carver had started his undergraduate career, bestowed upon him an honorary doctorate. This action legitimized the "Doctor Carver" title many people used to address him already.

❧

Along with his research and lecturing, Carver remained a valued consultant to the peanut industry. His most significant client was Tom Huston, whose Tom Huston Company packaged and sold Tom's Peanuts and other snack foods. In 1929 Huston offered the professor a full-time job. Though Carver turned down the position, he helped Huston figure out how to grow the Virginia variety of peanuts the company preferred in soil that had previously supported only inferior types.

Virginia peanuts grown in the deep South were immature or rotten when harvested. Company researchers believed the problem was a fungus in those regions. The senior horticulturist at the Department of Agriculture argued that the fungus was a secondary symptom caused by something else.

After examining a ruined crop of peanuts in the field, Carver thought the problem was a combination of several varieties of fungus, each causing a different kind of damage. The senior researcher at Huston thought Carver was right. Huston printed five thousand copies of a pamphlet detailing Carver's findings titled "Some Peanut Diseases."

Scientists and others who saw Carver only as "the peanut man" challenged his scientific conclusions, so Huston hired a respected researcher to review Carver's work. Meanwhile, the Department of Agriculture did its own survey and found that more than 20 percent of the crop was being lost, including Virginia peanuts, directly on account of the fungus, just as Carver had said. The department developed treatments that dramatically reduced crop loss and boosted farmers' profits. In time the government recognized Carver as a collaborator.

Digging Out of
Desperate Times

The collapse of world markets beginning in the fall of 1929 sent the economy on a downward spiral lasting more than three years. Farmers were in some of the worst economic shape of anyone. Between 1929 and 1932, farm prices fell 53 percent. Furthermore, eleven thousand banks failed in four years and, in the era before federal deposit insurance, bank failure often wiped out depositors' life savings.

Desperate financial times added to the value of Dr. Carver's work. Throughout the 1930s Carver added further to the lists of products derived from peanuts, sweet potatoes, and pecans, then branched out into other crops. He experimented with making paper from wheat, matting and rope from okra, and commercial starch from artichokes. All the while his media image grew, achieving a sort of mythical status.

One colorful and oft-quoted description of Dr. Carver came

from the October 1932 issue of the *American Magazine* and was reprinted in *Reader's Digest*. James Saxon Childers visited the professor at Tuskegee and wrote a sympathetic feature article about the gentle old scientist. His first impression of Carver remains one of the best of many similar descriptions.

The stooped old Negro shuffled along through the dust of an Alabama road at a curiously rapid rate. He was carrying an armful of sticks and wild flowers.

The sticks I could understand—he would use them for kindling—but I had never before seen an old black man ambling along the road at nine o'clock in the morning with swamp roses, wild geranium, and creeping buttercups mingled with a lot of dry sticks.

When I got a little closer to him I saw that he was wearing a saggy coat which originally might have been a green alpaca, but which the sun had faded until I couldn't be sure about the color; there were so many patches that I couldn't even be certain about the material.

The old man was walking towards . . . one of the buildings of Tuskegee Institute, the famous school for Negroes at Tuskegee, Ala. His thin body bent by the years, his hair white beneath a ragged cap, he seemed pathetically lost on the campus of a great modern educational institution. Poor old fellow; I had seen hundreds just like him. Totally ignorant, unable even to read and write, they shamble along through the dust of Southern roads in search of any little odd job that will earn enough food to keep them alive, enough clothes to cover their tired old bones.

At the entrance of the building toward which we were both walking, the old Negro turned in. "He's probably the janitor," I told myself, "and I'm sincerely glad that they've given him a job of some kind."

I stepped into the hallway. I saw a trim little secretary hurry

toward the bent old Negro. I heard her say to him, "That delega-
tion from Washington is waiting for you, Doctor Carver."[11]

The professor's public profile reached a new high with the news
in 1933 that one of his peanut oil mixtures could "evidently" cure
polio. Medical researchers had identified the polio virus in 1908 but
had so far found no effective treatment against it. Once a person
began showing symptoms, there was nothing doctors could do to
reverse or halt the damage.

The flurry of stories about Carver and polio treatment began
when Carver treated an eleven-year-old boy named Foy Thompson.
Foy was weak and underweight, and his parents thought Carver's
therapeutic massage technique might help him. Carver began treating Foy with what he called "muscle building" peanut oil massages.
In a month Foy gained thirty-one pounds.

An Associated Press reporter came to Tuskegee in late 1933 for
more details. The professor insisted, "It has been given out that I
have found a cure. I have not, but it looks hopeful."[12] Even so, the
clamor for his "miracle cure" continued for some time.

Toward the end of the 1930s, Carver began to travel less, make fewer
speeches, and spend less time on prospective commercial projects.
By 1938 the old professor had grown noticeably slower and weaker.
He spent weeks at a time in the hospital.

Around that time, the school started planning a museum to
honor Carver. Frederick Douglass Patterson, Tuskegee's third
president, realized Carver's publicity value and believed a museum
would not only honor a great teacher, scientist, and humanitarian
but bring attention and donations to the school as well. The George
Washington Carver Museum opened July 25, 1939, with more than
two thousand guests attending the dedication.

For all his notoriety as a beloved public figure, Professor Carver remained a second-class American, subject at a moment's notice to the legal racial discrimination that endured as a legacy of Reconstruction. In September, six weeks after his gala museum opening, Carver and an assistant named Austin Curtis took the train to New York, where the professor had been invited to appear on the radio program *Strange as It Seems*. The show was based on a popular syndicated comic strip featuring bizarre or unusual stories similar to its rival, *Ripley's Believe It or Not*.

When Carver and Curtis arrived at the elegant New Yorker Hotel where Curtis had made reservations, the registration clerk eyed the pair and told them there was no vacancy. Curtis refused to leave and called a contact at the publisher Doubleday, Doran and Company, which was preparing a biography of Carver.

Only after a vice president of Doubleday called the New Yorker and threatened to sue was Dr. Carver, friend of President Roosevelt, shown to his room, following six hours of sitting in a chair in the washroom hallway.

His accolades continued. In 1939 Carver was awarded one of three Roosevelt Medals given that year by the Theodore Roosevelt Association to honor accomplishments in fields reflecting TR's work and interests. Carver also accepted honorary memberships in the American Inventors Society, the Mark Twain Society, and the National Technical Society. Even Hollywood came calling. Metro-Goldwyn-Mayer, the film powerhouse that would distribute *Gone with the Wind* that same year, contacted Carver about a film biography of his life and career. He declined.

Late in his life, Professor Carver developed a close friendship with industrialist and inventor Henry Ford, one of the wealthiest and most prominent businessmen in America. Ford constructed a school for families on his Georgia plantation and named it the George Washington Carver School. He also set up a nutritional laboratory in Carver's honor.

A LEGACY OF HOPE

When he was a boy, a doctor had told Carver he shouldn't expect to live to twenty-one, yet he was still working and planning for the future at age eighty, though he walked now only with difficulty and spent much of his time in a wheelchair.

As his physical infirmities progressed, Professor Carver focused most intently on his historical legacy. Three projects in particular held his attention. The first was the George Washington Carver Foundation, established on February 10, 1940, to carry on his research.

Carver's second order of business was expanding the Carver Museum. Many who knew him as a scientist and teacher had no idea he was such an accomplished artist. Within a year the museum held seventy-one of his paintings, the largest number ever collected in one place. Henry Ford dedicated the expanded museum facilities on November 17, 1941.

The third project Carver took on was a biography, to be published by Doubleday, Doran and Company. The manuscript was written by Rackham Holt, the penname of Margaret Van Vechten Saunders Holt, a book critic, editor, and biographer. The first draft was completed by the summer of 1940, but after two years of refining and expanding, the work was still unfinished. On October 14, 1942, Carver wrote to Holt, prodding her to finish the revisions and get the book to press as soon as possible, adding, "I would like to have it come out while I am still able to see it."

❦

In June 1942 Carver went to visit Henry Ford in Dearborn and tour his company's research and engineering labs. The two were inseparable during their time together, with the gaunt industrialist, nearing eighty himself, showing his famous friend around day after day. Newspapers nationwide ran a photo of the white-haired old professor serving Ford a weed salad.

The trip to Michigan was to be his last. A few days after returning to Tuskegee, Carver slipped and fell on a patch of ice when he was opening the door to his museum. He never fully recovered from the fall. Shortly after New Year's he drifted off to sleep and never woke up. Professor Carver died at 7:30 p.m. on January 5, 1943.

The *New York Times* led its obituary section the next day with the headline, "Dr. Carver Is Dead; Negro Scientist," and a photo of Carver. The notice touched on his work with peanuts, his remarkable childhood, and his long list of accolades and honors. It made special mention of the faith that had guided and comforted him for so long.

At Carver's funeral three days later, Reverend C. W. Kelley read condolences and wishes from around the world. The professor was buried near Booker T. Washington. Forever connected in the public mind, they now rested only a short distance apart.

❧

George Washington Carver is largely forgotten today, displaced as a symbol of black achievement by men and women invested more in high-profile confrontation than in the patient, incremental progress Carver represented. Even the Carver Museum, dedicated to keeping the professor's memory alive, fell on hard times. In 1947 it was heavily damaged by fire. The building itself withstood the blaze, as did many of the scientific displays. The great tragedy was Carver's paintings. Of the seventy-one in the collection, only a handful survived, making a George Washington Carver canvas one of the most rare in the art world. The museum was rebuilt, further enlarged, and reopened in 1951.

In the generations since Carver's death, the world has been transformed into a place he would scarcely recognize. Still, for all the differences, some core elements of Carver's legacy stand resolutely unchanged. His commitment to training scientists at Tuskegee is alive and strong. The school of veterinary medicine there has trained 70 percent of black veterinarians in America. After Jonas

Salk developed a polio vaccine in 1953, Tuskegee provided more than six hundred thousand vaccine cultures worldwide, helping fulfill Carver's dream of defeating this terrible disease. And Dr. Carver's agricultural experiment station continues strong. Student scientists, under contract to NASA, are developing ways to grow sweet potatoes in outer space to feed astronauts on their way to Mars.

Of all the experiments and programs and peanut products George Washington Carver left behind, his greatest gift is a legacy of hope: a timeless message to black and white, rich and poor, that God made us all and has given us everything we need to find our sunlit place in the Creator's world.

To learn more about George Washington Carver, read John Perry's *George Washington Carver* (Nashville: Thomas Nelson, 2011) from the Christian Encounters Series.

9 | SERGEANT YORK

(1887–1964)

by John Perry

If this country fails, it will fail from within. I think we've just got to go back to the old time religion, shouting as though the world is on fire. Maybe people will realize we've gotten onto some wrong roads and return to the old paths.

—ALVIN YORK

The tiny, isolated settlement of Pall Mall, Tennessee, was founded in the Wolf River Valley on land used as hunting ground for generations of Shawnee, Cherokee, Creek, and Chickasaw. Around 1800 the first white settlers moved into the valley, including a twenty-four-year-old homesteader named Coonrod Pile. By the time Fentress County was formed in 1823, Coonrod owned tens of thousands of acres and was one of the wealthiest men in the region.

After Coonrod died in 1849, his riches were split among his eight children. One son, Alvin York's ancestor Elijah, supported the Union during the Civil War along with many other Tennesseans in the officially Confederate state. When U.S. general Ambrose Burnside marched his forces through Pall Mall, one of his soldiers named Brooks fell in love with Elijah's daughter, Nancy. The two married and had an infant daughter named Mary.

Uriah York was another Union sympathizer from Tennessee, a U.S. Army veteran who'd fought in the Mexican War. He went north to Kentucky to join the Union army, leaving his wife and son, William, behind. When a Confederate posse came looking for him, he hid in a canebrake, but later caught pneumonia and died.

William York and Mary Elizabeth Brooks grew up as neighbors. In time their acquaintance ripened into love, and the two were married in 1881. He was eighteen and she was fifteen.

The Yorks had eleven children in nineteen years; feeding so many mouths was a constant struggle. To supplement his meager income as a farmer, William taught himself blacksmithing and had a steady business in iron and woodworking. Once the two oldest boys were out of the house, William passed down the craft to his next son, Alvin Cullum, born December 13, 1887.

While still in his teens, Alvin earned a reputation as an incredible shot. Even among superlative marksmen his performance was unsurpassed. Shooting competitions honed hunting skills that the men and boys used almost every day. Alvin loved hunting from the time he was old enough to carry a gun. Boys in the valley often had a lightweight .22 by the age of ten.

Crops and livestock, cooking, canning, and household chores left little time for amusement, yet the hearty people of Pall Mall made their own fun. There were picnics at the Methodist church, and once in a while a dance in somebody's barn. With a fiddle accompaniment and perhaps an improvised rhythm section of washboard and spoons, neighbors would dance the night away.

Alvin sometimes enjoyed these festivities to a fault; those who knew him were wary of his behavior when he'd had too much to drink.

A MOTHER'S PRAYER

Life was hard in the Wolf River Valley, and the York family struggled even by valley standards. They owned seventy-five acres of farm land seven miles from the Kentucky line, just enough to scratch out a living for Alvin, his mother, and eight younger brothers and sisters. Two older brothers were married and on their own, leaving Alvin head of the household.

Days he worked his own land and hired out to help neighboring farmers. Nights he spent at his father's smithy.

Folks called him "Big 'Un." He was a burly, barrel-chested ox of a man, muscles grown taut and strong from a lifetime of steadying a plow and wielding a hammer. His head was topped with a thick, unruly thatch of red hair. Using his legendary shooting skills, he could drop five birds with five rifle shots.

When Big 'Un got into a fight, he fought big. Sometimes with his fists, sometimes with a knife—but always to win. When he drank, he drank big. Alcohol made him even more of a fighter, so that after a night of moonshine whiskey, Alvin was likely to fight anybody on any terms.

His father would have been disappointed but not surprised. Alvin had been a handful even as a boy. He hadn't gotten any milder by the time William York died in 1911, likely from pneumonia. That loss seemed to make Big 'Un even more boisterous and disruptive. People in the Wolf River Valley felt sorry for Mother York.

Mary Brooks York was the most mild-mannered, hardworking, God-fearing woman anybody in the community ever knew. She'd been a devoted wife and mother. Her father and husband had been responsible, sober family men. But Alvin had a mind of his own. Most men his age were already married and had families. Here he was in his late twenties, still single and wild as a billy goat, likely headed for jail or an early grave. All Mother York could do for her boy was pray. And she prayed hard day after day, year after year.

She was praying on New Year's Eve, 1914, when Alvin was out drinking as usual. As she sat in her rocker, with a few coals still burning in the kitchen fireplace, the soft glow of a kerosene lamp lit the room.

At last she heard Alvin's unsteady steps on the front porch and looked up as he opened the door, letting in a blast of icy December wind. As many times as he'd come home like this, she had never waited up for him before. Seeing her sitting there gave him a shock. Their eyes met. Alvin looked away and stared at the floor, shame working its way through the alcoholic fog.

"When are you going to be a man like your father and grandfather?" she asked softly.

Hearing his mother's voice, Alvin sensed a strange, unfamiliar feeling. The years of drinking and fighting flashed through his mind. The waste and emptiness of his life stood out as never before. It was like seeing himself clearly for the first time, and what he saw deeply saddened him.

His knees gave way. Kneeling beside Mother York's chair, he put his head in her lap and started to cry. She was crying too; it was the first time he'd ever seen her weep. He had disappointed his mother and the God she served so faithfully. He felt his heart being deeply changed.

When he finally found his voice, he said, "Mother, I promise you tonight that I will never drink again as long as I live. I will never smoke or chew again. I will never gamble again. I will never cuss or fight again. I will live the life God wants me to live."

And so, New Year's Day 1915 marked the beginning of a new life for Alvin York. Recalling the moment years later, he said, "God just took ahold of my life."[1]

Yes, the Lord got ahold of him in that quiet, lamplit cabin as the New Year dawned, and He never let go.

⁓

After his New Year's conversion, Alvin was hungry to know more about God and Christ. Though he had the Bible, his mother's example, and a few ministers in the community for guidance, he felt he needed more. Alvin wanted to explore the teaching of the Christian faith, and looked forward to the next church revival. Evangelists came to the valley once in a while, but their visits were rare.

To get in or out of the Wolf River Valley, visitors had to make a tough climb over steep hills. On foot it was hard to travel the twelve miles to the county seat of Jamestown and back between sunrise and dark. Few outsiders braved the trek, which made Alvin all the more anxious to welcome the next traveling evangelists to Pall Mall.

Early in 1915, Melvin H. Russell came to preach at Wolf River Methodist Church, the only church in the valley. He was a circuit-riding minister who traveled from one isolated rural community to the next, holding weeklong revivals. Brother Melvin was a minister of the Church of Christ in Christian Union, a spiritual cousin of the Pentecostal church. His host for the week was Pastor Rosier C. Pile, lay preacher, postmaster, and unofficial leader of the community. York could scarcely wait to learn more about what the Bible taught and how to apply it in his own life. Once the preaching got under way, Russell warned his audience in vivid terms about the terrors of punishment in hell and the joys of happiness in heaven for all who followed Christ.

Sunday morning, the last day of the revival, the preacher invited all who wanted to give their lives to Jesus to come down front. Alvin's family, especially Mother York, watched with thanksgiving and pride as he walked forward and asked God to forgive him for his years of sinful behavior.

Alvin began faithfully attending the Methodist church and studied the Bible diligently. By the time Melvin Russell came back to preach again in December, Alvin had become one of the most faithful and active members of the congregation. Russell and two other pastors came over Bald Mountain from the north on December 29. Before the first service W. W. Loveless, one of Russell's associates, saw a burly, redheaded man walking toward him. York was there to lead the singing.[2]

At the end of the week, Loveless established a new congregation of the Church of Christ in Christian Union in Pall Mall. The twenty-seven charter members elected Rosier Pile as first elder and Alvin York as second elder.

Sixty-seven people came to revival that week. One of them was fifteen-year-old Gracie Williams, a shy, blue-eyed blonde who, like Alvin, had been born in the valley and whose family had lived there for generations. Gracie had known Alvin all her life.

Until lately, Gracie hadn't been the least interested in Alvin. He was rude and violent, drank too much, and fought all the time. As little as she cared for him, her father cared even less. Over the past year, though, Big 'Un was a changed man. He'd quit drinking and fighting. Not only did he come to church, he led the singing. Now he was second elder in a new congregation. In time, Alvin asked Gracie to marry him.

ONWARD CHRISTIAN SOLDIER

The world of Alvin York was slowly changing in other ways as well. In 1916 the *Fentress County Gazette* reported that a highway was coming through town. Federal Aid Road 28, also called the Dixie Short Route, would run across Tennessee on its way from the Gulf Coast to St. Louis, ending Pall Mall's long isolation. There were also two railroads planning extensions into the county, which meant residents no longer had to go fifty miles by horse and wagon to catch the nearest train.

These projects promised steady work for local men, and Alvin soon joined the Dixie Short Route crew, earning $1.60 for a ten-hour day spent cutting trees, breaking rocks, and hauling gravel. He still found time to hunt with his coon dogs and to compete in the shooting matches he enjoyed and excelled in. It was a good life. To top it all off, now he was in love with the most wonderful girl in the world, and the two of them had agreed to marry if Mr. Williams would give his consent. He could imagine building a house for his bride on his mother's land and spending the rest of his life happily raising a family on the banks of the Wolf.

That future disappeared in an instant on June 5, 1917, with the arrival of a little red postcard from Washington, D.C., ordering Alvin York to register with the local draft board. On April 6 the United States had declared war on Germany, which had been fighting against much of Europe since the summer of 1914 and threatened America's allies Britain and France.

Based on what he understood of Christ's message in the Bible, York, the former brawler, now opposed war in any form and petitioned for a military deferment as a conscientious objector. Because the Church of Christ in Christian Union was not a "religion or sect" recognized by the government, York's petition was denied.

Fentress County's first draft quota was called up on September 23, so Alvin knew it would only be a matter of time before his turn came. He was ordered to Jamestown for a physical. Alvin was in excellent health, twenty-nine years old, six feet even, and 170 pounds of rock-breaking, blacksmithing muscle. He passed.

Alvin shared the sad truth with his dear Gracie. They'd have to postpone getting married, but promised to stay true to each other and marry when Alvin came home.

Alvin kept his job on the road crew until November 10, when Pastor Pile himself brought a blue postcard out to him in the middle of the day while he was driving steel. The card directed Alvin to be ready for military service on twenty-four hours' notice. Four days later he was ordered to report for duty in the U.S. armed forces. He said good-bye to Gracie, his family, and friends; packed a small suitcase; and walked the twelve miles to Jamestown.

Alvin and the twenty others called up along with him spent the night in town, then traveled to the train station in Oneida. At 2:00 a.m. the line of southbound coaches came chuffing in. Alvin had never seen a train before. He stepped aboard and headed for Camp Gordon, near Augusta, where within another day he was no longer Alvin C. York, but Private York, serial number 1910421, United States Army.

⌒⌒⌒

After two months of basic training, York was assigned in February 1918 to Company G, 328th Battalion, 82nd Division. Unknown to Private York, his mother and Pastor Pile had pursued his appeal with the draft board. The War Department sent word that if he would fill out the proper forms, York could receive an exemption. However, when faced with the decision, York couldn't decide between holding to the belief that "Thou shalt not kill" and serving his country in defense of freedom. York asked his company commander for advice. Together they went to see their battalion commander, Colonel George Edward Buxton. The colonel, himself a committed Christian, told York to go home and think it over, reminding him that "if the watchman see the sword come, and blow not the trumpet, and the people be not warned; if the sword come, and take any person from among them . . . his blood will I require at the watchman's hand" (Ezekiel 33:6).

York returned to Pall Mall and struggled with his decision until the end of his ten-day leave. The last night, alone on a hillside, God gave him the assurance he needed. "As I prayed there alone," he later recalled, "a great peace kind of come into my soul . . . and I received my assurance. . . . I knowed I would go to war. I knowed I would be protected from all harm, and that so long as I believed in Him He would not allow even a hair of my head to be harmed."

Company G left for Camp Upton, New York, on April 19, 1918.

On May 1, York and the rest of the battalion boarded a Scandinavian ship for the sixteen-day voyage to Liverpool. York spent five days in England before joining the Allied forces in France. Then, on the night of June 26, Company G marched out of the village of Rambucourt to man the trenches for the first time.

During the summer of 1918, the 328th held Company G in reserve, assigning them to relatively quiet sections of the line, then rotating them to safe positions in the rear. The Great War in France had stalled at a line of trenches running more than three hundred miles across the country. The Germans had originally anchored their offensive line at Alsace in the east, then planned to sweep down from Belgium like a giant hinge, driving the French ahead of them. But the offensive had stalled, the two sides had dug in, and there they stayed month after month, shelling and being shelled. The Americans had entered the war to help the French and their English allies push the hinge back open and drive the Germans northward out of France. While leaders gathered their forces and made their plans, there was little for the new American arrivals to do.

Living conditions in the trenches were miserable almost beyond description. One machine gunner did his best: "Lice, rats, barbed wire, fleas, shells, bombs, underground caves, corpses, blood, liquor, mice, cats, artillery, filth, bullets, mortar, fire, steel: That is what war is." Even in so hellish a place, Private York was sure the Lord would take care of him. "There is no use of worrying about Shells," he wrote in his diary, "for you cant keep them from busting in your trench . . . if you can't alter things just ask God to help you."

On July 8 York was promoted to private first class. Within two months, the 328th Infantry Battalion headed for the town of St. Mihiel and their first taste of active frontline combat. This medieval town was at the southern tip of a salient, an isolated forward thrust the Germans had made into French-held territory during the first months of the war and held ever since. Faced with the huge numbers of American reinforcements pouring in, the German commanders realized they could never hold all their forward positions, and this was one they had decided to abandon. The Germans started their withdrawal on September 11. The next morning, American guns opened up on the retreating enemy, and the 328th advanced against the invaders they called "the Bosch." Alvin had been promoted a second time, to corporal, and was now a squad leader.

After only two days, the Allies chased the Bosch out of the St. Mihiel salient, and by September 16 the area was secure. It was the first time York had been on the offensive and the first time he saw anybody killed by enemy fire.

The Americans were reopening the hinge of the German battle line, swinging the western end of the front to make the line of battle run more north-south, forcing the Germans back across their prewar border with France. This meant a heavy concentration of offensive units to the north and west. Allied leaders planned to throw everything they had—160 divisions—at the enemy, staggering them so the Germans wouldn't know where the next strike would come. Six hundred thousand Americans and 225,000 French soldiers would stage a massive, all-out offensive in the Meuse-Argonne sector to defeat Germany before winter weather set in.

The 328th rested in St. Mihiel for a week, then headed for their assigned spot, sixty-five miles northwest at Mézières and Sedan, where there was an important railroad junction. To get there they had to cross the Meuse River and march through the dense Argonne Forest, supposedly bristling with Germans. As the weather turned cold and rainy, the 328th mustered with the rest of the 82nd American Division and prepared to chase the Bosch out of France for good.

At 5:30 on the morning of September 26, 1918, the first Allied soldiers marched into the Argonne Forest to begin what General

John J. Pershing, commander of the combined Allied forces, planned as the final offensive of the war. Retreating Germans gave ground easily until the Americans were in the thick of the forest. Beginning about two miles in, the high underbrush was booby-trapped with coils of barbed wire, and hidden machine guns spit deadly fire from every direction. The offensive stalled in the middle of the forest on October 1. After a few days of rest and resupply, fresh troops came up, including the 328th. On October 5, Corporal Alvin York marched into the forest to root out the enemy.

The closer York got to the action, the busier the road was. Rain drizzled down incessantly, turning the surface into knee-deep muck made deeper by supply trucks, mule-drawn wagons, and hundreds of thousands of infantry boots. As vehicles broke down and gun caissons slid into ditches, swearing soldiers slogged wearily around them. When horses dropped dead from exhaustion, soldiers pulled the wagons themselves.

York marched on. A machine gun nest hidden in the brush opened fire on the other side of the road, mowing down members of his company while Alvin watched in horror. To stop and fight enemies they couldn't see would only make them more of a target, so they hurried forward.

THE BATTLE FOR HILL 223

Reaching the northern part of the Argonne, the 82nd Division fell in behind the 1st Division as the 1st fought for what the field maps called Hill 223. Here, near the edge of the forest, was a hill the Germans wanted to hold on to. At the foot of its western slope was a narrow-gauge railroad that brought supplies to the front and carried wounded men and iron ore out. The Americans' immediate objective was to go over the hill and capture the rail line. The time of attack was set for 6:00 a.m., October 8, 1918. It was the day Alvin C. York would become one of the most famous soldiers in American history.[3]

The attack was supposed to begin with an artillery barrage, but gunners had trouble getting their field pieces in position because of the mud. It was also tricky forming up offensive ranks in the dark. Even as the horizon began to lighten, soldiers could scarcely see through the mist and fog. At ten minutes past six, the signal came to advance without artillery. It was only about a mile and a quarter from the crest down the slope to the railroad, but as soon as the Allied helmets appeared, enemy machine gun emplacements opened up. Men were cut down in waves that reminded Corporal York of a mowing machine going through a hayfield.

Battalions to the right and left were pinned down, which left the still-advancing 328th isolated ahead of the rest of the line. Company G was in the worst position of all and suddenly exposed to fire from three sides. The 1st Division, still ahead of the 328th, was stalled in a salient in front of them. The Germans began a pincer movement to cut off and surround the 1st, with Company G directly in the path of the pincer jaws at the salient base.

The company commander, Captain E. C. B. Danforth, could see that as long as the German machine gunners kept firing from the opposite hillside, the Allies on his line were helpless. They would either be butchered trying to advance through Spandau fire or be killed or captured in the pincer movement. He ordered a platoon sergeant to send out a patrol to see if they could do anything about those machine gun emplacements. The patrol was commanded by Corporal Bernard Early and included squads led by Corporals William C. Cutting, Murray Savage, and Alvin C. York. At 6:00 a.m. the three squads had totaled twenty-four men; by now there were seventeen soldiers left.

Early led his men away from the line of fire and into enemy territory, following a natural ravine that had been widened to form a shallow trench.

With no warning, two German stretcher bearers appeared out

of the high brush and mist. Seeing the Americans, they ran. When the Americans ordered them to stop, one obeyed, but the other kept running. The patrol took off after him, hoping to catch him before he could give them away. They'd only gone a short distance in pursuit before literally stumbling upon twenty or thirty members of a Prussian reserve division having their breakfast. The reservists had put their weapons aside to eat, and only one officer was armed. After a few shots, the Prussians surrendered, but as the Americans formed their POWs into a line, the officer shouted to the machine gunners, who opened fire. Within seconds, the deadly Spandaus had killed six Americans and wounded three. Corporal Cutting was hit three times, Corporal Early six times, and Corporal Savage, York's bunkmate, was killed by so many rounds his uniform was almost torn off. Every other soldier in Savage's squad was dead; York's squad had one dead.

That left seven privates and Corporal York to carry out their mission. As the ranking soldier, York took command of the remnants of his patrol and about two dozen prisoners.

When machine guns resumed firing, Corporal York noticed, as he watched the gunners, that "in order to sight me or swing their machine guns at me, the Germans had to show their heads above the trenches [actually the gun emplacements] and every time I saw a head I just teched it off." York yelled at the gunners to stop firing and surrender, but they kept shooting, so whenever a head popped up, York "teched it off" without a miss.

As the gunners fell, the shooting became less intense. Once the protective brush around York was shot up, he thought he might as well aim from a better position and stood, firing offhand. When he ran out of rifle ammunition, he switched to his own Colt .45.

A German lieutenant led a bayonet charge against York. York saw them coming. The corporal had six shots. He didn't miss, dropping all six attackers in rapid succession. Borrowing a lesson from his bird hunting days, he shot the last man first, then worked forward one at a time so the others would keep coming.

The corporal's next responsibility was to get his men and their prisoners safely back to their own lines. As the soldiers marched, they picked up more prisoners along the way, including a Lieutenant Vollmer, who could speak English. York ordered Vollmer to line up the prisoners and to command the others to surrender or else Vollmer would be the next one "teched off." Vollmer signaled for the remaining men to drop their arms. The group headed to the front, with Vollmer in the lead; York right behind him, with his Colt in the small of the German's back; followed by the other officer, along with two more officers they'd picked up on the way. Then came the three wounded Americans carried by POWs, the rest of the Germans, and the seven able-bodied American privates.

As they approached the American lines, York was relieved to meet a squad that Captain Danforth had sent searching for him. As soon as he saw them, York stepped in front of Vollmer to show his American insignia.

Back at headquarters, the battalion adjutant counted 132 German prisoners of war that York had captured almost single-handedly.

Writing that night in his diary, Corporal York ended his entry with reflections on his miraculous experience.

"You can see here in this case of mine where God helped me out. I had bin living for God and working for the church some time before I come to the army. So I am a witness to the fact that God did help me out of that hard battle . . . I never got a scratch."

THE MEDAL OF HONOR

On November 1 York was promoted to sergeant. Ten days later, he heard the long-awaited news that the war was over and the Armistice signed. On February 11, Sergeant York was awarded the Distinguished

Service Cross by General Pershing himself, who described York as "the greatest civilian soldier of the war." Military brass asked York if he'd be willing to make a speaking tour of American military installations in France, sharing his story and visiting with soldiers to keep up morale as restless troops counted the hours until they could go home.

York traveled the French countryside, telling his story, answering questions, and talking about his faith in Christ and how it saw him through the battle of Hill 223. The YMCA sponsored many of his talks, where hundreds of soldiers and locals would crowd in to hear. York's humility, enthusiasm for sharing his Christian testimony, and his natural gift as a storyteller made him a huge success.

On April 18, 1919, the 82nd Division held a historic review on the parade ground in the town of St. Silva. There Sergeant York received the Medal of Honor from the division commander, General George B. Duncan.

The following month, he shipped out from Bordeaux to New York aboard the USS *Ohioan* and, on May 22, stood at the rail as the ship sailed past the Statue of Liberty in New York Harbor.

"Take a good look at me, Old Girl," he said to Lady Liberty. "Because if you ever want to see me again, you'll have to turn around."

♋

The United States Congress awarded 118 Medals of Honor to men who served in World War I. The medal was bestowed in a ceremony; there would be an article in the hometown paper, perhaps some speeches and parades; and that was as far as the notoriety usually extended. Like most recipients, Alvin York had no personal interest in spreading his story. That the world ever learned of York's miraculous exploits is a miracle, the result of a fantastic chain of events.

The chain began with American painter and illustrator Joseph

Cummings Chase, who was in France on assignment for *World's Work* magazine, one of many publications scrambling to satisfy the American public's appetite for war news. After the Armistice, Chase interviewed and painted a number of American generals, including Major General George B. Duncan, commander of the 82nd Division. While painting Duncan's portrait, Chase engaged him in conversation. The general kept coming back to the story of a corporal in his command who'd captured 132 Germans single-handedly.

General Duncan told Chase he ought to paint York's portrait, too, and ordered the sergeant to report later that evening. Chase set to work.

Sometime after painting Sergeant York, Chase was riding in the back of an army truck with George Pattullo, a reporter for the *Saturday Evening Post*. Chase told him General Duncan's story about Corporal York. Pattullo happened to be on his way to the 328th, and as soon as he arrived, he interviewed the sergeant, then went with him and General Duncan back to Hill 223 on February 3, where York retraced his movements for Duncan and other officers.

Pattullo set to work on a long, detailed, highly descriptive and compelling feature article eventually titled "The Second Elder Gives Battle." In it he described how the corporal outfought the machine-gun battalion with his rifle and automatic pistol. "There were seven other Americans present at the fight, but it was York's battle and only York's. But for him not a man of them would have come out alive except as prisoners."[24]

Pattullo's feature made it to print in the April 26, 1919, issue of the *Saturday Evening Post*. The story made York a national hero.

⁓

By the time York landed in New York, financial offers had already started pouring in. A magazine offered ten thousand dollars for his autobiography. A vaudeville impresario offered him a thousand dollars a night for thirty nights to tell his story from the stage. There were rumors of a fifty-thousand-dollar movie offer, and even a wild tale that a New York socialite had offered him a mansion, a Cadillac, and a stipend for life to father her child.

But all Alvin wanted was to go home. On May 29, 1919, he was officially mustered out of the army at Fort Oglethorpe. The next day he took the Tennessee Central Railroad to Crossville, where every automobile in Jamestown waited to escort their hometown hero to his mother. Mother York and the rest of the family came from Pall Mall to greet Alvin in Jamestown. As soon as the motorcade clattered into view, the crowd started shooting off their guns in celebration. After a round of handshaking and well-wishing, Sergeant York and his mother headed over the mountain for home.

Money for a School

The wedding of Alvin York and Gracie Williams was the biggest event in Fentress County history. Reporters had known he was in love. Midweek they learned that Alvin and Miss Gracie would be wed on Saturday, June 7. When Governor Albert Roberts heard the news, he set his sights on performing the wedding himself.

National wire service reporters estimated the wedding day crowd in Pall Mall at three thousand, while Governor Roberts's staff put the number at five thousand. Whatever the count, it was by far the largest crowd ever gathered in the valley.

Alvin and Gracie moved in with Mother York and her younger children, and Alvin started building a house of his own next door. He went back to farming and hunting, yet scarcely a day went by without a stranger coming into town and asking for directions to the York cabin. Visitors arrived in a steady stream with more offers.

Alvin York was not an educated man, but he was intelligent. He realized that his notoriety gave him rare and valuable clout for whatever he wanted to accomplish. A few months after his return, York developed a vision for a free, year-round school with the facilities and the budget to attract top-quality teachers. (York had received about a third grade education in the ramshackle facilities available.) The new building would be sturdy and warm, so children without coats or shoes could come even in bad weather.

Meanwhile, Tennessee Railroad Commissioner George Welch began sorting through the movie offers that kept pouring in on York's behalf. He concluded that no producer would settle for the religious slant York insisted on. York believed movies were worldly and immoral and didn't want anything to do with them unless they focused on Christian topics. So Welch decided to put a book deal together instead. He also thought the idea of funding a school for the mountain children was a great one, and enlisted the Nashville Rotary Club to set up a speaking tour to raise money.

The first tour was a four-stage marathon covering the whole eastern half of the nation. Audiences clamored to hear about York's war experiences, but at first the sergeant insisted he wouldn't talk about Hill 223. He finally agreed to have someone else along to tell the story of his heroism in France, and then York would speak about his religious convictions and his dream of a school. The enterprise got off to a modest start in Chattanooga. Sergeant York (though discharged, he continued using his rank, and did so for the rest of his life) told his audience he wanted to raise $150,000 for a series of schools in the Tennessee mountains.

In three months he raised about forty thousand dollars in contributions and had pledges for fifty thousand more.

❦

Notoriety and school contributions aside, Alvin still had to earn a living. He not only had a wife to support, but their first baby was on the way as well. Alvin had very publicly turned down one fortune after another, then raised tens of thousands of dollars for his school, yet he had scarcely enough personal income to get by on.

On June 5, only a few weeks after Alvin and Gracie moved into their own cabin beside Mother York, their first child was born, a son. They planned to name him Alvin Jr., but the boy had hydrocephalus. He lived only four days, almost every minute of it in his mother's arms.

Within a month Gracie was expecting again, and York and Welch turned their attention to getting Alvin's book under way. Welch chose a well-connected New York writer named Sam K. Cowan, counting on Cowan's reputation with magazine and book publishers to help sell the story. On December 9, Cowan reported he'd received an offer from Funk & Wagnalls. On December 28, a contract was signed.

Sergeant York and His People was published on April 20, 1922, backed by a major marketing push and heavy advertising. But booksellers didn't want another war book; the ones they had were being sold at 75 percent off. Even so, sales took hold after a while, rose to a respectable level, and held steady.

It was a good season for Sergeant York and his family. His story was out now, told the way he wanted it; he was gradually collecting money to start building his school; and he and Gracie had a healthy new son, Alvin Jr. On Valentine's Day 1922 the young family moved into a beautiful new two-story clapboard home, a gift of the Nashville Rotary Club. Now York could pour all of his energy into getting his school up and running.

On March 26, 1926, York signed the charter of incorporation for the Alvin C. York Industrial Institute.[5] On May 8, in front of a roaring crowd, he turned over the first shovel of dirt on the school property.

By September, the county school board formally joined forces with York's new institute, consolidating the county high school with York's state-funded venture. On September 6, the school held its first day of classes in a county building on the edge of town. Across the highway a crew started clearing land for the new administration building, driving tractors donated by Henry Ford.

LEAN YEARS

By November, York's school was teaching seventy-five to eighty children a day. Meanwhile, sales of *Sergeant York and His People* were steady but still disappointing. The Roaring Twenties were in full swing, and the war seemed like ancient history. Furthermore, readers who were interested in York the hero wanted to hear about killing Germans, not about his religious conversion. His story wasn't novel anymore, and the crowds were smaller.

The Yorks' personal financial picture was dire. Though their new home was a gift, it wasn't fully paid for. His farm turned little if any profit, and there were few opportunities to make money in Pall Mall. As a result the sergeant was barely scraping by. He and Gracie had three sons now—Alvin Jr., George Edward Buxton, and Woodrow Wilson.

Alvin revisited the idea of a book about his life to raise money. To reach the sales he needed, he'd have to write about the war after all. He finally decided to sell the rights to the pocket diaries he had carried throughout his military career.

Tom Skeyhill was an Australian writer living in New York, a war veteran himself. Skeyhill was convinced he could use the war diary as the core of an autobiographical best seller, and York agreed. The writer spent the winter of 1927–28 in Fentress County. York showed Skeyhill the diaries, saying he would put them in a book if it would help get the school built.

Sergeant York: His Own Life Story and War Diary began its run as a serial on July 14, 1928, and was a tremendous success.

York also decided to hire Famous Speakers in New York to schedule his speaking trips and negotiate fees. Almost overnight the bureau improved Alvin York's finances. The first tour they planned guaranteed $500 a week for ten weeks. Later in the fall Alvin received enthusiastic receptions in Boston and New York. Even more excitement for York came on the morning of February 11, 1929, when, back in Jamestown, 108 students walked proudly through the front door of their new school building. Alvin York's dream was there at last in bricks and desks and chalkboards. Now he had to keep it alive while at the same time earning a living.

Speaking and writing were the keys to generating the income York Institute needed. As York planned future speaking tours, Tom Skeyhill came up with another publishing idea. He rewrote the York story into an adventure book for boys titled *Sergeant York: Last of the Long Hunters*.

Then came a family crisis. Little Sam Houston York, nineteen months old, died of meningitis in his mother's arms. She was already expecting her next child: Andrew Jackson York would be born the following April,[6] making four boys in the house.

That same month, *Last of the Long Hunters* went on sale, and York went on the road, speaking in North Carolina, Washington, New York, Illinois, Kansas, then back to New York.

⸎

Whatever upward trend York's writing and speaking income might have taken was dashed as the stock market crash of October 1929 worked its way through the economy to York Institute. Speaking dates, originally $250 a night, all but disappeared, and Famous Speakers dropped York's fee to $150. Sometimes his hosts couldn't pay him at all. Moreover, by 1938 there were seven children in the York household: Betsy Ross, Mary Alice, and Thomas Jefferson had joined the family. York Institute was rescued when the Tennessee legislature agreed to take over its funding.

The next few years were lean ones for York, who took a job with the Civilian Conservation Corps to make ends meet. One late February day in 1940, he received a telegram requesting a meeting to discuss "a historical document of vital importance to the country in these troubled times." War was raging again in Europe, and there was vigorous debate in America over whether the United States should get involved. The writer of the telegram had asked to meet with York before and was turned down flat. But circumstances were different now.

HOLLYWOOD COME CALLING

The request was from Jesse Lasky, former producer of the CBS network radio program *Gateway to Hollywood* and a thirty-year show business veteran. At one point he was business agent for the biggest stars on the stage, including Al Jolson. From there he climbed to the top of the theatrical ladder as a Broadway producer. Unfortunately, Lasky spent so much money on knockout shows that he went bankrupt. He then entered the fledgling motion picture business, forming Paramount Pictures with his brother-in-law, Samuel Goldwyn, Adolph Zukor, and Cecil B. DeMille.[7]

Lasky was forced out of Paramount in 1932 when he kept spending top dollar on movie production even as profits plummeted during the Depression. By 1940 Jesse Lasky, nearing sixty and seemingly past his prime, needed a job. He had been one of the thousands of cheering New York bystanders who watched Sergeant York's welcome-home parade in 1919. He'd offered York a movie contract then and several times over the years since, but the sergeant always turned him down. "Uncle Sam's uniform ain't for sale," he insisted.

Desperate, Lasky contacted York again, hoping world events would convince him to change his mind. With Europe at war, York thought America should send supplies and weapons to help the British. Others, including the famous aviator Charles Lindbergh, considered the war none of America's business and not worth the commitment of American resources. Lasky thought he could convince York that his story on film now, focusing on patriotism, bravery, and the price of freedom, would sway popular opinion to support aid for Britain and France.

Lasky was right. After refusing even to discuss a movie for twenty years, York was willing to think about it in the light of promoting pro-interventionism. He believed his story would show the power of faith in battle and stir America's deeply rooted patriotism and love of freedom to the point that the people would step up and help their failing allies.

It would also enable York to build another school he had long dreamed of, the York Bible Institute.

⸙

"Extra! Extra! Contract signed for Sergeant York movie!"

The newsboys were shouting the headlines even before York and Lasky actually signed their agreement. Though he still wasn't completely satisfied with the deal, the sergeant went ahead. Lasky gave York a personal check for twenty-five thousand dollars as an advance, with a promise of an additional twenty-five thousand later in the year.

Most of the movie was filmed at Sound Stage 6 on the Warner Bros. lot in Burbank, California, with Gary Cooper playing the part of York. Battle scenes were shot in a barley field in the Simi Valley, where tractors, dump trucks, and dynamite re-created the Argonne battle site. The scene of York being awarded the Medal of Honor was staged at Los Angeles city hall. The production concluded on May 3, 1941, coming in at just under $1.4 million. York and Lasky waited impatiently to see whether their dreams would come to life—Lasky's of boosting his sagging career, and York's of finishing the schools he had struggled twenty years to complete.

☙❦❧

York arrived at New York's Pennsylvania Station on July 2 to attend the most widely anticipated movie premiere of the year. Above the Astor Theater on Broadway one of the biggest electric signs ever built—four stories high and half a block long—featured two alternating images of actor Gary Cooper: a mountaineer holding a muzzle loader and a soldier sighting down his infantry rifle. Underneath, lights spelled out huge letters reading, "Gary Cooper in *Sergeant York.*" The last Hollywood movie with so many advance ticket sales had been *Gone with the Wind.*[8]

Sergeant York was a smash hit. Influential columnists and critics of the day hailed it as a masterpiece. Dorothy Kilgallen called it "one of the greatest entertainments of all time." Louella Parsons declared *Sergeant York* "one of the finest pictures of any year."

Thanks to the Warner Bros. publicity machine, York gained a powerful platform for his pro-interventionist position, and his national profile was higher than it had been in decades. Soon he accepted the offer of a weekly inspirational radio show. The *Chicago Sun* hired him to write a daily syndicated newspaper column. York visited military bases, spoke at war bond rallies, endorsed the Red Cross, and chaired the Fentress County draft board.

Sergeant York was the highest-grossing picture of 1941 and garnered eleven Oscar nominations, winning two—Best Actor for Gary Cooper and Best Editing for editor William Holmes.

THE OLD TIME RELIGION

Alvin York joined an exuberant, grateful nation celebrating the end of the war in the summer of 1945. But a year later, York suffered a mild stroke. He refused to go to the hospital and spent a few days in bed, resuming his routine even though he felt numb on his right side. He kept a busy schedule—farming and cattle operations, visiting the Institute, and entertaining the usual noon crowd around his dinner table.

But the sergeant's stroke slowed him a bit, and two more, one late in 1948 and another in the spring of 1949, left him dependent on a walking stick. Despite his disability and advancing age, York remained keenly interested in world events and relished any opportunity to sound off on the news of the day. He consistently supported a position of deterrence through strength, especially in dealing with the Communists. Force, he said, was the only language a nation understood once it turned its back on God.

On February 24, 1954, Alvin York collapsed unconscious on the floor in his farmhouse from a cerebral hemorrhage. The sergeant was paralyzed from the waist down and confined to bed for the rest of his life. On top of his medical problems, the Internal Revenue Service came calling, claiming York owed tens of thousands of dollars in taxes on his movie royalties. York had given most of the fortune away, but had no records to prove it. Eventually a nationwide appeal brought in enough donations to settle his tax bill.

Even bedridden, York entertained a steady stream of friends, relatives, and complete strangers who came to the big white house on the bank of the Wolf River to pay their respects. On December 13, 1963, Alvin York celebrated his seventy-sixth birthday with an enormous dinner that was a highlight of the year in Pall Mall. He warned the crowd that day that America was veering from the path that had brought so many years of peace and prosperity. "If this country fails," he said, "it will fail from within. I think we've just got to go back to the old time religion."[9]

When York arrived at Veterans Hospital in Nashville in August 1964, it was his eleventh hospital stay in two years. The old veteran was simply worn out and ready to go. Gracie and their son George, now a Nazarene minister, were with him for what turned out to be his final trip out of the valley. Soon York fell into a coma[10] and on September 2, died without regaining consciousness.

Three days later, Alvin Cullum York was honored and laid to rest before a crowd of eight thousand, the largest gathering in Wolf River history, surpassing the wedding crowd of forty-five years before. President Lyndon Johnson sent Lieutenant General Matthew B. Ridgeway, leader of the 82nd Airborne during World War II and later commander of NATO, as his personal representative. A band and honor guard from the 82nd assisted with the graveside proceedings. Six soldiers carried the casket from the church to the cemetery as the band played York's favorite hymn, "Onward Christian Soldiers."[11]

Gracie died twenty years later, on September 27, 1984, at the age of eighty-four.

⁓

York Agricultural Institute has a current enrollment of 650. The four-hundred-acre campus (reported to be the largest high school campus in the world) includes a working farm and a park. The school received a National Blue Ribbon of Excellence in 1989, and in 1992 *Redbook* magazine designated York Institute one of the best rural schools in America.

The original brick building in which York took such pride still stands, but was replaced in 1981 by modern classrooms. In 2009 the state turned the building, along with five hundred thousand dollars, over to the nonprofit Sergeant York Patriotic Foundation, which hopes to preserve it. The sergeant's three surviving children, George, Andrew, and Betsy, maintain a keen interest in the school, the historic building, and their father's legacy.

That legacy has dimmed over time. When Sergeant Alvin York came home to a hero's welcome in 1919, his was the biggest ticker-tape parade in New York history up to that time. Day after day his name appeared in the *New York Times*. He was an international celebrity. Today most Americans younger than fifty have never heard of him. Yet the example he set is powerful and compelling. York's faith transformed his life, and that transformation had a ripple effect that eventually touched millions. The spiritual journey of this humble backwoods farmer took him into the presence of prime ministers and presidents. It made him a household name for two generations. And his life is still a reminder that the power of faith can equip even the meekest and most modest of us for a great work that we scarcely dare to dream of.

To learn more about Sergeant York, read John Perry's *Sergeant York* (Nashville: Thomas Nelson, 2010) from the Christian Encounters Series.

10 | WILLIAM F. BUCKLEY JR.

(1925–2008)

by Jeremy Lott

A man related to me . . . that Buckley's writings on religion had turned the tide of his agnostic mind toward belief.

—SHAWN MACOMBER

When sons are named for their fathers, they are often called by different names to avoid undue confusion. So it was with William F. Buckley Jr., born on November 24, 1925, to Aloïse Steiner-Buckley and William Frank Buckley. The father was known as "Will," so the third of his sons became "Bill."

Bill Buckley's parents left a heavy imprint on their son's character, his politics, his religion, and his ambition. When Will Buckley died in 1958, Bill wrote that it was to his father's "encouragement" that Bill's magazine *National Review* "owes its birth and early life."

Will Buckley was both Irish and Catholic, but the Irish clan he hailed from had been Protestant. According to family lore, Will's grandfather (Bill's great-grandfather) had been part of the landed Protestant gentry in Cork County, Ireland. Orangemen normally paraded through his land annually to celebrate the supremacy of the English king over the Catholics of Ireland. When Buckley took a Catholic bride, he asked that his fellow Protestants not march across his land. He didn't want to disturb the missus. The Orangemen attempted to march anyway, and Buckley bloodied the first man to cross the property line.

After that incident, great-grandfather Buckley felt it best to leave Ireland, and the Buckleys bounced around for generations: Canada, San Diego, Texas, Connecticut, Mexico, New York (where Bill was born), Britain, France, various points in Latin and South America. The children were educated in different languages depending on the locale at the time—Bill spoke Spanish and French before English.

Will bought an estate called Great Elm in Sharon, Connecticut, in 1923, where many of the Buckley children spent a few formative years. Bill left Great Elm at age thirteen to go to a British Jesuit boarding school.[1]

Will Buckley was an observant but quiet Catholic with prominent Protestant ancestors. His children might have assimilated into some form of Protestantism if it weren't for his wife, Aloïse. It was she who inspired an intense piety in many of her children.

When Aloïse died at the age of one hundred in 1985, Bill began her moving obituary: "My mother worshiped God as intensely as the saint transfixed. And his companionship to her was that of an old and very dear friend."

Will and Aloïse produced ten bustling Buckley children, from 1918 to 1938: Aloise, John, Priscilla, James, Jane, William, Patricia, Reid, Maureen, and Carol.

Creeping Secularism

Buckley came to Yale in 1946 after a two-year stint as a second lieutenant in the army. Along with his luggage, he said, "I brought with me a firm belief in Christianity and a profound respect for American institutions and traditions." To his disappointment, he discovered that something wrong was being done in the name of "academic freedom," producing "one of the most extraordinary incongruities of our time: the institution that derives its moral and financial support from the Christian individualists and then addresses itself to the task

241

of persuading the sons of these supporters to be atheistic socialists."[2] He would soon write a book addressing this very grievance. But in the meantime, Buckley became the very Yaliest of Yalies. With his tall frame, quick wit, piercing eyes, and full, toothsome smile, Buckley quickly won many of his fellow students over to whatever cause he was currently spearheading. He was, you could say, the "big man on campus." Bill was an excellent debater. He became a member of the university's famous, secret Skull and Bones society and was unanimously elected chairman of the *Yale Daily News*. Buckley could never be accused of being on the fringe of campus activity. He was well liked and right in the thick of it.

After his graduation from Yale, Buckley stayed on at Yale to teach Spanish, his first language. Soon he would find himself working, albeit briefly, for the CIA. His professor, Willmore Kendall, had been part of the Office of Strategic Services (OSS) during World War II. The OSS became the CIA in the postwar years as the American government readied itself for the long struggle against the Soviet Union.

It was while undergoing evaluation by the CIA and teaching at the university that Buckley wrote *God and Man at Yale*, a mid-century survey of the religious and economic content of undergraduate classes at his alma mater. According to Sam Tanenhaus, Bill Buckley's official biographer, this book contained the seeds of what grew into the conservative movement.

God and Man at Yale documented creeping secularism in the religion and social science and philosophy courses and other academic institutions and student associations. It deplored that creep, along with the tendency of Yale's professors, administrators, and economists to encourage the visible hand of the state to take hold of more of the U.S. economy, to redistribute wealth, and to regulate competition among businesses.

His choice of words really riled up the critics.

The *Atlantic Monthly* ran a scathing review in November 1951 by

Yale alum McGeorge Bundy, titled "The Attack on Yale."[3] In it, he called Buckley's effort a "savage attack" and found the book "dishonest in its use of facts, false in its theory, and a discredit to its author." He charged that Buckley "holds views of a peculiar and extreme variety, both on economics and on the organization of a university."

Bundy also threw in some old-fashioned Catholic baiting for good measure. *God and Man at Yale* is not a large-C Catholic work. Even so, Bundy tried to use Buckley's religion to hang him, finding it "most remarkable of all" that Buckley would urge "a return to what he considers to be Yale's true religious tradition" without disclosing "he himself is an ardent Roman Catholic." (Oddly enough, the book was almost consistently faulted in the Catholic press. The liberal Catholic lay magazine *Commonweal* even accused Buckley of advocating "anti-papal economics.")

It was during this same period that Buckley married Patricia "Pat" Taylor, from the wealthy Taylor clan of Vancouver, British Columbia.

Pat was Anglican and would not convert to marry Bill, but she did consent to having any Buckley children raised Catholic. They tied the knot in the summer of 1950 in a large wedding conducted by the Catholic archbishop of Vancouver and later blessed at the Taylor residence by an Anglican divine.

❧

The CIA wanted Buckley as a deep-cover agent. He was trained in spycraft in Washington, DC, and then sent by the CIA to Mexico City, which at the time was a hotbed of international intrigue. Yet, even though Buckley's training had been extensive, he didn't have the chance to use it much. He spent most of his time encouraging anti-Communists to run for leadership in Mexican student organizations and editing a book by Eudocio Ravines, a Peruvian former Communist, about Communist designs for world domination.

It was becoming more and more obvious that Bill's talents could be put to better use back in America. Even so, he and Pat might have stuck it out for more than the nine months that they lasted there. What finally forced their hand was the *New York Times* best-seller list.

Buckley did not have a contract when he undertook to write *God and Man at Yale*. He had simply written and sent it to the upstart conservative publisher Henry Regnery, founder of the firm that bears his name. Regnery promptly accepted it and published the book while Bill was in Mexico City.

It sold better than expected. Far better. The hostile reviews made people, especially students, want to see what all the fuss was about. It climbed the charts.

It was not feasible for Bill to stay a deep-cover agent in Mexico while his name was being splashed all over American newspapers. So he quit the CIA to come back to the United States and enter the contest of ideas, full-time.

McCarthy's Cause

For Bill and Pat Buckley, the early 1950s were a time of frustration and flux. Bill thought many of the reviews of *God and Man at Yale* were so outlandish because there were so many more liberal journals than nonliberal ones. Two of these nonliberal magazines, though, the *Freeman* in Chicago and the *American Mercury* in New York, reviewed his book favorably, and both offered him jobs.

He took the assistant editor post at the *American Mercury*. The magazine had been founded in the 1920s by H. L. Mencken and had featured the writing of some of America's notable writers, from Ernest Hemingway to Theodore Dreiser. But the magazine changed hands regularly, and the acquisitions led to several editorial turnovers, which changed its editorial nature.

When Bill came on in 1952, it was a more explicitly right-wing magazine than it had been, and as it drifted into genuine neo-Nazism, that political turn would eventually prove its undoing. Buckley worked there only a few months and left over the fact that one of its articles had been "spiked"—not published because of editorial caprice.

On September 28, 1953, Pat delivered a son, Christopher Taylor Buckley. The next May she suffered her second tubal pregnancy, the first having taken place while in Mexico City, reducing her already considerably lowered chances of conception to zero. The Buckleys had wanted a large family, but "providence," Bill said, had other ideas. It didn't immediately inform them what it had up its sleeve.

⎿

After the success of *God and Man at Yale* and the failure of Bill's attempt to keep a regular magazine journalism job, Henry Regnery suggested that Bill write a book on conservative philosophy. Instead Buckley proposed his one and only cowritten book, with Yale debate partner and brother-in-law L. Brent Bozell Jr. (The Brent Bozell who founded Media Research Center and appears regularly on television is his son.) It would be about the controversies surrounding the man of the moment, the communist-hunting Wisconsin senator Joseph McCarthy. The volume finally appeared in 1954, one month before the infamous Army-McCarthy hearings that led to McCarthy's censure, downfall, and death.

From the outset, the purpose of *McCarthy and His Enemies* was to vindicate the movement that the Wisconsin senator represented and only secondarily the man himself. The case for McCarthy was never that he was perfect, or even always prudent, but that he was onto something important and that his accusations didn't amount to a "witch hunt." The problem of Communist infiltration in the U.S. government was very real, argued Buckley and Bozell, and should be dealt with publicly.

Buckley later reflected, while promoting his novel *The Redhunter*, on how much McCarthy had done to cause his own undoing.

McCarthy was impulsive, drunken, violent, and possibly a morphine addict. He was condemned by colleagues and died an early death in 1957. But Buckley couldn't shake the conviction that McCarthy's cause was essentially right and just. At a conference in the summer of 2009 sponsored by the Portsmouth Institute about the religious side of Bill Buckley, Clark Judge charged that "Bill's understanding of the Communist challenge was informed of his Catholicism, reflecting a quality of moral insight almost entirely lost on the Protestant establishment of the day."[4] But that may be going a bit far. There were plenty of staunch Protestant anti-Communists in the 1950s. The revivalist Reverend Billy Graham was very much invested in the struggle against Communism. Screen Actors Guild president Ronald Reagan, raised in a fundamentalist Disciples of Christ congregation, was struggling against reds and naming names before Buckley graduated from Yale.

But Catholics felt especially committed to the struggle against Communism. Rome viewed Moscow as the champion of a rival, false, malevolent creed, and masses featured prayers for the conversion of Russia. Most American Catholic politicians—from John F. Kennedy to Eugene McCarthy—were staunch anti-Communists.

Still, it's possible to lean too hard on Buckley's religion as an explanation for his thoughts on Communism. The Buckleys had been isolationists until Pearl Harbor. After the war, they decided that the threat of expansionist Communism posed by the Soviet Union was great enough to justify a massive military buildup, serious cloak-and-dagger initiatives, and, of course, a public campaign to fight Communist infiltration of the U.S. government.

NATIONAL REVIEW AND YELLING STOP!

Bill Buckley wanted a magazine, but he didn't want to start one from scratch. He made offers to take over the *Freeman* and *Human Events* and was rebuffed. Incredibly, he also attempted to buy *Commonweal* despite the magazine's earlier harsh criticism of his views.

Before Buckley, America had been a country with diverse strains of free-market liberal, anti-Communist, and traditionalist thinking. Buckley sought to gather those all under the sail of "conservatism" and fix the newly cast conservative cannons on collectivism, liberalism, and Communism, but he had no illusions that such a thing could be accomplished without other parallel institutions that did not yet exist.

National Review was thus one of only several foundings in which Bill Buckley played a vital part. This magazine would serve as a springboard for Buckley's countless public campaigns, and help to catapult him on to other things.

He also helped to start the conservative youth organization Young Americans for Freedom in 1960. The first meeting was held at his parents' estate in Sharon, Connecticut, and the organization's charter document, the so-called Sharon Statement, bears the indelible stamp of Buckley's politics and personality.

Then there was the Conservative Party of New York. Buckley and a group of Republicans who were disgusted with the tilt of their own state party established this group as an alternative for voters.

National Review in the early years was not much like the *National Review* of today. It still has the same blue frame on every cover, an idea stolen from *Time* magazine and tweaked. And it is still broadly concerned with issues of conservative orthodoxy. But it does not have the same spirited independence that it enjoyed early on.

It would be hard to imagine *National Review* not endorsing the Republican candidate for president. George W. Bush got the magazine's guarded and then enthusiastic endorsements, as well as a big pat on the back on the way out. John McCain, who had been a thorn in the side of movement conservatives and almost switched parties, also got the thumbs-up.

But *National Review* declined to formally endorse Eisenhower in 1956 and again withheld its endorsement from Richard Nixon in the 1960 election. In fact, the sort of moderate "modern Republicanism" that Ike and Nixon represented was the target of much ridicule by Buckley and company. The kids today might call them hard-core.

The magazine and the movement it hoped to represent "stands athwart history, yelling Stop, at a time when no one is inclined to do so, or to have much patience with those who so urge it."[5] By no one, they meant American society's elites. They explained that "literate America [had] rejected conservatism in favor of radical social experimentation." The editors also believed that the domestic growth of government "must be fought relentlessly" and came out swinging against "Social Engineers," "intellectual cliques," "bipartisanship," "union monopolies," and "world government." Communism, said *National Review*, was "the [twentieth] century's most blatant force of Satanic utopianism." And "coexistence" was judged "neither desirable nor possible nor honorable; we find ourselves irrevocably at war with communism and shall oppose any substitute for victory."

This mission statement was a collective expression of the editors. And it thanked the "more than one hundred and twenty investors [who] made this magazine possible." But the principal investor was Bill Buckley. His father put up $100,000 in 1955 dollars to help get *National Review* off the ground, and Bill owned all the voting shares in the corporation. He made many of the edits and all the final calls for what went into the magazine.

৵৵৵

Buckley and his editorial team lost no time in identifying national political figures they thought could advance the conservative agenda. According to conservative historian and Goldwater biographer Lee Edwards, "Senator Barry Goldwater of Arizona was an outspoken conservative Republican who attracted national attention in the late fifties by calling the Eisenhower Administration's excessive spending a 'betrayal' of the public trust and for exposing trade union corruption in widely televised congressional hearings."[6]

Buckley fastened onto Goldwater and promoted him relentlessly. He was one of the people who worked to draft Goldwater to enter the race for the Republican presidential nomination in 1960. Goldwater eventually let his name be considered, though he never thought he had a chance at winning or of securing the vice presidential slot, and he was right. No matter. The real prize was down the road in 1964, and Buckley and nearly the entire *National Review* crew were pulling for him.

Through the early 1960s, Buckley used his magazine, his new weekly column syndicated by the *Washington Star*, and his regular speeches to promote the candidacy of Goldwater.

Then came JFK's fatal visit to Dallas on November 22, 1963, and Lyndon Johnson became president. Goldwater was convinced there was no chance that he could be elected over Johnson, and Buckley agreed.

Goldwater ran anyway, barely won a brutal primary fight with liberal Republican and New York governor Nelson Rockefeller, and ran one of the most honest, uncompromising general election campaigns the world has ever seen. He refused to pander to audiences, talked of drastically reducing the size and scope of the federal government, and said that he would approach the Cold War with a will to win.

The result was an Electoral College bloodbath. Lyndon Johnson carried forty-four states for 486 votes to Goldwater's 52 votes.

WFB FOR MAYOR

Undeterred by this national repudiation of his conservative position, Bill Buckley decided to run for public office himself. His famous 1965 campaign for mayor of New York began as a joke. *National Review* was running an article by Buckley on the reforms that New York City should pursue. An editor suggested that they call attention to this by putting "WFB for Mayor" on the cover. Then the magazine started getting calls and inquiries of where people might sign up, and one thing led to another . . .

That's the official story, and it's partly true. But really, Buckley ran for mayor because of a feud he had with the very liberal New York Republican John Lindsay. When Lindsay captured the mayoral nomination of the Republican Party, Buckley announced that he would stand for office on the Conservative ticket, the party he had helped found to oppose liberal members of the state GOP. He said he was running because, though the "main candidates" for mayor agreed that New York was in trouble, they were "resolutely opposed to discussing the reasons why it is in crisis."

Among other things, Buckley spoke out against the crime problem in New York and proposed to actually do something about it. "We need . . . a much larger police force," he said. Buckley was willing to expand the police force by cutting elsewhere because "the protection of the individual against the criminal is the first and highest function of government."

On other topics, Buckley promised to defang the city's unions and order police to protect workers who cross picket lines, drastically scale back welfare payments and introduce a yearlong residency requirement for receiving them, and scrap the minimum wage.

The *New York Times* editorialized dismissively, "William F. Buckley Jr., leading apostle of Goldwaterism on the Eastern Seaboard, has offered himself as the Conservative Party candidate for mayor. He regards New York as a city to be saved from crisis and . . . himself as the man to do it. Whether New York is also ready for Mr. Buckley is another matter."

Of course he didn't win. When the vote totals came in that November, they looked like this:

CANDIDATE	VOTE
John Lindsay	44.9 percent
Abe Beame	40.9 percent
Bill Buckley	13.3 percent

Lindsay proved to be an awful mayor. He greatly expanded welfare programs and grew the city's bureaucracy. By the time he left office, crime and high taxes had driven about a million New Yorkers out of the city. Historian Vincent Cannato titled his book about the Lindsay years *The Ungovernable City*, and that certainly seemed to be the case. New York City almost filed for bankruptcy in 1975 and had to be bailed out by the federal government.

Despite Buckley's poor showing in the polls, his candidacy set certain things in motion that helped New York recover from the crisis. It nudged the Republican Party in the direction of law and order and fiscal sanity. Lindsay managed to win a second term as mayor in 1969 as a Liberal, not a Republican. The next year, Bill's brother James Buckley won a three-way race for a Senate seat as a Conservative against Democrat Richard Ottinger and liberal Republican Charles Goodell. Jim Buckley won the three-way race and captured the Republican nomination in the next election.

The conservative threat pushed the politics of the state to the right for the other parties as well. Running for reelection in 1976 as the Republican nominee, Buckley lost to Democrat Daniel Patrick Moynihan, but only after Moynihan defeated the very liberal feminist Bella Abzug in the Democratic primary. Abzug then went on to lose in the Democratic mayoral primary to the much more conservative Ed Koch.

∽⁖∾

Critics have intimated that Bill Buckley used his run for mayor to launch his television career. Buckley claimed the opposite was true, that the mayoral race actually slowed him down. In fact, Buckley delayed his television-hosting career to run for mayor. But it is undeniably true that he milked the mayoral run for all it was worth.

On August 4, 1965, Buckley had traveled to Washington, DC, and held a press conference at the National Press Club headquarters. The reason given for the trip was to make a point about federal overreach into the affairs of state and local governments. Buckley eventually got around to complaining about that, but the real purpose of the event was greater publicity through novelty.

Rather than take questions from reporters, Buckley interviewed himself—literally. He stood at the podium and pretended to be two people, turning his neck from one side to the other as he changed personas—from Bill Buckley the interviewer to Bill Buckley the political candidate, and back. He used the self-interrogation to introduce his book *The Unmaking of a Mayor*. In Buckley's final 2008 novel, *The Rake*, roguish lead Ruben Castle does something similar.

MEDIA MATRIX

At last, a year after his mayoral run, Buckley's *Firing Line* debuted in April 1966. It is remembered now as a forum for civilized debate and long conversation by the attention span–shortened standards of modern television, but it was a very different show in the beginning from the show that it became.

Buckley's program eventually found a home on PBS and lasted thirty-three years—longer than any other American public affairs show. In the early years, it was broadcast on commercial television and was more like the intellectual prize fight of the week, with Bill Buckley going up against—and bloodying—famous liberals.

There is a certain undeniable attraction to those early broadcasts. *Firing Line*, with its bare set—usually just Buckley and an opponent or two sitting in swivel chairs, rigorous introductions, and enforced manners (Buckley called everybody by honorifics and expected the same)—was one of the purest exchanges of ideas television audiences ever witnessed.

It was formal, and it was brutal, so much so that several prominent politicians refused to go on *Firing Line*. The question was put to Buckley, "Why doesn't Bobby Kennedy go on your show?" "Why does baloney fear the grinder?" he replied.

If that's all *Firing Line* had ever been—a smart, opinionated host running roughshod over his guests—then it would be remembered only as a more literate precursor to *Crossfire*-like cable shows and conservative talk radio. Buckley wasn't always happy with how the early shows came off. So he changed things up considerably. He sought a wider variety of guests and topics, and tried to be less abrasive.[7]

The new approach made for some of the best television in the history of broadcasting. Buckley only partially captured this in his 1989 book *On the Firing Line*, where he wrote of Muhammad Ali arguing for his sincerity in converting to the Nation of Islam. Even before the draft board tried to reclassify him and send him to Vietnam, Ali said, he divorced his first wife because "she wouldn't wear her dresses long."

Ali spelled out exactly how much money that cost him: "It cost me two hundred and fifty thousand dollars. I'm paying twelve hundred dollars a month now in alimony. I paid nearly ninety-six thousand dollars in lawyers' fees. Now if that's not sincerity, I don't know what is."[8]

It probably shouldn't surprise us, though, that Buckley's most famous television exchange was not part of his television show. As a guest commentator for ABC at the 1968 Republican and Democratic conventions, Bill appeared opposite the expatriate gay left-wing novelist Gore Vidal, and it was obvious from the opening bell that the two loathed each other. Buckley even made fun of Vidal's novels. In turn, Vidal threw any charge at Buckley that he thought might stick.

One outrage that Buckley managed to inspire among many conservative Christians was over the fact that he allowed himself to be interviewed by—and wrote for—*Playboy*.

Buckley initially claimed that he did so because he wanted to reach the magazine's large audience. He ultimately stopped writing for the publication because he concluded, from the paucity of responses, that most people really don't read it for the articles after all. But while contributing to the magazine, Buckley attacked *Playboy* in his other writings.

When *Playboy* asked Buckley how he could "be so sure" that his theological dogmas wouldn't "crumble sooner or later," Buckley reached deep into the Old Testament and found a passage from the book of Job: "I know that my Redeemer liveth."[9]

Buckley's controversial streak over the years was not limited to the pages of *Playboy*.

In August 1957, *National Review* ran its most infamous unsigned editorial, titled "Why the South Must Prevail."[10] It argued that "the white community in the South is entitled to take such measures as are necessary to prevail, politically and culturally, in areas which it does not predominate numerically" because "for the time being, it is the advanced race" and the "claims of civilization supersede those of universal suffrage."

Bill Buckley biographer John Judis tells us that Bill not only approved but also penned that editorial, which "crossed the line between constitutionalism and racism."[11] This defense of the subjugation of blacks proved indefensible—not in the long run of American history, but right away. Buckley was forced to eat some Jim Crow in the very next issue.

Brent Bozell pointed out in the pages of *National Review* that the position of the editors flatly contradicted the Fifteenth Amendment, which the magazine claimed to revere. The amendment reads:

1. The right of citizens of the United States to vote shall not be denied or abridged by the United States or by any State on account of race, color, or previous condition of servitude.
2. The Congress shall have power to enforce this article by appropriate legislation.

Buckley's editorial damaged his reputation and the reputation of his magazine. Still, he remained outspoken about the issues that mattered to him. On the topic of abortion, his writings stressed that science clearly showed that there was a unique human life in the womb from the earliest days of pregnancy, and that the protection of innocent human life from violence was a bedrock commitment of all civilized nations. In 1974, his brother Jim introduced in the Senate, and Bill supported, a human life amendment to the United States Constitution that would have overturned *Roe v. Wade*.

NIXON YES, NIXON NO

John Judis has argued that Bill Buckley's public career is divided into two distinct phases: the wilderness years and the establishment years. In the first phase, he was a dedicated, serious critic of the political and cultural establishment—a voice crying out in the wilderness. In the second phase, Buckley was part of that establishment—more like King Ahab's court prophets.

The best evidence for this is Buckley's on-again, off-again support for Richard Nixon. Leading up to the 1968 election, Buckley told reporters that he would back "the most right, viable candidate." That was a departure from *National Review*'s and his position that it would be best to hold out for a real conservative.

After the LBJ landslide of 1964, the flood of new federal programs that were rammed through the overwhelmingly Democratic Congress, and the buildup but endless dithering over how to fight the Vietnam War, Bill Buckley thought it was important to back a winner who could at least put the brakes on. And he believed that the man who could do that was the man his magazine had declined to endorse in 1960: Richard Nixon.

Buckley endorsed Nixon in 1968, throwing the weight of *National Review* behind him. He believed that Nixon could pull the election off—and he did.

Nixon didn't leave Buckley's support for him unrewarded. He gave Buckley a post on the advisory board of the United States Information Agency, and he appointed him as a delegate to the United Nations, a position that Buckley turned into the book *A Delegate's Odyssey*. He also supported Bill's brother Jim in his successful bid for the U.S. Senate.

But to Buckley's dismay, Nixon went along with many liberal initiatives on domestic policy, and even dreamed up new ones— including affirmative action, the Environmental Protection Agency, and wage and price controls. In foreign policy he derecognized Taiwan, recognized China, stepped up the Vietnam War, and then effectively sued for peace.

In August 1971 Buckley convened an influential group in New York City that issued a statement publicly suspending his support of Nixon, which made the front page of the *New York Times*. In March 1972 he declined his reappointment by the president to the U.S. Advisory Commission on Information.[12]

Then came Watergate.

The burglary by government-sponsored thieves revealed during the Watergate trials did not surprise Bill Buckley one bit. He'd known for nearly a year of the revelations to come and had to pretend shock as events unfolded. He wrote about this dilemma in *Nearer, My God*.

Howard Hunt was Buckley's old boss from the CIA and one of the Nixon White House "plumbers"—contract dirty tricks operatives—who got caught breaking into the Democratic National Committee headquarters in the Watergate Hotel in June 1972.

On December 8, 1972, while the case was winding its way through the courts, Hunt's wife, Dorothy, died in a plane crash. Buckley learned from the nightly news that he had been named executor of her will.

Not long after, "Howard came by with his second daughter ([my] godchild, whom I had never before laid eyes on) to my apartment in New York. In a few hours he recounted the entire story of Watergate." Hunt put Buckley "about nine months ahead of the news as, day by day, it would develop."

Buckley's old boss "knew that in a matter of months he'd be in jail, leaving his orphaned children, aged twenty-three, twenty, sixteen and seven, unchaperoned," and so turned to his former underling to help look after them. Bill and Pat Buckley did what they could to help Hunt's family.[13]

Meanwhile, Buckley distanced himself from Nixon by speaking out against the president's policies, calling for Nixon's resignation at the end of 1973, and encouraging Senator Jim Buckley to call for Nixon's resignation in January 1974. Jim did so in March.

AGENT BLACKFORD OAKES

When Bill Buckley was presented with a contract to write a novel in 1974, he wasn't sure he was up to it. He had never written fiction, and he had recently learned that a manuscript by former Nixon speechwriter and *New York Times* columnist William Safire had been rejected by his publisher. Buckley suspected politics was behind the rejection, and he worried that his own politics could make things difficult in a new writing market.

Even so, Buckley went to Gstaad, Switzerland, for the winter of 1974–75 and produced the whole novel in about six weeks. The next year *Saving the Queen* hit bookstores. It was a commercial and critical success.

The central character in *Saving the Queen* and of Buckley's next nine novels was Blackford Oakes, a dashingly handsome Yale student from the class of 1951 (Buckley was class of 1950), a veteran of World War II who didn't want to get drafted into the Korean War, and, thus, a rookie recruit to the CIA. Much of Oakes's training was based on the training his creator had actually received.

Buckley would try for the rest of his life to deny that Oakes was his fictional doppelganger—to little success. He protested to the *Paris Review* in 1996 that Oakes is an "engineer," a "Protestant," and "a pilot, which I was not." Oakes was also a career officer in the CIA, said Buckley, "and I'd quit after nine months." He did admit some similarities:

> **BUCKLEY**: It is quite true that he's conservative. . . . And he's also pro-American. And we're both bright, sure.
> **PARIS REVIEW**: And you're both admirers of Bill Buckley.
> **BUCKLEY**: Exactly![14]

Both Oakes and Buckley came from conservative families with prewar isolationist politics. Both were educated during their teens in English boarding schools and had a rough time of it. And both became dedicated anti-Communists who would do whatever they possibly could to hurt the Soviet Union. Most of the differences boiled down to this: Oakes could do what Buckley could not. "There's a little touch of James Bond in his experiences, which there never was in mine," Buckley told *Paris Review*. In the first novel, Oakes not only beds the Queen of England; he manages to convince a Communist mole to kill himself to save both Moscow and Her Royal Highness from embarrassment.

Over the next eighteen years, in nine more novels and then in a surprise late addition in 2005, Buckley told more of these stories, all designed to make America the good guys and to "celebrate the Cold War." In fact, Buckley's goal in writing the Blackford Oakes novels was not only to entertain the reader, but also to make a polemical point: for all their many faults and awful mistakes, America was doing the right thing in seeking to destroy organized Communism.

Bill Buckley entered the high point of his fame in 1977, the year the Woody Allen movie *Annie Hall* was released. The film is the story of a romance that goes sour between a neurotic left-wing comedian named Alvy and his girlfriend, Annie (played by Allen and Diane Keaton).

In the "spider scene," Annie asks Alvy to come over to her apartment to dispose of a "big black spider in the bathroom." He grouses, then asks for a magazine to use as a weapon. And he is shocked by her choice of literature:

ALVY: What is this? What are you—since when do you read the *National Review*? What are you turning into?

ANNIE: Well, I like to try to get all points of view.

ALVY: It's wonderful. Then why don'tcha get William F. Buckley to kill the spider?[15]

A FRIEND OF PRESIDENTS

According to old *National Review* hand Richard Brookhiser, Buckley harbored doubts that Ronald Reagan would be able to seize the Republican nomination in 1980, but he kept those to himself—mostly.

Reagan taped an episode of *Firing Line* in January 1980, in which Buckley had resolved to ask Reagan "very direct questions on the assumption not that he was a *candidate* for President, but that he *was* President," and that's what he did. After explaining the setup, Buckley referred to Reagan as "Mr. President" for the whole show, "someone who, one year and one week later, was inaugurated President."

Over the years, Buckley managed to become friends with this man who would become president. In fact, in the foreword to Buckley's posthumously published book, *The Reagan I Knew*, son Christopher wrote that though the late president (whom he called an "elusive personality") "tended, famously, to shy away from personal intimacy," he thought it was "entirely possible that Pup [Christopher's name for his father] may have gotten as close to him as one could."[16]

Reagan was close to Buckley's ideal president for several reasons, one of which was that the former actor and California governor had been a charter subscriber of *National Review*. Reagan was a fusionist conservative, a pro-lifer, and a dedicated anti-Communist. He tried to cut taxes and regulation, rein in government spending, and build up the military so that the U.S. government could have more flexibility in dealing with the USSR.

Reagan pulled off some of that. He slashed top marginal tax rates and slowed down the growth of government. And there were no large wars on his watch.

Buckley forcefully criticized Reagan in the 1980s over Reagan's nuclear arms reduction talks with Soviet president Mikhail Gorbachev and Reagan's offer to share Strategic Defense Initiative "Star Wars" antimissile technology with the Russians once America got it up and running.

These concessions had struck Buckley as extremely unwise, but he said his piece and ultimately trusted that Reagan would do the right thing. He believed in Reagan because of what Reagan believed.

The USSR, Reagan publicly declared, in defiance of all the diplomatic censors, was an "evil empire."

Buckley was insistent that the heat should be kept on the Soviet Union regarding Communism's goal to produce a socialist heaven on earth. A serious nuclear exchange would make that impossible. Since Christians believe in an afterlife and do not need an earth in order to reach Paradise, and since most Americans are professing Christians of one stripe or another, he believed the threat of nukes could be the ultimate trump card.

Buckley also believed that other measures would contribute to Communism's downfall, and he was more than happy to back a president who worked to frustrate Soviet ambitions.

SHAPING A LEGACY

Buckley endorsed fellow Yalie and vice president George H. W. Bush in 1988, and he announced his retirement as editor in chief of *National Review* in 1990. Neither of those choices has aged well.

Bush proved to be a competent but uninspiring president. He oversaw the transition from the Communist to the post-Communist world. He won a crushing victory in Iraq. And then he lost in his reelection bid to a little-known Southern governor. He also enraged conservatives for a whole number of reasons—from raising taxes to disappointing pro-lifers.

Meanwhile, Buckley handed *National Review* into the capable hands of veteran British journalist John O'Sullivan, but he never really let go. From the reader's point of view, he was about as big a presence in the magazine as he had ever been. He retained all voting stock in the company, and his sister Priscilla was the longtime managing editor.

O'Sullivan didn't have the same resources as Buckley, which created problems. He brought on or regularly published several writers who wanted to change the magazine's and conservatism's stance on immigration. Reaganites had been broadly supportive of immigration, but this new crop of writers marshaled new evidence and arguments that essentially unchecked immigration was bad for America's fiscal health and culture.

This led to predictable clashes among conservatives, libertarians, and other members of the right-wing coalition. O'Sullivan wasn't as adept at mollifying aggrieved parties as was Buckley, and in 1996 Buckley fired him. He replaced O'Sullivan with a dark horse candidate, Rich Lowry, a onetime staff writer who would eventually consolidate his control over the whole *National Review* enterprise.

In later years, fans and foes could see changes in Buckley's conservatism. At his urging *National Review* came out in favor of drug legalization. Buckley also took some baby steps away from the foreign policy advice of many hawkish conservatives. He said that America should certainly be a great military power, and he supported the First Gulf War, but he rejected the progressive "Wilsonian" approach to foreign policy, which seeks above all else to make the world safe for democracy. Several conservatives beat the drums against China in the early 2000s. Buckley wasn't one of them.

After initially supporting a return trip, he also denounced the 2003 invasion of Iraq. Buckley argued that the lack of weapons of mass destruction proved the opponents of the war had been right. He said that if America were a parliamentary democracy, the choice of war and its mismanagement would have cost Prime Minister George W. Bush his job.

He wasn't completely untouched by the attacks of September 11, 2001. He was, of course, all for invading Afghanistan and crushing al-Qaeda and similar Islamic terrorist groups, but he had some skepticism for a broader war on terror, and that skepticism grew over time.

The last decade or so of Buckley's life was largely about discharging obligations. *Nearer, My God*, his book about Catholicism, appeared in 1997, because—he suggested in interviews—he owed it to God. The book was an entertaining, digressive consideration of the faith.

Buckley folded *Firing Line* in 1999, after more than fifteen hundred episodes, because he didn't "want to die onstage."

And in 2004, at the age of seventy-nine, Bill Buckley finally relinquished ownership of *National Review* to a board of trustees, including his son Christopher.

William F. Buckley Jr. was found dead on February 27, 2008. His body was slumped over his desk in the sprawling garage-office of his Stamford, Connecticut, home. His health had been failing for some time from emphysema and assorted hazards of old age as he worked to finish his book about his old friend Ronald Reagan. Buckley's final labor, *The Reagan I Knew*, was released October 2007.

The funeral was held at St. Patrick's Cathedral in Manhattan on April 4. Christopher told the gathered crowd of thousands, "We talked about this day, he and I. He said, 'If I'm still famous, try to get the cardinal to do the service at St. Patrick's. If I'm not, just tuck me away in Stamford.'" He waited two beats, surveying the crowd, and added, "Well, Pop, I guess you're still famous."

To learn more about William Buckley Jr., read Jeremy Lott's *William F. Buckley Jr.* (Nashville: Thomas Nelson, 2010) from the Christian Encounters Series.

NOTES

CHAPTER 1: SAINT PATRICK

1. Jocelin (12th century–1199), *The Life and Acts of St. Patrick*, trans. Edmund L. Swift (public domain), chap. 5.
2. Patrick, *The Confession of St. Patrick*, part 1, http://www.ccel.org/ccel/ patrick/confession.txt (public domain).
3. Ibid., part 27.
4. Ibid.
5. Philip Freeman, *Ireland and the Classical World* (Austin: University of Texas Press, 2001), 46.
6. Ibid., 99.
7. Ibid.
8. Liam de Paor, *Saint Patrick's World: The Christian Culture of Ireland's Apostolic Age* (Dublin: Four Courts Press, 1993; US: University of Notre Dame Press, 1997), 27.
9. Patrick, *Confession*, part 1.
10. Ibid.
11. Liam de Paor, *Saint Patrick's World*, 100. See also Wikipedia, s.v. "Saint Patrick," under the heading "In his own words," http://en.wikipedia .org/wiki/Saint_Patrick.
12. Patrick, *Confession*, part 2.
13. Ibid., part 16.
14. Ibid.
15. Patrick, *Confession*, part 17.
16. Liam de Paor, *Saint Patrick's World*, 23.
17. Patrick, *Confession*, part 16.
18. Ibid., part 23.

19. Ibid.
20. Ibid.
21. Ibid., part 24. The use of the word learned comes from Maire B. de Paor's *Patrick: Pilgrim Apostle of Ireland*.
22. Patrick, St. *Patrick's Epistle to the Christian Subjects of the Tyrant Coroticus*, in *The Most Ancient Lives of Saint Patrick*, ed. James O'Leary (public domain). Hereinafter referred to as *Epistle*.
23. Patrick, *Confession*, part 1.
24. Ibid., part 9.
25. Ibid.
26. E. A. Thompson, *Who Was Saint Patrick?* (Suffolk, UK: Boydell, 1985; Rochester: Boydell, repr. 1999), 44. Citations are to the 1999 edition.
27. Patrick, *Confession*, part 10.
28. Ibid., part 26.
29. Ibid., part 27.
30. Ibid.
31. Ibid., part 32.
32. Ibid., part 26.
33. Ibid., part 29.
34. For more on some of these legends, see Liam de Paor, *Saint Patrick's World*; Jocelin, *The Life and Acts of St. Patrick*, chap. 32; and MacEvin, *The Tripartite Life*, part 1, in O'Leary, *The Most Ancient Lives of Saint Patrick* (public domain).
35. Patrick, *Confession*, part 38.
36. Ibid., part 50.
37. Ibid., part 51.
38. Ibid., part 52.
39. Ibid., part 41.
40. Ibid., part 42.
41. Liam de Paor, *Saint Patrick's World*, 187.
42. Patrick, *Confession*, part 15.
43. Ibid., part 48.
44. Ibid., part 58.
45. Ibid., part 55.
46. Patrick, *A Letter to the Soldiers of Coroticus*, part 1, para. 2, in *The Confession of Saint Patrick and Letter to Coroticus*, transl. John Skinner, with a foreword by John O'Donohue (New York: Image, 1998), 3.
47. O'Leary, *Epistle*.
48. *Letter*, 2.

49. O'Leary, *Epistle.*

50. Ibid.

51. Ibid.

52. Ibid.

53. Ibid.

54. Ibid.

55. According to tradition, the apostle Thomas took the gospel as far as India. There is no historical evidence to prove (or disprove) that Thomas made the trip. The idea may have originated in the apocryphal Acts of Thomas, a third-century Gnostic work. In any case, in the sixteenth century, the "first" Catholic missionaries to India were surprised to find a long-established community of Christians already there—Christians who traced their spiritual lineage through Thomas.

56. Peter Brown, *The World of Late Antiquity* (London: Thames & Hudson, 1971; New York: W. W. Norton, 1989; citations are to the Norton edition), 87.

57. Ibid., 112.

58. Patrick, *Confession*, part 4.

59. Ibid., part 40.

60. Ibid., parts 40, 41.

Chapter 2: Galileo

1. Michael Sharratt, *Galileo: Decisive Innovator* (Cambridge: Cambridge University Press, 1994), 22–23.

2. Stillman Drake, *Galileo at Work: His Scientific Biography* (New York: Dover Publications, Inc., 1978), 448.

3. Stillman Drake, "Vincenzio Galilei," in *Dictionary of Scientific Biography*, ed. Charles Coulston Gillispie (New York: Charles Scribner's Sons, 1972), 249.

4. Sara Bonechi, *How They Make Me Suffer . . . A Short Biography of Galileo Galilei*, trans. Anna Teicher (Florence: Institute and Museum of the History of Science, 2008), 13.

5. Sharratt, *Galileo: Decisive Innovator*, 26.

6. Stillman Drake, *Galileo: A Very Short Introduction* (Oxford: Oxford University Press, 2001), 1.

7. Drake, *Galileo at Work: His Scientific Biography*, 2–3.

8. James Reston Jr., *Galileo: A Life* (Washington, D.C.: Beard Books, 2000), 14.

9. The chapters are called "books." The forty-seventh fact of Book I is what we now call the Pythagorean theorem.

10. Drake, *Galileo at Work*, 3.
11. Ibid., 21.
12. Bonechi, *How They Make Me Suffer*, 17.
13. Thomas S. Kuhn, *The Copernican Revolution: Planetary Astronomy in the Development of Western Thought* (Cambridge: Harvard University Press, 1957), 111.
14. Reston, *Galileo: A Life*, 26.
15. Sharratt, *Galileo: Decisive Innovator*, 61.
16. Paul F. Grendler, *The Universities of the Italian Renaissance* (Baltimore: The Johns Hopkins University Press, 2002), 40.
17. Drake, *Galileo: A Very Short Introduction*, 30.
18. Drake, *Galileo at Work*, 45.
19. Sharratt, *Galileo: Decisive Innovator*, 73.
20. Dava Sobel, *Galileo's Daughter* (New York: Walker & Co., 1999), 23.
21. Sharratt, *Galileo: Decisive Innovator*, 73.
22. Drake, *Galileo at Work*, 74–75.
23. Ibid., 74.
24. Ibid., 75.
25. Sobel, *Galileo's Daughter*, 22.
26. Drake, *Galileo at Work*, 104; Annibale Fantoli, *Galileo: For Copernicanism and for the Church*, trans. George V. Coyne, 3rd ed., vol. 6, Studi Galileiani (Vatican City: Vatican Observatory Publications, 2003) 65.
27. Drake, *Galileo at Work*, 105.
28. Ibid., 106.
29. Ibid., 118.
30. Ibid.
31. Ibid., 138–39.
32. Stillman Drake, *Discoveries and Opinions of Galileo* (New York: Anchor Books, 1957), 36.
33. Sobel, *Galileo's Daughter*, 36.
34. Ibid., 37–38.
35. William R. Shea and Mariano Artigas, *Galileo in Rome: The Rise and Fall of a Troublesome Genius* (Oxford: Oxford University Press, 2003), 35.
36. Sharratt, *Galileo: Decisive Innovator*, 91.
37. Ibid., 92.
38. Shea and Artigas, *Galileo in Rome*, 45.
39. Ibid., 44.
40. Sobel, *Galileo's Daughter*, 44–45.
41. Fantoli, *Galileo: For Copernicanism and for the Church*, 125.
42. Ibid., 135.
43. Sharratt, *Galileo: Decisive Innovator*, 98.

44. Fantoli, *Galileo: For Copernicanism and for the Church*, 128.
45. Ibid.
46. Verses 12–13, The New American Standard Bible, 1995 Update (La Habra, California: The Lockman Foundation), 1996 (emphasis added).
47. Drake, *Galileo: A Very Short Introduction*, 69.
48. Maurice A. Finocchiaro, *The Essential Galileo* (Indianapolis: Hackett Publishing Company, 1989), 104.
49. Ibid., 106.
50. Ibid., 104.
51. Sharratt, *Galileo: Decisive Innovator*, 110.
52. Ibid.
53. Ernan McMullin, "Galileo on Science and Scripture," in *The Cambridge Companion to Galileo*, ed. Peter Machamer (Cambridge: Cambridge University Press, 1998), 281.
54. Finocchiaro, *The Galileo Affair*, 134–35.
55. Sharratt, *Galileo: Decisive Innovator*, 111.
56. Fantoli, *Galileo: For Copernicanism and for the Church*, 169.
57. Ibid.
58. Finocchiaro, *The Galileo Affair*, 134.
59. Finocchiaro, *The Essential Galileo*, 137–38.
60. Shea and Artigas, *Galileo in Rome*, 75.
61. Fantoli, *Galileo: For Copernicanism and for the Church*, 174.
62. Ibid., 176–177.
63. Shea and Artigas, *Galileo in Rome*, 81.
64. Fantoli, *Galileo: For Copernicanism and for the Church*, 175.
65. Shea and Artigas, *Galileo in Rome*, 81.
66. Ibid., 81–82.
67. Sharratt, *Galileo: Decisive Innovator*, 90.
68. Drake, *Discoveries and Opinions of Galileo*, 227.
69. Sharratt, *Galileo: Decisive Innovator*, 137.
70. Sobel, *Galileo's Daughter*, 4.
71. Sharratt, *Galileo: Decisive Innovator*, 151.
72. Fantoli, *Galileo: For Copernicanism and for the Church*, 215.
73. Sharratt, *Galileo: Decisive Innovator*, 144.
74. Stillman Drake, "Galileo and the Church," in *Essays on Galileo and the History and Philosophy of Science* (1999), 162.
75. Ibid.
76. Shea and Artigas, *Galileo in Rome*, 131–32.
77. Drake, "Galileo and the Church," 163.
78. Drake, *Galileo: A Very Short Introduction*, 88.
79. Fantoli, *Galileo: For Copernicanism and for the Church*, 246.

80. Drake, "Galileo and the Church," 163.
81. Ibid., 164.
82. Fantoli, *Galileo: For Copernicanism and for the Church*, 247.
83. Drake, *Galileo at Work*, 336.
84. Shea and Artigas, *Galileo in Rome*, 157.
85. Fantoli, *Galileo: For Copernicanism and for the Church*, 252.
86. Galileo Galilei, *Dialogue Concerning the Two Chief World Systems: Ptolemaic and Copernican*, ed. Stephen Jay Gould, trans. Stillman Drake, The Modern Library Science Series (New York: The Modern Library, 2008), 6.
87. Shea and Artigas, *Galileo in Rome*, 121.
88. Sharratt, *Galileo: Decisive Innovator*, 169.
89. Galilei, *Dialogue Concerning the Two Chief World Systems: Ptolemaic and Copernican*, 538.
90. Galileo Galilei and Maurice A. Finocchiaro, *Galileo on the World Systems: A New Abridged Translation and Guide* (Berkeley: University of California Press, 1997), 82.
91. Reston, *Galileo: A Life*, 237.
92. Drake, *Galileo at Work*, 348.
93. Ibid., 342.
94. Maurice A. Finocchiaro, "That Galileo Was Imprisoned and Tortured for Advocating Copernicanism," in *Galileo Goes to Jail: And Other Myths About Science and Religion*, ed. Ronald L. Numbers (Cambridge: Harvard University Press, 2009), 77.
95. Ibid., 73.
96. Fantoli, *Galileo: For Copernicanism and for the Church*, 332–33.
97. Drake, *Galileo at Work*, 417.
98. Shea and Artigas, *Galileo in Rome*, 194.
99. Fantoli, *Galileo: For Copernicanism and for the Church*, 337.
100. Shea and Artigas, *Galileo in Rome*, 195.
101. Allan-Olney, *The Private Life of Galileo: Compiled Principally from His Correspondence and That of His Eldest Daughter*, 262.
102. Ibid.
103. Fantoli, *Galileo: For Copernicanism and for the Church*, 347.
104. Michael Segre, "The Never-Ending Galileo Story," in *The Cambridge Companion to Galileo*, ed. Peter Machamer (Cambridge: Cambridge University Press, 1998), 389.
105. Paolo Galluzzi, "The Sepulchers of Galileo: The 'Living' Remains of a Hero of Science," in *The Cambridge Companion to Galileo*, ed. Peter Machamer (Cambridge: Cambridge University Press, 1998), 418.
106. Drake, *Galileo at Work*, 436.

107. Fantoli, *Galileo: For Copernicanism and for the Church*, 351.

108. Ernan McMullin, ed., *The Church and Galileo* (Notre Dame: University of Notre Dame Press, 2005), 6.

CHAPTER 3: ANNE BRADSTREET

1. Augustine Jones, *The Life and Work of Thomas Dudley: The Second Governor of Massachusetts* (Boston: Houghton, Mifflin, 1900), 42. Hereafter cited as *Thomas Dudley*.

2. *The Works of Anne Bradstreet in Prose and Verse*, ed. John Harvard Ellis (Charlestown, MA: Abram E. Cutter, 1867), 4. Hereafter cited as *Works*.

3. Samuel Eliot Morison, *Builders of the Bay Colony* (Boston: Northeastern University Press, 1981, repr.), 54–55.

4. John Woodbridge, "To my dear Sister, the Author of these Poems," in *Works*, 5, 86–88.

5. *Works*, 4.

6. Ibid.

7. Meaning he did not conform to the ceremonies of the Church of England.

8. John Cotton, "God's Promise to His Plantation" (1630), ed. Reiner Smolinski, 1; http://digitalcommons.unl.edu/etas/22 (Libraries at University of Nebraska-Lincoln); Thomas Gamble, *Data Concerning the Families of Bancroft, Bradstreet, Brown, Dudley . . . in England and America, 1277 to 1906 AD* (Savannah, GA: n.p., 1906), 43.

9. Alice Morse Earle, *Margaret Winthrop* (New York: Charles Scribner's Sons, 1895), 115.

10. Alexander Young, *Chronicles of the First Planters of the Colony of Massachusetts Bay, 1623–36* (Boston: Little & Brown, 1846), 310, Thomas Dudley's words.

11. Earle, *Margaret Winthrop*, 200.

12. Robert Charles Winthrop, *Life and Letters of John Winthrop*, vol. 2 (Boston: Little, Brown, 1869), 4–5.

13. Jones, *Thomas Dudley*, 58.

14. Frederick Weis, *The Colonial Clergy and the Colonial Churches of New England* (Lancaster, MA: n.p., 1936), 74.

15. Morison, *Builders of the Bay Colony*, 78.

16. Ibid., 78.

17. Jones, *Thomas Dudley*, 79.

18. Ibid.

19. *Works*, xxl, xv; see http://www.firstchurchboston.org/events/ category; http://www.masshist.org/findingaids/doc.cfm?fa=fa0030; Charlotte Gordon, *Mistress Bradstreet: The Untold Life of America's First Poet* (New York: Little, Brown, 2005), 112.

20. See http://www.masshist.org/findingaids/doc.cfm?fa=fa0030.

21. Jones, *Thomas Dudley*, 91.

22. Young, *Chronicles of the First Planters*, 325.

23. Alice Morse Earle, *Customs and Fashions in Old New England* (New York: Charles Scribner's Sons, 1893), 148–49.

24. Michael Sletcher, ed., *New England* (Westport, CT: Greenwood Press, 2004), 237–38.

25. Winthrop, *Life and Letters*, 2:38.

26. Morison, *Builders of the Bay Colony*, 82.

27. Jones, *Thomas Dudley*, 98, 105; Massachusetts Bay Colony marker, http://freepages.genealogy.rootsweb.ancestry.com.

28. Eve LaPlante, *American Jezebel* (San Francisco: HarperSanFrancisco, 2004), 72–74.

29. *Works*, xxxiii; Poets of Cambridge, U.S.A., Anne Bradstreet, http:// www.harvardsquarelibrary.org/poets/bradstreet.php; historic markers, Cambridge, MA, http://www.cambridgema.gov/~Historic/ markers.html#stations; Jones, *Thomas Dudley*, 124.

30. Later they moved to Ipswich, and then Samuel was a founder of Salisbury, where he was in the General Court for several years. Mary died in childbirth, after which Samuel had two more wives. Samuel and his family last settled in New Hampshire, where he was a preacher.

31. *Works*, 5, 391–92.

32. See http://www.1911Encyclopedia.org/William_Prynne; http://www .british-civil-wars.co.uk/biog/prynne.htm.

33. *Works*, 381–85.

34. Ibid.

35. Morison, *Builders of the Bay Colony*, 135; Leland Ryken, *The Puritans as They Really Were* (Grand Rapids: Zondervan, 1990), 2.

36. Morison, *Builders of the Bay Colony*, 289.

37. Earle, *Customs and Fashions in Old New England*, 316–17.

38. Jones, *Thomas Dudley*, 181–82.

39. Gamble, *Data Concerning the Families*, 59.

40. Jones, *Thomas Dudley*, 211.

41. *Works*, 394.

42. Ibid., 394–95.

43. Ibid., 395–98.

44. Nelson Manfred Blake, *A History of American Life and Thought* (New York: McGraw-Hill, 1963), 56.

45. *Works*, 370–81.

46. Morison, *Builders of the Bay Colony*, 333, 335–36.

47. John Josselyn, *New-England's Rarities* (Boston: William Veazie, 1865), 96, 115; Josselyn's first trip to New England took place in 1638.

48. Ibid., 141–47.

49. James M. Volo and Dorothy D. Volo, *Family Life in 17th- and 18th-Century America* (Westport, CT: Greenwood Press, 2006), 209–11.

50. Elizabeth Ferszt, "'Transatlantic Dame School?: Anne Bradstreet's Early Poems as Pedagogy" (Ph.D. diss., Ferris State University, 24 January, 2008).

51. *Works*, 330–43.

52. Ibid., 369.

53. Jones, *Thomas Dudley*, 320.

54. Gamble, *Data Concerning the Families*, 48; Ipswich Historical Society, *Dudley and Bradstreet* (Salem, MA: Salem Press, 1903), 29.

55. Ibid., 468; Louis Mitchell et al., eds., *Woodbridge Record: Being an Account of the Descendants of the Rev. John Woodbridge* (New Haven: n.p., 1883), 6.

56. George Ballard, *Memoirs of Several Ladies of Great Britain* (Oxford: W. Jackson, 1752), 251.

57. Gordon, *Mistress Bradstreet*, 253.

58. *Works*, 365–67.

59. Ibid., 20.

60. Ibid., 21.

61. Ibid., 23–24, September 30, 1657.

62. Perry Miller and Thomas Johnson, eds., *The Puritans: A Sourcebook of Their Writings* (Toronto: General Publishing, 2001), 631.

63. Eve LaPlante, *American Jezebel*, 225.

64. George Edward Ellis, *Puritan Age and Rule in the Colony of the Massachusetts Bay, 1629–1685* (New York: Ben Franklin, 1970), 409–44.

65. LaPlante, *American Jezebel*, 253–54.

66. *Works*, 27.

67. Gamble, *Data Concerning the Families*, 51.

68. *Works*, 32–33.

69. Gamble, *Data Concerning the Families*, 51; Ellis, *Puritan Age and Rule*, 500, 504; *Works*, 32n.

70. *Works*, 42–43.

CHAPTER 4: JOHN BUNYAN

1. *Wikipedia*, s.v., Harrowden, Bedfordshire, http://en.wikipedia.org/wiki/Harrowden,_Bedfordshire.
2. Roger Sharrock, *John Bunyan* (London: Macmillan, 1968), 11.
3. Ola Winslow, *John Bunyan* (New York: The Macmillan Company, 1961), 10.
4. http://www.bedford.gov.uk/Default.aspx/Web/ElstowVillage.
5. John Pestell, *Travel with John Bunyan* (Day One Publications, 2002), 12.
6. Ibid., 10.
7. Ibid.
8. *The Life of John Bunyan by Edmund Venables*, p. 1, http://books.jibble.org/1/0/3/1037/1037/TheLifeofJohnBunyanbyEdmundVen-1.html.
9. *The Dictionary of National Biography* (1886), 275.
10. From the 11th edition of the *Encyclopedia Britannica* (New York: 1910).
11. Winslow, *John Bunyan*, 8.
12. Ibid.
13. Ibid., 11.
14. John Bunyan, *Grace Abounding to the Chief of Sinners* (London: Simpkin, Marshall and Co., 1863), 7.
15. George W. Latham, ed., *The Pilgrim's Progress by John Bunyan* (Chicago: Scott, Foresman and Company, 1906).
16. See the fine article about chapbooks posted on the Web site of the Lily Library at the University of Indiana: http://www.indiana.edu/~liblilly/chapbook.shtml.
17. John Mullan and Christopher Reid, eds., *Eighteenth-Century Popular Culture: A Selection* (Oxford University Press, 2000), 146.
18. Margaret Spufford, *Small Books and Pleasant Histories: Popular Fiction and Its Readership in Seventeenth-Century England* (London: Cambridge University Press, 1985), 49.
19. John Bunyan, *A Few Sighs from Hell* (1658).
20. See George Offor, ed., *The Works of John Bunyan*, vol. 3 (London: Blackie and Son, 1856), 711.
21. A point made powerfully by C. S. Lewis in his *Selected Essays*, ed. Walter Hooper (Cambridge University Press, 1969), 147.
22. John Bunyan, *Grace Abounding and The Pilgrim's Progress*, ed. Roger Sharrock (London: Oxford University Press, 1966), 8.
23. Richard L. Greaves, *Glimpses of Glory: John Bunyan and English Dissent* (Stanford, California: Stanford University Press, 2002), 7.
24. From Thomas Babington Macaulay's biographical essay on Bunyan in the *Encyclopedia Britannica*, submitted in May 1854.

25. Bunyan, *Grace Abounding and The Pilgrim's Progress*, 8–9.
26. John Brown, *John Bunyan: His Life, Times and Work* (London: Wm. Isbister Limited, 1885), 41.
27. Ibid., 42.
28. Greaves, *Glimpses of Glory*, 11.
29. Ibid.
30. Ibid., 19.
31. Ibid., 11.
32. Ibid., 12. See specifically, Luke, *Letter Books*, 22, 25, 27–28, 37, 54, 56, 74, 82, 84, 91, 94–95, 593; BL., Add MS 61,681, fol. 111r; CSPD, 1644–45, 66.9. For the summary of conditions Bunyan and his fellow soldiers faced, see Greaves, *Glimpses of Glory*, 13–15.
33. Ibid.
34. Ibid.
35. Bunyan, *Grace Abounding and The Pilgrim's Progress*, 10.
36. See Brown, *John Bunyan*, 54; emphasis added.
37. Ibid.
38. Bunyan, *Grace Abounding and The Pilgrim's Progress*, 10.
39. Ibid.
40. Ibid., 10–11.
41. Ibid., 11–12.
42. Ibid., 12.
43. Ibid.
44. Ibid., 12–13.
45. Ibid., 13.
46. Bunyan, *Grace Abounding and The Pilgrim's Progress*, 13.
47. Ibid., 13–14.
48. Ibid., 14–15.
49. Ibid., 16–17.
50. Ibid.
51. Greaves, *Glimpses of Glory*, 34.
52. In the past, tuberculosis was called consumption, because it seemed to consume people from within, with a bloody cough, fever, pallor, and long, relentless wasting.
53. Bunyan, *Grace Abounding and The Pilgrim's Progress*, 81.
54. Ibid., 84.
55. See John Bunyan, *The Pilgrim's Progress*, Library of Classics (London & Glasgow: Collins, n.d.), 47–48.
56. Brown, *John Bunyan: His Life, Times and Work*, 96.
57. Ibid., 115.

58. Greaves, *Glimpses of Glory*, 57.
59. M. Hersen, S. M. Turner, and D. C. Beidel, eds., *Adult Psychopathology and Diagnosis*, 5th ed. (Hoboken, NJ: John Wiley & Sons, Inc., 2007).
60. Brown, *John Bunyan*, 111. Here, Brown wrote: "On the earnest desire of the Church, and after some solemn prayer to the Lord, with fasting, [Bunyan] was more particularly called forth and appointed to a more ordinary and public preaching of the Word."
61. Sharrock, *John Bunyan*, 49.
62. The Elstow parish church records contain the following regarding Bunyan's two daughters by his first wife: "Mary, the daughter of John Bonion, was baptized the 20th day of July, 1650." "Elizabeth, the daughter of John Bonyon, was born 14th day of April, 1654." See Brown, *John Bunyan*, 96. Bunyan's sons by his first wife, John and Thomas, were likely born between 1654 and 1658.
63. Greaves, *Glimpses of Glory*, 142.
64. Ibid., 136.
65. Ibid., 98–99.
66. Ibid., 138.
67. John Bunyan, "A Relation of the Imprisonment . . . ," in John Stachniewski, ed., *Grace Abounding and Other Spiritual Autobiographies, with Anita Pacheco* (Oxford: Oxford University Press, 1998), 99.
68. Brown, *John Bunyan*, 152.
69. Greaves, *Glimpses of Glory*, 135.
70. Brown, *John Bunyan*, 152.
71. Greaves, *Glimpses of Glory*, 137.
72. Brown, *John Bunyan*, 190.
73. Ibid.
74. See Brown, *John Bunyan*, 162–68; and John Howard, *State of the Prisons in England and Wales*, 3rd ed. (1785), 283.
75. Brown, *John Bunyan*, 163.
76. Ibid., 167.
77. Bunyan, *Grace Abounding and The Pilgrim's Progress*, 133–34.
78. Brown, *John Bunyan*, 168.
79. Ibid.
80. Bunyan, *Grace Abounding and The Pilgrim's Progress*, 100. Wording has been changed slightly, for clarity.
81. From Perry Keenlyside's introductory essay for the Naxos Audio Book edition of *The Pilgrim's Progress* (1999).
82. See Greaves, *Glimpses of Glory*, 210; and page liv of W. R. Owens, ed., John Bunyan, *The Pilgrim's Progress* (Oxford's World Classics, 2003).

83. Greaves, *Glimpses of Glory*, 220.

84. Ibid., 342.

85. Victorian biographer John Brown's summary of the plot of *The Pilgrim's Progress*, is as fine a synopsis as has been written. See his *John Bunyan*, 267–72.

86. Ibid., 266, 272.

87. Ibid., 273.

88. Ibid.

89. See Brown, *John Bunyan*, 275–81.

90. The first American edition of *The Pilgrim's Progress* was published by Samuel Green of Boston in 1681.

91. Sharrock, *John Bunyan*, 49.

92. Ibid.

93. Sharrock, *John Bunyan*, 49–50. See also Brown, *John Bunyan*, 358–59.

94. George Offer, ed. *The Whole Works of John Bunyan*, vol. 2 (London: Blackie and Son, 1862), 709.

95. Brown, *John Bunyan*, 386–87.

96. Greaves, *Glimpses of Glory*, 598.

97. Brown, *John Bunyan*, 390.

Chapter 5: Johann Sebastian Bach

1. Much of this section's material is drawn from Philippe Ariés, *A History of Private Life, vol. 3: Passions of the Renaissance*, ed. Roger Chartier; transl. Arthur Goldhammer (Cambridge and London: Belknap Press of Harvard Univ. Press, 1981).

2. See Albert Schweitzer, *J. S. Bach*, transl. Ernest Newman (New York: Macmillan, 1950).

3. Paul S. Jones, "J. S. Bach and Musical Hermeneutics: An Evangelical Composer/Preacher," *Singing and Making Music: Issues in Church Music Today* (Philadelphia: P & R Publishing, 2006), http://home.comcast.net/~pjones25/articles/Bach_Hermeneutics.htm.

4. "Bach always understood his positions as Cantor, Music Director, and Organist to be offices founded by King David in I Chronicles" (Ibid.).

5. Ibid.

6. Vitally interested in his ancestry, Johann Sebastian Bach compiled a genealogy in 1735. See Johann Nikolaus Forkel, *Johann Sebastian Bach: His Life, Art, and Work*, translated with notes and appendices by Charles Sanford Terry (London: Constable and Co., 1920). Bach began to collect documents about his family's history in the 1730s, a project

continued by sons Wilhelm Friedemann and especially Carl Philipp Emanuel. These papers, and the assistance of C. P. E. Bach, aided Forkel in the publication of the first biography of J. S. Bach in 1802. This section relies on Forkel's book.

7. Ibid., 38–39.

8. Ibid.

9. Robin Leaver, et al., *Bach, the Evangelist*, a roundtable discussion on *Encounter*, a Radio National/Australian Broadcasting Corporation program, October 22, 2000, featuring Leaver, John Kleinig, and Michael Marissen.

10. Christoph Wolff, *Bach: The Learned Musician* (NY: W. W. Norton, 2000), 251.

11. Leaver, roundtable discussion.

12. Pamela Urfer, writer and executive producer, *A Life Worth Living: J. S. Bach's 60th Birthday Party*, Peter Homer, dir. (Purfer Productions, 2000). This video production imagining a family reunion provides an utterly charming, genuine, and trustworthy portrayal of the family life of the Bachs.

13. Ibid., 424.

14. Forkel, *Bach: His Life, Art, and Work*, 6 et seq.

15. Wolff, *Bach: The Learned Musician*, 8.

16. Schweitzer, *J. S. Bach*, 1:115.

17. Theodore Hoelty Nickel, ed., *The Little Bach Book* (Valparaiso: Valparaiso University Press, 1950), 77–78.

18. B minor was Bach's favorite key in which to compose (Spitta, *Johann Sebastian Bach*, 1:414).

19. Research in the 1930s revealed that it was more than the aforementioned boyhood eyestrain that damaged Bach's eyes. Though the cause and actual malady remain unknown, it seems likely that he suffered infection at the hands of the doctor. See Bert Lenth, "Bach and the English Oculist," *Music and Letters*, a periodical of Oxford University Press, 1938, XIX(2): 182–98.

20. See H. C. Zegers, MD: "The Eyes of Johann Sebastian Bach" in *Archives of Ophthalmology* 23, no. 19 (October 2005): 1427–30.

21. The illustration appears in Hans T. David and Arthur Mendel, eds., *The New Bach Reader: A Life of Johann Sebastian Bach in Letters and Documents*, revised and expanded by Christoph Wolff (New York: W. W. Norton, 1998), 374.

22. Clemens Romijn, in liner notes accompanying "The Complete Works of Johann Sebastian Bach," *Bach Edition* (Brilliant Classics), www.brilliantclassics.com.

CHAPTER 6: JANE AUSTEN

1. Irene Collins, *Jane Austen: The Parson's Daughter* (London: Hambledon Press, 1998), 122.

2. Deidre Le Faye, *Jane Austen: A Family Record*, 2nd ed. (Cambridge: Cambridge Univ. Press, 2004), 13, 17.

3. Collins, *Parson's Daughter*, 4.

4. Ibid., 6, 8.

5. Ibid., xix–xx.

6. Ibid., 13.

7. Ibid., 59.

8. George Austen to Francis Austen, in Collins, *Parson's Daughter*, 48.

9. George Austen, quoted in ibid., 45.

10. Le Faye, *Jane Austen*, 10.

11. George Austen to Mrs. Walter, in Le Faye, *Jane Austen*, 23.

12. Le Faye, *Jane Austen*, 140.

13. Ibid., 139–40.

14. Caroline Austen, "My Aunt Jane Austen: A Memoir," in *A Memoir of Jane Austen and Other Family Recollections*, ed. Kathryn Sutherland, Oxford World Classics (Oxford: Oxford Univ. Press, 2002), 175.

15. Collins, *Parson's Daughter*, 48.

16. Ibid., 9.

17. Henry Austen, "Memoir of Miss Austen," in Sutherland, *A Memoir of Jane Austen*, 153–54.

18. Collins, *Parson's Daughter*, 40.

19. Ibid., 26. A copy of *Goody Two-Shoes* with "Jane Austen" written on the front page still exists.

20. Anna Lefroy to James Edward Austin-Leigh, in Anna Lefroy, "Recollections of Aunt Jane," in Sutherland, *A Memoir of Jane Austen*, 183.

21. Collins, *Parson's Daughter*, 112.

22. Caroline Austen, "My Aunt Jane Austen: A Memoir," in Sutherland, *A Memoir of Jane Austen*, 170.

23. Jane Austen to James Edward Austen, in *Jane Austen's Letters*, new ed., ed. Deirdre Le Faye (Oxford: Oxford Univ. Press, 1997), 323.

24. Jane Austen to Cassandra Austen, in Le Faye, *Letters*, 352.

25. William Dereiewicz, *Jane Austen and the Romantic Poets* (New York: Columbia Univ. Press, 2005), 7.

26. Collins, *Parson's Daughter*, 62–63.

27. Le Faye, *Jane Austen*, 47, 59; Claire Harman, *Jane's Fame: How Jane Austen Conquered the World* (Edinburgh: Canongate, 2009), 16.

28. Jane Austen, quoted in Collins, *Parson's Daughter*, 133.

29. Harman, *Jane's Fame*, 13.

30. David Cecil, *A Portrait of Jane Austen* (London: Penguin, 1980), 59.

31. Ibid., 60.

32. Ibid.

33. Jane Austen, "Love and Friendship," in *Catherine and Other Writings*, eds. Margaret Anne Doody and Douglas Murray, Oxford World Classics (Oxford: Oxford Univ. Press, 1993), 78.

34. Mary Russell Mitford, quoted in Cecil, *Portrait*, 67.

35. Collins, *Parson's Daughter*, 112.

36. Ibid., 113.

37. Ibid., 131; Jane Austen to Cassandra Austen, 5 September 1796, Le Faye, *Letters*; Jane Austen to Cassandra Austen, 15–16 September 1796, Le Faye, *Letters*.

38. Jane Austen to Cassandra Austen, 9–10 January 1796, Le Faye, *Letters*; Jane Austen to Cassandra Austen, 14–15 January 1796, Le Faye, *Letters*.

39. Le Faye, *Jane Austen*, 111, 100–11.

40. Jane Austen, quoted in Cecil, *Portrait*, 120.

41. Collins, *Parson's Daughter*, 195.

42. Henry Austen, "Memoir of Miss Austen," in Sutherland, *A Memoir of Jane Austen*, 153.

43. Jane Austen to Cassandra Austin, 12–13 May 1801, in Le Faye, *Letters*, 84.

44. Jane Austen, "An Evening Prayer," Republic of Pemberley, www .pemberley.com/janeinfo/ausprayr.html.

45. Jane Austen to Cassandra Austen, in Le Faye, *Letters*, 188.

46. Jane Austen to Cassandra Austen, 31 May 1811, in Le Faye, *Letters*, 191–92.

47. Cecil, *A Portrait of Jane Austen*, 90.

48. Collins, *Parson's Daughter*, 224–26.

49. Le Faye, *Jane Austen*, 145.

50. Jane Austen to Francis Austen, in Le Faye, *Letters*, 95–98.

51. Collins, *Parson's Daughter*, 232–33.

52. Ibid., 208.

53. Jane Austen to Cassandra Austen, 5–6 May 1801, in Le Faye, *Letters*, 82; Jane Austen to Cassandra Austen, in Le Faye, *Letters*, 223.

54. Jane Austen to Francis Austen, in Le Faye, *Letters*, 217.

55. Caroline Austen, "My Aunt Jane Austen: A Memoir," in Sutherland, *A Memoir of Jane Austen*, 171.

56. Ibid., 169.

57. Jane Austen to Cassandra Austen, 21–22 May 1801, in Le Faye, *Letters*, 86.

58. Harman, *Jane's Fame*, 38.

59. Cecil, *Portrait*, 156.

60. Jane Austen to Cassandra Austen, in Le Faye, *Letters*, 291.

61. Cassandra Austen to Fanny Knight, in Le Faye, *Letters*, 344.

62. Review of *Sense and Sensibility*, quoted in Claire Tomalin, *Jane Austen: A Life* (New York: Vintage, 1997), 220.

63. See Mary Waldron, "Critical responses, early," in *Jane Austen in Context*, ed. Janet Todd (Cambridge: Cambridge Univ. Press, 2005), 83–91.

64. Sir Walter Scott, quoted in David Cecil, *A Portrait of Jane Austen* (London: Penguin, 1980), 181.

65. Waldron, "Critical responses," 89–90.

66. Thomas Babington Macaulay, quoted in Austen-Leigh, "Memoir," 104.

67. Henry James, quoted in Claudia Johnson, "Austen cults and cultures," in *The Cambridge Companion to Jane Austen*, eds. Edward Copeland and Juliet McMaster (Cambridge: Cambridge Univ. Press, 1997), 211.

68. Rudyard Kipling, "The Janeites," http://ebooks.adelaide.edu.au/k/kipling/rudyard/debits/chapter14.html.

69. Virginia Woolf, "Jane Austen," *The Common Reader*, http://ebooks .adelaide.edu.au/w/woolf/virginia/w91c/chapter12.html.

Chapter 7: D. L. Moody

1. R. B. Cook, *The Life, Work and Sermons of Dwight L. Moody* (Baltimore: R. H. Woodward Company, 1900), 15.

2. D. L. Moody, *The Works of D. L. Moody, Volume 2: Anecdotes* (Chicago: Fleming H. Revell, 1900), 10.

3. J. Wilbur Chapman, *The Life and Work of D. L. Moody* (Philadelphia: International Publishing Co., 1900), 46.

4. Paul Moody and A. P. Fitt, *The Shorter Life of D. L. Moody* (Chicago: BICA, 1900), 10.

5. W. H. Daniels, *D. L. Moody and His Work* (Hartford: American Publishing Co., 1875), 7.

6. D. L. Moody, C. F. Goss, et al., *Echoes from the Pulpit and Platform* (Hartford: Worthington and Co., 1900), 601.

7. "[Moody's] total schooling was the equivalent of a fifth-grade education today," from Dr. David Maas, "The Life & Times of D. L. Moody," *Christian History* magazine, January 1, 1990, Issue 25.

8. Chapman, *Life and Work of D. L. Moody*, 52–53.

9. J. C. Pollock, *Moody* (New York: Macmillan, 1963), 5–6.

10. Moody, Goss, et al., *Echoes from the Pulpit and Platform*, 224–25.

11. William R. Moody, *The Life of D. L. Moody* (New York: Fleming H. Revell Company, 1900), 35.

12. Stanley N. Gundry, *The Wit and Wisdom of D. L. Moody* (Chicago: Moody Press, 1974), 7.

13. Pollock, *Moody*, 7.

14. Ibid.

15. This story appears on pages 55–56 of Chapman, *Life and Work of D. L. Moody* (Toronto: The Bradley-Garretson Company, 1900).

16. Kimball's account appears in Chapman, *Life and Work of D. L. Moody*, 75–76.

17. Ibid., 46.

18. Moody and Fitt, *Shorter Life of D. L. Moody*, 23.

19. Ibid., 25.

20. As quoted on page 23 of Pollock, *Moody*.

21. William R. Moody, *D. L. Moody*, 30.

22. Pollock, *Moody*, 25–26.

23. As quoted in G. T. B. Davis, *Dwight L. Moody: The Man and His Mission* (K. T. Boland, 1900).

24. As quoted in Pollock, *Moody*, 26.

25. Ibid.

26. Lyle W. Dorsett, *A Passion for Souls* (Chicago: Moody Press, 1997), 65–66.

27. i.e., quarantine zone.

28. W. H. Daniels, *D. L. Moody and His Work*, new ed., rev. (Hartford: American Publishing Company, 1877), 34.

29. *The Dictionary of American Biography*, vol. 7, ed. by Dumas Malone (New York: Charles Scribner's Sons, 1962), 103.

30. Ibid.

31. Information supplied by the National Park Service and posted on the Web site for Ken Burns's miniseries *The Civil War* at: http://www.pbs .org/civilwar/war/map4.html.

32. Ibid.

33. Moody, Goss, et al., *Echoes from the Pulpit and Platform*, 164–66.

34. Ibid., 45.

35. Pollock, *Moody*, 24.

36. Ibid.

37. Ibid., 29.

38. As quoted on page 29 of Pollock, *Moody*.

39. Charles Morris, ed., *Famous Orators of the World and Their Best Orations* (Philadelphia: The John C. Winston Co., 1902), 290.

40. L. T. Remlap, ed., *"The Gospel awakening." Comprising the sermons and addresses, prayer-meeting talks and Bible readings of the great revival meetings conducted by Moody and Sankey*, 20th ed. (Chicago: Fairbanks and Palmer Publishing Co., 1885), 66–67.

41. Ibid., 67–68. Italics added.

42. Dorsett, *A Passion for Souls*, 151.

43. Pollock, *Moody*, 88.

44. H. D. Northrop, *The Life and Labors of Dwight L. Moody* (Chicago: A. B. Kuhlman Company, 1899), 332.

45. R. Moody, *The Life of Dwight L. Moody*, 145–46.

46. Dorsett, *A Passion for Souls*, 177.

47. Ibid.

48. W. R. Moody, *The Life of Dwight L. Moody*, 161.

49. Ibid., 161–62.

50. Ibid., 162.

51. Ibid., 164.

52. W. R. Moody, *The Life of Dwight L. Moody*, 190.

53. Ibid., 198–99.

54. Ibid., 199.

55. Ibid., 199–200.

56. W. R. Moody, *The Life of Dwight L. Moody*, 251.

57. Ibid., 320.

58. Ibid.

59. Ibid., 321.

60. Ibid., 322.

61. Ibid., 323.

62. Ibid., 327.

63. Ibid., 330, 333.

64. A paraphrase of Luke 12:48 (NASB): "From everyone who has been given much, much will be required."

65. W. R. Moody, *The Life of Dwight L. Moody*, 333.

66. Ibid.

67. Ibid., 333–35.

68. Moody Bible Institute, http://www.moodyministries.net/crp_MainPage.aspx?id=62.

69. This mission statement quote is part of an article posted online by the Moody Bible Institute, http://www.moodyministries.net/crp_MainPage.aspx?id=790.

70. As quoted in Stanley and Patricia Gundry, eds., *The Wit and Wisdom of D. L. Moody* (Chicago: Moody Press, 1974), 43.
71. A point well made by Goss in his biographical sketch of Moody in Moody, Goss, et al., *Echoes from the Pulpit and Platform*, 58. Here Goss speaks of Moody and Sankey "battling with the hoary customs and prejudices of the past" during their first great evangelistic campaign in Britain in 1872.
72. Cook, *Life, Work and Sermons of Dwight L. Moody*, 200.
73. William R. Moody, *The Life of Dwight L. Moody*, 545.
74. Pollock, *Moody*, 312.
75. Ibid.
76. Ibid.
77. Chapman, *The Life and Work of D. L. Moody*, 263.
78. Ibid., 263–64.
79. William R. Moody, *The Life of Dwight L. Moody*, 548–49.
80. Ibid., 549–50.
81. Ibid., 552.
82. Ibid., 552–53.
83. From the article "D. L. Moody; A Life of the Great Evangelist—Written by His Son," from the Wednesday, May 19, 1900, edition of the *New York Times*, Saturday Review of Books and Art, Page BR16, 785 words.

CHAPTER 8: GEORGE WASHINGTON CARVER

1. Robert P. Fuller, "The Early Life of George Washington Carver," Washington DC: National Park Service, 26 November 1957.
2. John Perry, *Unshakable Faith* (Sisters: Multnomah, 1999), 139.
3. Linda O. McMurry, *George Washington Carver* (Oxford: Oxford Univ. Press, 1981), 49.
4. Ibid., 116.
5. Perry, *Unshakable Faith*, 240.
6. Ibid., 286–87.
7. Ibid., 299.
8. All quotations from the hearing transcript are in R. Kremer, ed., *George Washington Carver in His Own Words* (Columbia: University of Missouri Press, 1987), 103–13.
9. "Men of Science Never Talk That Way," *New York Times*, 20 November 1924, 22, col. 6.

10. Kremer, *George Washington Carver in His Own Words*, 129–30.
11. James Saxon Childers, "A Boy Who Was Traded for a Horse," *American Magazine*, October 1932, 24ff.
12. McMurry, *George Washington Carver*, 243–47.

Chapter 9: Sergeant York

1. John Perry, *Sgt. York: His Life, Legend & Legacy: The Remarkable Untold Story of Sgt. Alvin C. York* (Nashville: Broadman & Holman, 1997), 39.
2. Ibid. See pages 41ff. for the full account of the revival.
3. The account of York's battle for Hill 223 is taken from official reports and eyewitness affidavits collected years later by Warner Bros. screenwriters working on the film script. These documents are at the Warner Bros. Film Archive on the campus of the University of Southern California–Los Angeles. Quotations from York within the account are from the war diary in York and Skeyhill, *Sergeant York*.
4. From George Pattullo, "The Second Elder Gives Battle," *Saturday Evening Post*, April 26, 1919, 1ff.
5. In time, the school's name was changed.
6. The account of Sam Houston's death was given to the author by Sam's older brother, George Edward York.
7. Jesse L. Lasky's story from his autobiography, *I Blow My Own Horn* (Garden City: Doubleday & Co., 1957).
8. Accounts of the film premieres in New York and Washington are from the Warner Bros. archives, and from media reports quoted in Perry, *Sgt. York*, 265–72.
9. Perry, *Sgt. York*, 319.
10. This account of York's last days from an author interview with his son George Edward.
11. "Sergeant York, War Hero, Dies," *New York Times*, September 3, 1964, 1.

Chapter 10: William F. Buckley Jr.

1. William F. Buckley Jr., *Miles Gone By: A Literary Autobiography* (Washington, DC: Regnery, 2004), 1–9.
2. Much of the text relating to Buckley's *God and Man at Yale* draws extensively from the introduction to the 25th anniversary edition of that book.
3. McGeorge Bundy, "The Attack on Yale," *Atlantic Monthly*, November

1951, http://www.theatlantic.com/magazine/archive/1969/12/
the-attack-on-yale/6724/.

4. Clark Judge, "Remarks to the Portsmouth Institute," June 20, 2009.

5. Quotations in this section are from "Our Mission Statement,"
   National Review, November 19, 1955. This mission statement can be
   viewed online at: http://www.nationalreview.com/articles/223549/
   our-mission-statement/william-f-buckley-jr.

6. Lee Edwards, "The Conservative Consensus: Frank Meyer, Barry
   Goldwater, and the Politics of Fusionism" (Heritage Foundation First
   Principles #8), January 22, 2007, http://www.heritage.org/research
   /nationalsecurity/fp8.cfm.

7. The Hoover Institution has put together a large archive of Buckley's
   shows. Information, clips, transcripts, and such can be found at http://
   hoohila.stanford.edu/firingline/. Also, many of the episodes are
   available for purchase through sites such as Amazon.com, and clips of
   these shows that zero in on choice moments can be found on YouTube.

8. William F. Buckley Jr., *On the Firing Line: The Public Life of Private
   Figures* (New York: Random House, 1989), 93–97.

9. Buckley, *On the Firing Line*, xxxvii.

10. "Why the South Must Prevail," *National Review*, August 24, 1957.

11. John B. Judis, *William F. Buckley, Jr.: Patron Saint of the Conservatives*
    (New York: Simon & Schuster), 138–39.

12. William F. Buckley Jr., *Overdrive* (Boston: Little Brown, 1981), 195–202.

13. William F. Buckley Jr., *Nearer, My God: An Autobiography of Faith*
    (Orlando: Harcourt, 1997), 217–21.

14. "The Art of Fiction No. 146," *The Paris Review*, summer 1996, http://
    www.parisreview.com/viewinterview.php/prmMID/1395.

15. Woody Allen, *Annie Hall*, 1977.

16. Christopher Buckley, in William F. Buckley, *The Reagan I Knew*, xii
    (foreword).

INDEX

Close Encounters of the Christian Kind

www.ChristianEncountersSeries.com

JANE AUSTEN
9781595553027
EBOOK: 9781418555214

JOHANN SEBASTIAN BACH
9781595551085
EBOOK: 9781595553911

ANNE BRADSTREET
9781595551092
EBOOK: 9781595554291

WILLIAM F. BUCKLEY
9781595550651
EBOOK: 9781595554307

JOHN BUNYAN
9781595553041
EBOOK: 9781418555221

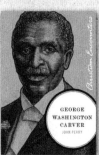

GEORGE WASHINGTON CARVER
9781595553034
EBOOK: 9781595554048

WINSTON CHURCHILL
9781595553065
EBOOK: 9781418555238

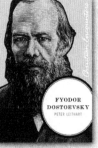

FYODOR DOSTOEVSKY
9781595550347
EBOOK: 9781595554093

Close Encounters of the Christian Kind

www.ChristianEncountersSeries.com

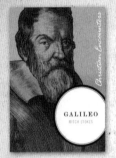

GALILEO
9781595550316
EBOOK: 9781595553935

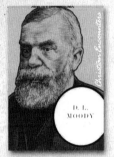

D. L. MOODY
9781595550477
EBOOK: 9781595553782

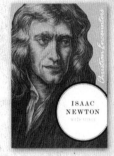

ISAAC NEWTON
9781595553034
EBOOK: 9781418555290

SAINT FRANCIS
9781595551078
EBOOK: 9781401604509

SAINT NICHOLAS
9781595551153
EBOOK: 9781595553768

SAINT PATRICK
9781595553058
EBOOK: 9781418584252

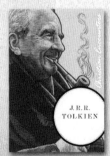

J. R. R. TOLKIEN
9781595551078
EBOOK: 9781595554031

SERGEANT YORK
9781595550255
EBOOK: 9781595553775